Great Debates on the European Convention on Human Rights

Great Debates in Law

Series Editor
Jonathan Herring, Professor of Law, University of Oxford

Commercial and Corporate Law
Andrew Johnston & Lorrain Talbot (eds)

Company Law (2nd edition)
Lorraine Talbot and Andreas Kokkinis

Contract Law (3rd edition)
Jonathan Morgan

Criminal Law (4th edition)
Jonathan Herring

Employment Law (2nd edition)
Simon Honeyball

Equity and Trusts
Alastair Hudson

EU Law
Jeremias Adams-Prassl and Sanja Sanja Bogojevic

European Convention on Human Rights (2nd edition)
Fiona de Londras & Kanstantsin Dzehtsiarou

Family Law (2nd edition)
Jonathan Herring, Rebecca Probert & Stephen Gilmore

Gender and Law
Rosemary Auchmuty (ed)

Jurisprudence (2nd edition)
Nicholas J McBride & Sandy Steel

Medical Law and Ethics (2nd edition)
Imogen Goold & Jonathan Herring

Tort Law
Jonathan Morgan

Land Law (3rd edition)
David Cowan, Lorna Fox O'Mahony & Neil Cobb

Great Debates on the European Convention on Human Rights

Second Edition

Fiona de Londras
and
Kanstantsin Dzehtsiarou

•HART•
OXFORD • LONDON • NEW YORK • NEW DELHI • SYDNEY

HART PUBLISHING

Bloomsbury Publishing Plc

Kemp House, Chawley Park, Cumnor Hill, Oxford, OX2 9PH, UK

1385 Broadway, New York, NY 10018, USA

Bloomsbury Publishing Ireland Limited, 29 Earlsfort Terrace, Dublin 2, D02 AY28, Ireland

HART PUBLISHING, the Hart/Stag logo, BLOOMSBURY and the Diana logo are trademarks of Bloomsbury Publishing Plc

First published in Great Britain 2025

1

A catalogue record for this book is available from the British Library.

A catalogue record for this book is available from the Library of Congress.

ISBN: PB: 978-1-35045-619-8
ePDF: 978-1-35046-927-3
ePub: 978-1-35046-928-0

Typeset by Compuscript Ltd, Shannon
Printed and bound in Great Britain by TJ Clays

For product safety related questions contact productsafety@bloomsbury.com

To find out more about our authors and books visit www.hartpublishing.co.uk. Here you will find extracts, author information, details of forthcoming events and the option to sign up for our newsletters.

Contents

Long Contents vii
List of Abbreviations xi
Table of Cases xiii

1. The Convention, the Court and the Heart of the Matter 1
2. Sovereignty and Authority 33
3. Admissibility 55
4. Evolution or Revolution? Interpretation of the Convention by the European Court of Human Rights 81
5. Accounting for Difference: Proportionality and the Margin of Appreciation 105
6. The Convention in Times of Insecurity 131
7. Socio-Economic Rights and the European Convention on Human Rights 161
8. Implementing the Convention: The Execution of Judgments of the Court 183

Index 213

Long Contents

Contents v
List of Abbreviations xi
Table of Cases xiii

1. The Convention, the Court and the Heart of the Matter **1**
Debate 1. Is the European Court of Human Rights Legitimate? 1
Debate 2. Has the Court Entered into the Age of Subsidiarity? 10
Debate 3. Should the Court be Further Reformed? 13
Debate 4. Who Are the Judges of the Court? 20
Debate 5. What Is the Role of the Registry within the Structure of the Court? 25
Debate 6. What Are the Consequences of Expulsion from the Council of Europe? 30
Conclusion 31
Further Reading 32

2. Sovereignty and Authority **33**
Debate 1. Who Has the Final Word in Human Rights Cases: The Court or the Contracting Parties? 33
Debate 2. What Is the Relationship between the EU and the ECHR? 41
Debate 3. Should the EU Accede to the ECHR? 46
Debate 4. What Is the Relationship between the ECHR and Other Sources of International Law? 49
Conclusion 54
Further Reading 54

3. Admissibility **55**
Debate 1. How Do Admissibility Criteria Affect the Court's Legitimacy? 57
Debate 2. Who Can Apply to the Court? 60
Debate 3. How Significant Must Disadvantage Be? 68
Debate 4. How Much Discretion Should the Court Have in Deciding Admissibility? 70
Debate 5. How Does Admissibility Relate to Effectiveness? 76
Conclusion 79
Further Reading 79

4. Evolution or Revolution? Interpretation of the Convention by the European Court of Human Rights **81**
Debate 1. Is Evolutive Interpretation of the Convention Necessary? 82
Debate 2. How Does the Court Determine the Moment of Evolution? 89
Debate 3. Is Evolution Necessarily Progressive? 99
Conclusion 103
Further Reading 103

5. Accounting for Difference: Proportionality and the Margin of Appreciation **105**
Debate 1. Do We Need a Proportionality Analysis for Rights Adjudication? 107
Debate 2. Should National Authorities Have a Margin of Appreciation in Respect of Human Rights Protection? 117
Debate 3. What are the Boundaries of the Margin of Appreciation? 121
Conclusion 128
Further Reading 129

6. The Convention in Times of Insecurity **131**
Debate 1. Does the ECHR Apply in War? 132
Debate 2. Does the ECHR Have Extraterritorial Effect? 135
Debate 3. Should Rights Be Suspended in Times of Emergency? 145
Debate 4. Does the Convention Protect People from 'Everyday Insecurity'? 153
Conclusion 159
Further Reading 159

7. Socio-Economic Rights and the European Convention on Human Rights **161**
Debate 1. Should the ECHR Be Used to Protect Socio-Economic Rights? 162
Debate 2. Can the ECHR Protect Socio-Economic Wellbeing in a Time of Austerity? 170
Debate 3. Can the Right to Non-Discrimination Promote Socio-Economic Equality? 175
Conclusion 181
Further Reading 181

8. Implementing the Convention: The Execution of Judgments of the Court **183**
Debate 1. What Remedies Can the Court Order? 184
Debate 2. Must Respondent States Execute Judgments of the Court? 193
Debate 3. Should Non-Respondent States Give Effect to Judgments of the Court? 204
Debate 4. Are Advisory Opinions Effective in Embedding the Principles of the Convention Domestically? 208
Conclusion 210
Further Reading 211

Index **213**

List of Abbreviations

CDDH	Steering Committee for Human Rights
CEO	Chief Executive Officer
CJEU	Court of Justice of the European Union
CLR	Centre for Legal Recourses
ECB	European Central Bank
ECHR	European Convention on Human Rights
ECtHR	European Court of Human Rights
ECJ	European Court of Justice
EU	European Union
HUDOC	Human Rights Documents (ECHR case-law database)
ILO	International Labour Organisation
IMF	International Monetary Fund
KFOR	Kosovo Peacekeeping Forces (NATO)
LGBTQI	Lesbian, Gay, Bisexual, Transgender, Queer (or Questioning), Intersex
NATO	North Atlantic Treaty Organization
NGO	non-governmental organisation
PACE	Parliamentary Assembly of the Council of Europe
TRNC	Turkish Republic of Northern Cyprus
TWAIL	Third World Approaches to International Law
UK	United Kingdom
UN	United Nations

UN HRC	United Nations Human Rights Committee
UNMIK	United Nations Mission in Kosovo
US	United States
USSR	Union of Soviet Socialist Republics
VCLT	Vienna Convention on the Law of Treaties

Table of Cases

European Court of Human Rights and European Commission on Human Rights

A v Croatia App no 55164/08 (ECtHR, 14 October 2010) 155

AA v Greece App no 12186/08 (ECtHR, 22 July 2010) 168

A and B v Georgia App no 73975/16 (ECtHR, 10 February 2022)....................... 155

A and Others v the United Kingdom [2009] ECHR 301 ...... 148, 152–53

A, B and C v Ireland [2010] ECHR 2032 .... 6, 92–93, 97–98, 123

Abdulaziz, Cabales and Balkandali v the United Kingdom, 28 May 1985, Series A no 94.................... 179

Ádám and Others v Romania App nos 81114/17, 49716/18, 50913/18, 52370/18, 54444/18, 54475/18, (ECtHR, 13 October 2020) 176

Advisory Opinion on Certain Legal Questions Concerning the Lists of Candidates Submitted with a View to the Election of Judges to the European Court of Human Rights (No 1), 12 February 2008 208

Advisory Opinion on Certain Legal Questions Concerning the Lists of Candidates Submitted with a View to the Election of Judges to the European Court of Human Rights (No 2), 22 January 2010 208

AE v Bulgaria App no 53891/20 (ECtHR, 23 May 2023)....... 158, 176

Agrotexim and Others v Greece [1999] ECHR 42 65–66

Airey v Ireland [1979–80] 2 EHRR 305 .... 162, 165

Aksoy v Turkey [1996] ECHR 68 152

Al-Dulimi and Montana Management Inc v Switzerland [2016] ECHR 576 51–52

Al Jedda v the United Kingdom [2011] ECHR 1092 .... 51–52, 137, 140

Al-Khawaja and Tahery v the United Kingdom [2011] ECHR 2127 34–35

Al-Skeini and Others v the United Kingdom [2011] ECHR 1093 .... 137, 139–40

Alekseyev v Russia App nos 4916/07, 25924/08 and 14599/09, (ECtHR, 21 October 2010)................. 109–10

Amuur v France, 25 June 1996, Reports of Judgments and Decisions 1996-III 74
Ananyev and Others v Russia [2012] ECHR 21 172
Anchugov and Gladkov v Russia [2013] ECHR 638 38
Animal Defenders International v the United Kingdom [2013] ECHR 362 125–26
Assanidze v Georgia [2004] ECHR 140 186
Association for the Defence of Human Rights in Romania – Helsinki Committee on behalf of Ionel Garcea v Romania [2015] ECHR 309 65
Avotiņš v Latvia App no 17502/07 (ECtHR, 23 May 2016) 44
Azinas v Cyprus App no 56679/00 (ECtHR, 20 June 2002) 199
Baka v Hungary App no 20261/12 (ECtHR, 23 June 2016) 194
Bankovic' and Others v Belgium and Others [2001] ECHR 890 .... 50, 79, 136–40, 142–43
Basu v Germany, App no 215/19 (ECtHR, 18 October 2022) 176
Bayatyan v Armenia [2011] ECHR 1095 .... 90, 92, 206
Behrami and Behrami v France and Saramati v France, Germany and Norway App nos 71412/01 and 78166/01 (ECtHR, 2 May 2007) 50–51, 79
Bevacqua and S v Bulgaria [2008] ECHR 498 154–55
'Blondje' v the Netherlands [2009] ECHR 1495 76
Bock v Germany [2010] ECHR 139 72
Bosphorus Hava Yollari Turizm ve Ticaret Anonim Sirketi v Ireland [2005] ECHR 440 .... 42–46, 49, 52
Branko Tomašic' and Others v Croatia App no 46598/06 (ECtHR, 15 January 2009) 155
Brannigan and McBride v the United Kingdom [1993] ECHR 21 150–52
Budina v Russia [2009] ECHR 1104 170
Burden v the United Kingdom [2008] ECHR 356 61–62
Burdov v Russia (No 2) [2009] ECHR 86 189–90
Burmych and Others v Ukraine (striking out) [2017] ECHR 894 190–91
Calmanovici v Romania [2008] ECHR 1907 37
Campbell and Cosans v the United Kingdom, 25 February 1982, Series A no 48 153
Cannavacciuolo And Others v Italy [2025] ECHR 29 .... 122, 189
Capital Bank AD v Bulgaria [2005] ECHR 752 66
Capuano v Italy [1987] ECHR 10 59
Carter v Russia [2021] ECHR 766 143
Case 'Relating to Certain Aspects of the Laws on the Use of Languages in Education in Belgium' (merits), 23 July 1968, Series A no 6 179
Catan and Others v the Republic of Moldova and Russia [2012] ECHR 1827 109
Centre for Legal Resources on behalf of Valentin Câmpeanu v Romania [2014] ECHR 972 64
Chapin and Charpentier v France [2016] ECHR 504 6
Christine Goodwin v the United Kingdom [2002] ECHR 588 86–88
Ciorap v Moldova (No 2) [2010] ECHR 1138 74
Civek v Turkey [2016] ECHR 207 155
Communauté Genevoise D'action Syndicale (Cgas) v Switzerland App no 21881/20, (ECtHR, 27 November 2023) 148
Cossey v the United Kingdom [1990] ECHR 21 86

Costello-Roberts v the United Kingdom, 25 March 1993, Series A no 247-C 153
Costa and Pavan v Italy [2012] ECHR 2040 6
Cruz Varas and Others v Sweden, 20 March 1991, Series A no 201 95
Cyprus v Turkey App no 25781/94 (12 May 2014) 137, 186
D v the United Kingdom [1997] ECHR 25 163
Daddi v Italy App no 15476/09 (ECtHR, 2 June 2009) 59
Daniel Faulkner v the United Kingdom [2016] ECHR 823 70
Dániel Karsai v Hungary App no 32312/23 (ECtHR, 2 September 2024) 88
Dareskizb Ltd v Armenia [2021] ECHR 760 150
Demir and Baykara v Turkey [2008] ECHR 1345 ..... 95, 166
Demopoulos and Others v Turkey [2010] ECHR 306 58
Denmark and Others v Greece ('The Greek Case') (1970) 12 CD 186 ..... 148, 150
De Souza Ribeiro v France [2012] ECHR 2066 58
De Wilde, Ooms and Versyp v Belgium (Article 50) [1972] ECHR 1 185
DH and Others v the Czech Republic [2007] ECHR 922 180
Dian v Denmark App no 44002/22 (ECtHR, 21 May 2024) 102–03
Dickson v the United Kingdom [2007] ECHR 1050 124
Di Mauro v Italy [1999] ECHR 63 59
Dobri v Romania App no 25153/04 (ECtHR, 14 December 2010) 153
Drijfhout v Netherlands [2011] ECHR 408 72
Duarte Agostinho and Others v Portugal and 32 others App no 39371/20, (ECtHR, 9 April 2024) 144
Dudek v Germany [2010] ECHR 1991 72
Dudgeon v the United Kingdom [1981] ECHR 5 ..... 62, 92, 125
EG v the Republic of Moldova App no 37882/13 (ECtHR, 13 April 2021) 111–12
Egmez v Cyprus [2000] ECHR 681 58
EM v Romania App no 43994/05 (ECtHR, 30 October 2012) 156
Eremia v the Republic of Moldova [2013] ECHR 601 156
Evans v the United Kingdom [2007] ECHR 264 ..... 6, 125
Fadeyeva and Others v Russia App no 50345/18 (ECtHR, 16 January 2025) 31
Fedotova v Russia, [2023] ECHR 55 91
Finger v Bulgaria [2011] ECHR 781 70
Finogenov and Others v Russia [2010] ECHR 589 63
Firth and others v United Kingdom [2014] EHRR 874 191
Folgerø and Others v Norway [2011] ECHR 2189 74–75
Fretté v France App no 36515/97 (ECtHR, 26 May 2002) 92
Frodl v Austria [2010] ECHR 508 ..... 37, 40, 100
Gaygusuz v Austria [1996] ECHR 36 ..... 174, 179
Georgia v Russia (II) [2021] ECHR 58 ..... 132, 135
Giacomelli v Italy [2006] ECHR 916 108
Grandrath v Germany App no 5591/72 (European Commission of Human Rights, 2 April 1973) 90
Greens and MT v the United Kingdom [2010] ECHR 1826 ..... 37, 191
GZ v Austria App no 5591/72 (European Commission of Human Rights, 2 April 1973) 90
Haas v Switzerland [2011] ECHR 2422 6

Hajduová v Slovakia App no 2660/03 (ECtHR, 30 November 2010) 155
Halime Kılıç v Turkey App no 63034/11 (ECtHR, 28 June 2016) 157
Hassan v the United Kingdom [2014] ECHR 936 133–35
Hatton and Others v the United Kingdom [2001] ECHR 565 128
Hirst v the United Kingdom (No 2) [2005] ECHR 681 ..... 35–39, 100, 127, 188, 191, 201
Idalov v Russia, no 5826/03 (ECtHR, 22 May 2012) 58
Ilias and Ahmed v Hungary App no 47287/15 (ECtHR, 21 November 2019) 45
Ilyushkin and others v Russia App nos 5734/08 et seq (ECtHR, 17 April 2012) 190
Inze v Austria, 28 October 1987, Series A no 126 176
Ionescu v Romania [2010] ECHR 1023 69
Ireland v the United Kingdom [1978] ECHR 1 151–52
Iribarren Pinillos v Spain App no 36777/03 (ECtHR, 8 January 2009) 153
Jahn and Others v Germany [2005] ECHR 444 174
Jaloud v the Netherlands [2014] ECHR 1292 ..... 133, 141
James and Others v the United Kingdom [1986] ECHR 2 119
Janowiec and Others v Russia App nos 55508/07 and 29520/09 (ECtHR, 16 April 2012) 121–22
Janowiec and Others v Russia [2013] ECHR 1003 122
Kalashnikov v Russia [2002] ECHR 596 153
Kalda v Estonia (No 2) [2022] ECHR 1052 ..... 36, 39
Kalinkin and others v Russia App no 34006/02 (ECtHR, 14 September 2006) 190
Kalucza v Hungary App no 57693/10 (ECtHR, 24 April 2012) 155
Kavala v Turkey [2019] ECHR 898 203
Kavala v Türkiye (infringement proceedings) App no 28749/18 (ECtHR, 11 July 2022) 203
Kiyutin v Russia [2011] ECHR 439 176
Klass and Others v Germany [1978] ECHR 4 62
Koch v Germany App no 497/09 (ECtHR, 19 July 2012) 6
Kolosovskiy v Latvia App no 50183/99 (ECtHR, 29 January 2007) 72
Kondrulin v Russia [2016] ECHR 772 65
Konstantin Markin v Russia App no 30078/06 (ECtHR, 7 October 2010) 115
Konstantin Markin v Russia [2012] ECHR 514 ..... 114, 166
Kontrová v Slovakia App no 7510/04 (ECtHR, 31 May 2007) 155
Korolev v Russia [2010] ECHR 1051 69
Koufaki and Adedy v Greece App nos 57665/12 and 57657/12 (ECtHR, 7 May 2013) 172
Kovačević v Bosnia and Herzegovina [2023] ECHR 625 181
Kreuz v Poland App no 28249/95 (ECtHR, 19 June 2001) 163
Kurt v Austria App no 62903/15 (ECtHR, 15 June 2021) 111, 158
L and V v Austria [2003] ECHR 20 99
LF v the United Kingdom App no 19839/21 (ECtHR, 24 May 2022) 173
Lacatus v Switzerland [2021] ECHR 37 102
Lakićević and Others v Montenegro and Serbia App nos 27458/06 and 3 others (ECtHR, 13 December 2011) 174

Lautsi and Others v Italy [2011] ECHR 2412 .... 101, 113, 122
Lawless v Ireland [1961] ECHR 2 .... 148, 151
Leonidis v Greece [2009] ECHR 5 153
Leyla Şahin v Turkey App no 44774/98 (ECtHR, 10 November 2005) 101
Lithgow and Others v the United Kingdom [1986] ECHR 8 109
Loizidou v Turkey (merits), 18 December 1996, Reports of Judgments and Decisions 1996-VI 136
Luczak v Poland App no 77782/01 (ECtHR, 27 November 2007) 173
Lukenda v Slovenia [2005] ECHR 682 58
Lustig-Prean and Beckett v the United Kingdom [1999] ECHR 71 178
MC v Bulgaria App no 39272/98 (ECtHR, 4 December 2003) 122
MG v Turkey App no 646/10 (ECtHR, 22 March 2016) 157
ML v Poland App no 40119/21 (ECtHR, 14 December 2024) 194
MSD v Romania App no 28935/21 (ECtHR, 3 December 2024) 122
MSS v Belgium and Greece App no 30696/09 (ECtHR, 21 January 2011) 168–70
Mamatkulov and Askarov v Turkey [2005] ECHR 64 94–95
Mammadov v Azerbaijan (No 2) App no 919/15 (ECtHR, 5 March 2018) 202
Manerov v Russia [2016] ECHR 19 185
Marckx v Belgium [1979] ECHR 2 .... 85, 87, 94, 185
Marguš v Croatia [2014] ECHR 523 95
Marshall v United Kingdom App no 41571/98 (ECtHR, 10 July 2001) 151
McDaid and Others v the United Kingdom App nos 34822/97 and five others, (European Commission of Human Rights, 9 April 1996) 58
McHugh and others v United Kingdom App no 51987/08 (ECtHR, 10 February 2015) 191
Mehmet and Suna Yigit v Turkey App no 52658/99 (ECtHR, 17 July 2007) 163
Mehmet Hasan Altan v Turkey [2018] ECHR 251 152
Mentzen v Latvia App no 71074/01 (ECtHR, 7 December 2004) 73
Micallef v Malta App no 17056/06 (ECtHR, 15 October 2009) 8
Michaud v France [2012] ECHR 2030 45
Modarca v Moldova [2007] ECHR 390 153
Moraru and Marin v Romania App nos 53282/18 and 31428/20 (ECtHR, 20 December 2022) 176
Mortier v Belgium [2022] ECHR 764 103
Murphy v Ireland [2003] ECHR 352 125
Murtazaliyeva v Russia [2018] ECHR 1047 12–13
NKM v Hungary App no 66529/11 (ECtHR, 14 May 2013)......... 173–74
Nada v Switzerland [2012] ECHR 1691 51–52
Nagovitsyn and Nalgiyev v Russia [2010] ECHR 1331 190
Nencheva and Others v Bulgaria [2013] ECHR 554 172
Nurcan Bayraktar v Türkiye App no 27094/20 (ECtHR, 27 June 2023) 176
O'Keeffe v Ireland App no 35810/09 (ECtHR, 28 January 2014)........... 11
OAO Neftyanaya Kompaniya Yukos v Russia [2009] ECHR 287 .... 66, 186
Odièvre v France App no 42326/98 (ECtHR, 13 February 2003) 125

Oleksandr Volkov v Ukraine [2013] ECHR 32 187
Oliari and Others v Italy [2015] ECHR 716 .... 6, 123
Opuz v Turkey [2009] ECHR 870 .... 156, 158, 172
Oršuš and Others v Croatia App no 15766/03 (ECtHR, 16 March 2010) 180
Osmanoğlu and Kocabaş v Switzerland App no 29086/12 (ECtHR, 10 January 2017) 112
Paez v Sweden, 30 October 1997, Reports of Judgments and Decisions 1997-VII 74
Pająk and Others v Poland App no 25226/18 (ECtHR, 24 October 2023) 176
Parrillo v Italy App no 46470/11 (ECtHR, 27 August 2015) 6
Paun Jovanović v Serbia App no 41394/15 (ECtHR, 7 February 2023) 176
Pešić and Others v Serbia App nos 48973/20, 54565/20 and 54676/20 (ECtHR, 5 January 2023) 148
Piskin v Turkey [2020] ECHR 902 151
POA and Others v the United Kingdom [2013] ECHR 600 75
Poznanski and Others v Germany (dec) App no 25101/05 (ECtHR, 3 July 2007) 72
Pretty v the United Kingdom [2002] ECHR 427 6
Proceedings under Article 46(4) in the case of Ilgar Mammadov v Azerbaijan App no 15172/13 (ECtHR, 29 May 2019) 202–03
Rees v the United Kingdom [1986] ECHR 11 86
Roman Zakharov v Russia App no 47143/06 (ECtHR, 4 December 2015) 63
S and Marper v the United Kingdom [2008] ECHR 1581 .... 108, 124
SAS v France [2014] ECHR 695 .... 93, 101, 110
Şahin Alpay v Turkey [2018] ECHR 253 152
Salgueiro da Silva Mouta v Portugal [1999] ECHR 176 176
Sanchez-Sanchez v The United Kingdom [2022] ECHR 925 150
Sander v the United Kingdom [2000] ECHR 194 178
Schalk and Kopf v Austria [2010] ECHR 1996 6
Scoppola v Italy (no 3) [2012] ECHR 868 .... 37–38, 100, 102
Scordino v Italy [2004] ECHR 412 59
Schwizgebel v Switzerland App no 25762/07 (ECtHR, 10 June 2010) 176
SD v Greece App no 53541/07 (ECtHR,11 June 2009) 168
Sejdić and Finci v Bosnia and Herzegovina App nos 27996/06 and 34836/06 (ECtHR, 22 December 2009) 177, 180–81
SH and Others v Austria App no 57813/00 (ECtHR, 3 November 2011) 88
Shamayev and Others v Georgia and Russia App no 36378/02 (ECtHR, 12 April 2005 16 September 2003) 75–76
Sheffield and Horsham v the United Kingdom [1998] ECHR 69 88
Sidabras and Džiautas v Lithuania App nos 55480/00 and 59330/00 (ECtHR, 27 October 2004) 179
Singh v France [2008] ECHR 1906 73
Soering v the United Kingdom [1989] ECHR 14 .... 5, 62
Söyler v Turkey App no 29411/07 (ECtHR, 17 September 2013) 39

Stec and Others v the United Kingdom [2006] ECHR 1162 179
Stichting Mothers of Srebrenica and Others v the Netherlands [2013] ECHR 739 50
Sufi and Elmi v the United Kingdom [2011] ECHR 1045 169–70
Sutherland v the United Kingdom App no 25186/94 (European Commission of Human Rights, 1 July 1997) 99
Tabesh v Greece App no 8256/07 (ECtHR, 26 November 2009) 168
Talpis v Italy App no 41237/14 (ECtHR, 2 March 2017) 157
Tańase v Moldova App no 7/08 (ECtHR, 27 April 2010) 92
Thlimmenos v Greece [2000] ECHR 162 180
Tkhelidze v Georgia App no 33056/17 (ECtHR, 8 July 2021) 176
Tyrer v the United Kingdom [1978] ECHR 2 .... 98–99, 153
Tysiac v Poland [2007] ECHR 219 6
Ukraine and the Netherlands v Russia App nos 8019/16, 43800/14, 28525/20 (ECtHR, 30 November 2022) 142–43
Ukraine v Russia (re Crimea) App nos 20958/14 and 38334/18 (ECtHR, 25 June 2024) 31, 135, 142
United Communist Party of Turkey v Turkey [1998] ECHR 1 126
Valiuliene v Lithuania [2013] ECHR 240 156
Verein KlimaSeniorinnen Schweiz and Others v Switzerland [2024] ECHR 304 .... 61, 66
VgT Verein gegen Tierfabriken v Switzerland [2001] ECHR 412 125
Vinter and Others v the United Kingdom [2013] ECHR 645 .... 92, 107
Vo v France [2004] ECHR 326 6
Volodina v Russia [2019] ECHR 539 158
Von Hannover v Germany [2004] ECHR 294 110
Von Hannover v Germany (No 2) [2012] ECHR 228 113
Vuckovic v Croatia App no 15798/20 (ECtHR, 12 December 2023) 154
Wa Baile v Switzerland App nos 43868/18 and 25883/21 (ECtHR, 20 February 2024) 176
Walesa v Poland [2023] ECHR 9344 189
Wieczorek v Poland [2009] ECHR 2025 174
Winterstein and Others v France, [2013] ECHR 98 163
Y and Others v Bulgaria App no 9077/18 (ECtHR, 22 March 2022) 158
Yumak and Sadak v Turkey [2008] ECHR 1887 124
Yuriy Nikolayevich Ivanov v Ukraine [2009] ECHR 1570 190
Z v Finland [1997] ECHR 10 120
Žegarac and Others v Serbia App no 54805/15 (ECtHR, 17 January 2023) 173
Zhdanov and Others v Russia [2019] ECHR 565 72

UK Supreme Court and House of Lords

In the matter of an application by Siobhan McLaughlin for Judicial Review [2018] UKSC 48 207
R (Daly) v Secretary of State for the Home Department [2001] UKHL 26 115
R v Horncastle [2009] UKSC 14 34
R (HS2 Action Alliance Ltd) v Secretary of State for Transport [2014] UKSC 3 196

R v Special Adjudicator, ex parte Ullah [2004] UKHL 26 207–08
Secretary of State for Defence v Al-Skeini & Others [2007] UKHL 26 139
Thoburn v Sunderland CC [2002] 4 All ER 156.................... 196
Whaley v Lord Advocate [2004] SC 78 162

Russian Constitutional Court

Decision of the Constitutional Court of the Russian Federation from 14 July 2015 N 21-П 'in the case of verification of constitutionality of Article 1 of the Federal Law "On Ratification of the Convention For the Protection of Human Rights and Fundamental Freedoms and Its Protocols", sections 1 and 2 of Article 32 of the Federal Law "On International Treaties of the Russian Federation", sections 1 and 4 of Article 11, subsection 4 of section 4 of Article 392 of the Civil Procedural Code of the Russian Federation, Sections 1 and 4 of Article 13, subsection 4 of section 3 of Article 311 of the Arbitration Procedural Code of the Russian Federation, sections 1 and 4 of Article 15, subsection 4 of section 1 of Article 350 of the Administrative Court Proceedings Code of the Russian Federation, and subsection 2 of Section 4 of Article 413 of the Criminal Procedural Code of the Russian Federation in relation to the request of the group of the members of state Duma (parliament)' 38
The Judgment of the Russian Constitutional Court as to the Possibility of Execution of the Judgment of the ECtHR in the case of *Anchugov and Gladkov v Russia*... 39

Court of Justice of the European Union

Bosphorus Hava Yollari Turizm ve Ticaretas v Minister for Transport, Energy and Communications and Others ECLI:EU:C:1996:312......... 43
Costa v Ente Nazionale Energia Elettrica (ENEL) [1964] ECR 585 41
Internationale Handelsgesellschaft mbH v Einfuhr- und Vorratsstelle für Getreide und Futtermittel [1970] ECR 1125 .... 42, 115
Joined Cases C-293/12 and C-594/12 *Digital Rights Ireland* [2014] OJ C175/07 44
Joined Cases C-402/05 and C-415/05P *Kadi and another v European Union Council* ECLI:EU:C:2008:461 44
Nold v Commission ECLI:EU:C:1974:51 42
Opinion 2/13 *Accession of the European Union to the European Convention for the Protection of Human Rights and Fundamental Freedoms* ECLI:EU:C:2014:2454 46–48
Opinion 2/94 [1996] ECR I-1759.................................... 46
Rutili v Ministre de l'Interieur [1975] ECR 1219 42

UN Human Rights Committee

Singh v France, HRC, 26/09/2013, CCPR/C/108/D/1928/2010... 73

Constitutional Court of Germany

Görgülü 2 BvR 1481/04 (14 October 2004) BVerfGE 111, 307....................... 196
BVerfGE 3, 383 (1954).................... 115

Supreme Court of Israel

HCJ 2056/04 *Beit Sourik Village Council v The Government of Israel* PD 24 [2004] 115

Supreme Court of Canada

R v Oakes [1986] 1 SCR 103 115

European Committee of Social Rights

European Roma Rights Centre v Bulgaria Complaint No 48/2008 (Decision 31 March 2009) 167
Federation of Employed Pensioners of Greece (IKA-ETAM) v Greece, Complaint 76/2011 174
General Federation of Employees of the National Electric Power Corporation (GENOP-DEI) and Confederation of Greek Civil Servants' Trade Unions (ADEDY) v Greece, Complaint 66/2011 174

Italian Constitutional Court

Judgments Nos 348 and 349 (24 October 2007) (It) 195
Judgment No 49 (26 March 2015) (It) 196

1

The Convention, the Court and the Heart of the Matter

Throughout this book, we will consider specific debates about the European Convention on Human Rights (the Convention or ECHR), the rights it protects, and the ways in which states might be said to justifiably or legally infringe, or otherwise limit, those rights. All of these debates connect with a larger question: *is the system of human rights protection under the ECHR legitimate?* This question is deceptively complicated, not least because of the complexity of legitimacy as an analytical category. That is what we start with in this chapter, which in turn acts as a gateway into key frameworks, concepts and actors that will help the reader to engage with the debates we outline in the chapters that follow. Having considered the different frameworks for understanding legitimacy vis-à-vis the ECHR and European Court of Human Rights (the Court or ECtHR), we go on to outline the institutional framework of the ECHR, including the judiciary and the Registry.

Debate 1

Is the European Court of Human Rights Legitimate?

The ECtHR was created to ensure that the Contracting Parties to the Convention comply with the human rights enshrined in it. This mission almost inevitably leads to the fact that from time to time the Court will find these Parties in violation of the Convention. In some cases, rather than resolving the underlying domestic problems that caused the violation, a state will dispute the Court's legitimacy and, thus, its finding of a violation. While most courts' legitimacy is questioned at one point or another, the ECtHR is particularly susceptible to claims of illegitimacy because it can be mistakenly perceived as a 'foreign court', it protects vulnerable and sometimes unpopular groups of people, and it identifies the human rights-related implications of policy decisions that may have significant political and popular support. Furthermore, the Court is only one of the actors with responsibility for developing and protecting ECHR rights: national governments, legislatures and courts share that responsibility. It is thus to be expected that some good-faith questions of (il)legitimacy would arise.

Broadly speaking, legitimacy can be understood across four broad categories: input legitimacy, output legitimacy, outcome legitimacy and perceived legitimacy. In simple terms, *input legitimacy* relates to the processes by which decisions are made. In the context of the Convention and its enforcement, this includes matters such as the mechanisms for the appointment of key actors (such as judges), the independence enjoyed by those actors, procedural regularity in the workings of the Court, and mechanisms and processes of textual change to the Convention itself (such as the agreement of new Protocols). *Output legitimacy*, on the other hand, relates to the quality of the outputs of the process itself, which, in this context, means the judgments of the Court. In that respect, any legitimacy analysis must look at both the methodological rigour and the quality of the reasoning employed, considering whether a case develops, applies or reinforces a right in a way that is sensible and effective for the Convention system and rights enjoyment generally. *Outcome legitimacy* is considered by reference to the outcome of the Convention and case law per se – what are the *outcomes* of the Convention's application in real terms? In other words, is the Convention *effective* by reference to both the Convention per se and the judgments of the Court enforcing and implementing that Convention? Does it lead to resolution of the rights violations identified by the Court, and to the general improvement of rights protection across the Council of Europe member states?

Finally, *perceived legitimacy* relates to perceptions of the Court by its key stakeholders, such as Contracting Parties or the public at large. In this respect, the accuracy of those perceptions is not relevant. Rather, perceived legitimacy is an important analytical framework, because an institution that starts with a legitimacy deficit (because, for example, it is not a democratic institution or because it is 'foreign') is likely to make decisions about how to exercise its powers (eg be innovative, evolve the Convention standards, wade into sensitive areas with enormous rights implications but which are politically sensitive, etc) by reference to its understanding of its perceived legitimacy. In other words, perceptions of legitimacy are likely to impact on the Court's willingness to flex its muscles (or not to do so), especially in sensitive contexts. In terms of perceived legitimacy, the Court requires 'diffuse support', meaning support for the institution itself, even if a state disagrees with some of the decisions that it makes. Where a court enjoys diffuse support, stakeholders will perceive it as a credible decision maker whose decisions should attract compliance even when individual judgments might be subject to some criticism. That in turn requires them to see it as legitimate.

What Are the Sources of ECtHR Legitimacy?

The ECHR is an international treaty that is designed to impact, shape and restrict what states can do in respect of the people who are within their jurisdiction.[1] In other words, it has the capacity to reach into what was conventionally thought to be the most sovereign of spaces – the *domestic sphere* – and attempt to shape what happens there. Whilst that may seem to be a fairly standard feature of human rights law today (and it is), it was truly remarkable in the late 1940s and early 1950s when the Convention was introduced. It is useful to recall that the Universal Declaration on Human Rights was adopted in 1948, and that core instruments of international human rights law, such as the International Covenant on Civil and Political Rights and the International Covenant on Economic, Social and Cultural Rights, were not introduced until 1966.

Thus, at the time of its coming into force, the ECHR was purporting to do something truly extraordinary: to make individuals the subjects of international law, to shape the state's domestic activities, and to create a system of international adjudication making states accountable should they fail to adhere domestically to the principles they had signed up to internationally. Given this context, and given the fact that many claims of *illegitimacy* that are currently made against the Court and Convention, and which will be discussed throughout this book, are thinly disguised claims of unjustified interference in the domestic sphere, the debate surrounding the source of the Convention's legitimacy is an important one. Here we canvass five possible sources that will be returned to – implicitly and explicitly – in the debates and discussions considered in this book.

a. *Consent as a Basis for Legitimacy*

As with all international treaties, one of the core sources for the legitimacy of the ECHR is the consent of states. International law is largely built on the claim that all states consent to the international rules to which they signed up. Of course, we know that in many ways this 'consent' trope is a myth. Third World Approaches to International Law (TWAIL) scholars have convincingly shown how the principle of consent elides the coloniality of and imperialism of international law per se,[2] while criteria for admission to trading blocs – such as the requirement to ratify human rights treaties before being admitted – raises questions of non-military coercion. Within orthodox principles of international law, however, the assumption that all states enjoy sovereign equality, and thus all states *consent* to be bound by the treaties to which they are parties, prevails.

There are at least two reasons why original consent alone is an inadequate account of how and why the Convention and its system enjoy legitimacy. The first relates to the costs of withdrawing consent. Denouncing the Convention and leaving the Council of Europe brings with it serious damage to reputation, which most states would not want to suffer. In these circumstances, a state may

[1] Article 1, ECHR.

[2] For example Antony Anghie, "Rethinking International Law: A TWAIL Retrospective" (2023) 34(1) *European Journal of International Law* 7.

consider it less damaging to simply ignore adverse judgments of the ECtHR, or half-heartedly engage in quasi-implementation or routinely fall below the Convention standards for as long as possible, than to actually leave the Convention. Thus, whilst consent is the most basic ground of legitimacy and may well keep the system together in formalistic terms, it is unable to ensure the effectiveness of the Convention system on its own.

The second reason why consent is an inadequate basis for legitimacy on its own is the distance between what a state might originally have consented to and what the Convention now means, largely through the innovations of the Court in its judgments. In order to keep the ECHR up to date, practical and effective, the ECtHR uses techniques such as evolutive interpretation (discussed in chapter 4) to develop ECHR law, sometimes in directions that the signatories would never have envisaged at the time they originally consented to the Convention. Whilst it is possible to argue that states consented both to the Convention 'as text' and the Convention 'as applied' by the Court, it is clear that it is some states' perception that the Convention now is drastically different in meaning, reach and intention to the Convention they signed up to. Accordingly, this calls into question how far 'consent' takes us as a source of legitimacy in respect of the Convention and, perhaps especially, of the Court.

Despite these challenges consent remains important, and states parties to the Convention have ways to signal to the Court and the Council of Europe that they do not consent to a particular development. First, the Convention can be amended through Protocols. There have been 16 Protocols to the Convention that changed its text. Of course, in order to amend the Convention, the agreement of all 46 Contracting Parties is required. This is not easily achieved. Moreover, it is difficult to limit the capacity of the ECtHR to innovate by crude means such as amending the Convention text. An attempt to do that was made by Protocol 15, which introduced references to subsidiarity and the margin of appreciation to the Preamble of the Convention, although one might argue this has had more of a symbolic than tangible effect.[3] Second, the Contracting Parties can express their dissatisfaction by voicing their concerns in various ways. For instance, former UK Prime Minister, David Cameron, famously stated that the ECtHR should not deal with cases of minor importance.[4] More recently, comments from the UK Government about the inadequacy of the Court's procedure for interim measures[5] led to a change in the Court's practice

[3] Kanstantsin Dzehtsiarou, 'Much Ado About Nothing' (*ECHR Blog*, 17 April 2013) at www.echrblog.com/2013/04/ngo-reaction-to-draft-protocol-15-and.html; Helga Molbæk-Steensig, 'Subsidiarity Does Not Win Cases: A Mixed Methods Study of the Relationship Between Margin Of Appreciation Language and Deference at the European Court Of Human Rights' (2023) 36(1) *Leiden Journal of International Law* 83.

[4] Nicholas Watt, 'David Cameron calls for reform of European court of human rights' (*The Guardian*, 25 January 2012).

[5] Interim measures are regulated by rule 39 of the Rules of Court. Within the scope of interim measures, the ECtHR instructs the relevant parties not to worsen the situation in which the immediate risk to human rights exists. For more, see Kanstantsin Dzehtsiarou and Vassilis P Tzevelekos

in this area.[6] Third, states can express their concerns at the conferences dedicated to the future of the ECtHR.[7] In 2023, the future of the Court was discussed at the Summit of Heads of State and Government of the Council of Europe in Reykjavík. There, the states reaffirmed their commitment to the Court, but also emphasised the importance of the principle of subsidiarity, which we discuss below.[8]

b. Moral Purpose as a Basis for Legitimacy

Most would agree that the protection and promotion of human rights is, in and of itself, a desirable or morally admirable 'end', so that actions done in pursuit of that enjoy at least a presumption of legitimacy. Recall the context in which the Convention was introduced: drafted, agreed upon and ratified in the immediate aftermath of a war that had 'shocked the conscience of mankind' and ravaged the continent of Europe, this new human rights regime was intended and designed to protect against the future emergence of any analogous forms of totalitarianism, barbarism and state-inflicted cruelty. Seen in this light, there is an argument that the protection of human rights through application of the Convention gives the Court a certain moral purpose, character or nature.[9] The special purpose of human rights, and the commitment to their universal and equal protection, seen in this light, might be said to legitimate the Court's interference with decisions taken by sovereign states. Indeed, in many cases the Court has referred to the Convention's particular, rights-protecting character as underpinning its decision to take an evolutive, or otherwise innovative, approach to the development of Convention law.[10] Certainly, there are indications of such a view in the Preamble to the Convention itself, which states that fundamental freedoms are the foundation of justice and peace in the world. Of course, this is not to say that the mechanism by which the Convention protects human rights is necessarily either the morally preferable one or even morally defensible.

'Interim Measures: Are Some Opportunities Worth Missing?' (2021) 1 *European Convention on Human Rights Law Review* 1.

[6] European Court of Human Rights, *The Court Amends Rule 39 And The Practice Direction On Interim Measures* (ECHR 073, 2024) at https://hudoc.echr.coe.int/app/conversion/pdf/?library=ECHR&id=003-7911964-11013195&filename=Amendments%20to%20Rule%2039%20of%20the%20Rules%20of%20the%20Court%20and%20the%20Practice%20Direction%20on%20interim%20measures.pdf.

[7] See Conferences on the future of the European Court of Human Rights at https://edoc.coe.int/en/247-conferences-on-the-future-of-the-european-court-of-human-rights.

[8] Council of Europe, *Reykjavík Declaration. United Around Our Values* (2023), 4 at https://rm.coe.int/4th-summit-of-heads-of-state-and-government-of-the-council-of-europe/1680ab40c1.

[9] George Letsas, *A Theory of Interpretation of the European Convention on Human Rights* (Oxford University Press, 2007).

[10] See, for example, *Soering v the United Kingdom*, 7 July 1989, Series A no 161, para 87.

As will become clear throughout this book, there are issues about which there is profound moral disagreement across the Council of Europe, and which raise questions of the content and applicability of rights.[11] Abortion is, perhaps, an obvious example,[12] but so too are same-sex marriage,[13] the use of assisted reproductive technologies,[14] the right to choose the time and means of one's death,[15] and so on. When the Court, then, is asked to adjudicate upon such matters – as it is, from time to time – it must navigate murky waters and make decisions that are inconsistent with many people's moral values. In such cases there are strong arguments for saying that the Convention and the Court have no *prima facie* morality-related legitimacy in asserting, applying and promoting a human rights position; instead, for many, such questions are ones on which democratically elected and accountable politicians ought to make *policy*, and translate that policy into law.

Quite apart from these cases in which there is no agreed moral position – or notion of what is 'right' or 'wrong' – there are further question marks about the extent to which the Convention and the Court enjoy some form of morality-based legitimacy. The Convention primarily protects so-called civil and political rights, and pays remarkably little attention to socio-economic, cultural and group rights. Thus, whilst, for example, the right to a fair trial, to freedom of expression and to a private life are protected, the ECHR does not explicitly refer to a right to health, a right to food, a right to an adequate standard of living or a right to be free from poverty. It does not expressly recognise group and cultural rights, and it is constructed on a decidedly individualistic basis. One might question whether such a charter can really protect human rights in a way that not only prevents the state from engaging in cruelty of various forms, but also enables people to truly flourish.[16] We shall see in chapter 7 that some of these apparent substantive shortcomings have been mitigated through both the jurisprudence of the Court and the development of the European Social Charter, but still one might argue that the ECHR simply reinforces socio-economic inequalities – or at least does nothing positively to address them – and thus approaches human rights within a problematic, unequal and

[11] Jeremy Waldron, *Law and Disagreement* (Oxford University Press, 1999).

[12] See, for example, *A, B and C v Ireland* [2010] ECHR 2032; *Vo v France* [2004] ECHR 326; *Tysiac v Poland* [2007] ECHR 219.

[13] See, for example, *Chapin and Charpentier v France* [2016] ECHR 504; *Oliari and Others v Italy* [2015] ECHR 716; *Schalk and Kopf v Austria* [2010] ECHR 1996.

[14] See, for example, *Parrillo v Italy*, App no 46470/11 (ECtHR, 27 August 2015); *Costa and Pavan v Italy* [2012] ECHR 2040; *Evans v the United Kingdom* [2007] ECHR 264.

[15] See, for example, *Koch v Germany* [2012] ECHR 1621; *Haas v Switzerland* [2011] ECHR 2422; *Pretty v the United Kingdom* [2002] ECHR 427.

[16] See, for example, Liam Thornton 'The European Convention on Human Rights: A Socio-Economic Rights Charter?' in Suzanne Egan, Liam Thornton, Judy Walsh (eds), *Ireland and the European Convention on Human Rights: 60 Years and Beyond* (Bloomsbury, 2014) 227; Mashood Baderin and Robert McCorquodale, *Economic, Social, and Cultural Rights in Action* (Oxford University Press, 2007) 241–56.

statist paradigm. As a result, one might justifiably question whether the Convention's approach to rights protection really does endow it with sufficient moral purpose from which to derive legitimacy. It is however possible to argue that the status quo is a justifiable example of 'separation of responsibility' in international law. The Court was designed to ensure the most basic rights, which can often be realised simply by not interfering with people's private life, not torturing them or not preventing them from speaking. While the Court should ensure that this basic level is provided, other institutions, such as the European Committee of Social Rights, should be responsible for the gradual realisation of socio-economic rights, which almost inevitably stumble upon hard questions of redistribution of resources.

There are further accusations of exclusion or inadequacy that might be levied against the Convention. For example, there is a compelling argument to be made that the Convention, and its interpretation and application by the ECtHR, fails adequately to address the needs and rights of historically marginalised and subjugated groups such as women, the Roma, disabled people and religious minorities.[17] If this is the case, one might argue that the ECHR cannot solely draw on the claim of moral purpose to legitimate its overall operation.

Thus, whilst the moral purpose of rights protection provides some basis for a claim of legitimacy on the part of the Convention and its application by the Court, there are sufficient question marks about the morality of the Court's positions, and the inadequacy or incompleteness of the Convention system, for this to be an insufficient source of legitimacy in itself.

c. Method as a Basis for Legitimacy

We have already noted that input legitimacy relates to the processes by which decisions are made, so that the methods by which the ECtHR comes to its decisions might also be a source of legitimacy for the Convention and the Court. In this account, even an outcome on which there is, for example, profound moral disagreement might gain legitimacy from the process through which it has been reached. Thus, for the ECtHR, ensuring consistency, coherence, legal certainty and predictability is key to making a claim for legitimacy based on the method of decision making that is used. This is not particular to the Strasbourg Court. Indeed, ensuring that there is a clear and well-reasoned basis for the decision reached by a court, and ensuring consistency from one

[17] See, for example, Dia Anagnostou and Susan Millns, 'Individuals from Minority and Marginalized Groups before the Strasbourg Court: Legal Norms and State Responses from a Comparative Perspective' (2010) 16 *European Public Law* 393; Susana Martínez Guillem, 'European Identity: Across Which Lines? Defining Europe Through Public Discourses on the Roma' (2011) 4 *Journal of International and Intercultural Communication* 23; Lourdes Peroni and Alexandra Timmer, 'Vulnerable Groups: The Promise of an Emerging Concept in European Human Rights Convention Law' (2013) 11 *International Journal of Constitutional Law* 1056; Colin Harvey, 'Protecting the Marginalised: The Role of European Convention on Human Rights' (2000) 51 *Northern Ireland Legal Quarterly* 445.

case to another, is seen as elemental to the rule of law and judicial claims of legitimacy.[18]

Of course, the Court is not formally bound by any strict system of 'precedent',[19] but it does tend to refer to its previous judgments in its case law, and it will depart from its existing position only in exceptional cases. Thus, even without a formal system of precedent, an informal expectation that the ECtHR will follow its past jurisprudence operates. Indeed, as further discussed below, one of the ways in which a case can make its way to the Grand Chamber of the Court is where it does, or where it might, introduce an inconsistency or incoherence in the jurisprudence of the Court. Consistency and coherence in its case law is, then, something to which the Court gives close attention.

The method and quality of reasoning are also important to claims of input legitimacy. Thus, the Court provides the reasons for its decisions in a case, and in doing so tends to refer not only to its past judgments but also to the judgments of other courts and tribunals, to relevant reports, to states' practice and, sometimes, to scholarly work.[20] Of course, like most courts, it is occasionally criticised for the quality of its judgments, just as it is sometimes praised, but it is worth noting that the sheer workload facing the Court almost certainly creates significant challenges in ensuring that a high quality of reasoning is expressed in writing for every case that is decided before the Court. The Court's resources are extremely limited: its budget (which covers all non-capital costs from judicial salaries to the Registry) for 2024, for example, was slightly over €85 million;[21] by contrast, the budget for the Court of Justice of the European Union, which deals with a smaller number of cases, in 2023 was €487 million.[22] This gives some indication of how stretched the resources in the Court are, and thus how limited the support for judgment writing must be in terms of both time (for judges and Registry lawyers) and research support, so that the crucial administrative task of finding an appropriate balance between the quality of reasoning and speed of operations is a difficult one indeed.

Furthermore, the Court has developed, and applies, particular approaches to reasoning in its case law, which have the effect (and potentially also the

[18] See The Venice Commission. Rule of Law Checklist at www.venice.coe.int/images/SITE%20IMAGES/Publications/Rule_of_Law_Check_List.pdf. See also Jeremy Letwin, 'Why Completeness and Coherence Matter for the European Court of Human Rights' (2021) 2(1) *European Convention on Human Rights Law Review* 119.

[19] In *Micallef v Malta*, the Court stated that '[w]hile it is in the interests of legal certainty, foreseeability and equality before the law that the Court should not depart, without good reason, from precedents laid down in previous cases, a failure by the Court to maintain a dynamic and evolutive approach would risk rendering it a bar to reform or improvement': *Micallef v Malta*, App no 17056/06 (ECtHR, 15 October 2009), para 81.

[20] The examples are multiple. For analysis, see Kanstantsin Dzehtsiarou, 'What is law for the European Court of Human Rights?' (2018) 49 *Georgetown Journal of International Law* 89.

[21] ECHR Budget at www.echr.coe.int/Documents/Budget_ENG.pdf.

[22] CJEU 2023 At a Glance at https://curia.europa.eu/panorama/2023/en/at-a-glance.html#the-year-in-figures.

intention) of enhancing the legitimacy of its operations, its interpretation and application of the Convention, and the legitimacy of the entire ECHR system of rights protection. These techniques – such as proportionality, the margin of appreciation and extensive use of comparative law – are important ways in which the Court shows not only that it reasons its decisions carefully and rigorously, and takes states' national dynamics into some account, but also that it is willing to exercise self-restraint, and that its decisions can be benchmarked against those of other courts. We return to these questions of method in chapters 4 and 5.

Transparency is another feature of judicial method that can enhance the input legitimacy of a court. Unlike democratically elected institutions, courts are not accountable to the public, or at least not inasmuch as they can be voted out of office, for example. In many ways this is to ensure the independence and impartiality of judges. This lack of accountability can be compensated for by transparency in the adjudicatory process. Although deliberations of the judges are held behind closed doors, the hearings, when held, are open. In almost all cases the procedure is written; oral hearings are organised only for cases that are being heard in the Grand Chamber and a very small number of Chamber cases. The hearings are webcast on the Court's website. Almost all documents submitted by the parties and third parties are accessible by the public. Only internal judicial documents are confidential.

d. *Effectiveness as a Basis for Legitimacy*

We have already mentioned that output legitimacy is considered by reference to the outcome of the Convention and case law per se, that is it concerns whether or not the Convention actually 'works'. Where a system and instrument are effective, this adds to their legitimacy, particularly among stakeholders who might be highly reliant on the institution and system in question. Thus, effectiveness is a key indicator and source of legitimacy for the Convention and its system of enforcement.[23] However, in order to understand whether something is effective, we have to know what its purposes and objectives are, and in relation to the Convention this is something about which there is some disagreement. For some, the Convention exists now for the same reasons as it existed when it was first introduced: to act as a 'beacon to those at the moment in totalitarian darkness … [to] give them a hope of return to freedom'.[24] On this reading, the Convention is a safeguard in the most extreme of circumstances and not, necessarily, a set of human rights standards that can and do

---

[23] Shai Dothan, *Reputation and Judicial Tactics: A Theory of National and International Courts* (Cambridge University Press, 2015).

[24] Speech of Sir David Maxwell-Fyfe on the occasion of signing the European Convention on Human Rights, 4 November 1950. As quoted in Ed Bates, *The Evolution of the European Convention on Human Rights: From Its Inception to the Creation of a Permanent Court of Human Rights* (Oxford University Press, 2010) 5.

reach into every part of the state's domestic and, sometimes, overseas activities. However, that vision of the Convention's purpose reflects a limited and, arguably, outmoded concept of what human rights instruments are and are for. It also recognises only a certain kind of systemic oppression as needing or justifying the intervention of international standards.

Of course, it is impossible to see how Europe would have developed if no Convention had been signed in 1950, but the recent rise of far-right movements in Europe, development of illiberal democracies, and wars in Ukraine and Nagorno-Karabakh show that the Convention does not prevent war and totalitarianism. Furthermore, people across Europe continue to live under oppressive systems: LGBTQI people in parts of Europe are routinely persecuted, and even in 2025 attempts are being made to prohibit Pride marches through legislation. In some countries, Roma are not permitted to educate their children in a culturally appropriate manner. Muslim women are criminalised for their decision to dress in what they consider to be religiously appropriate ways. Asylum seekers are held in sub-standard detention centres. Victims of trafficking and sexual exploitation find themselves criminalised for 'illegal immigration' or participation in criminal activity. Trans people are denied respect and recognition for their gender identity. People are prosecuted for accessing abortion. Europe is rife with smaller and larger instances of oppression, abuse, detention and rights violation, and all too often domestic courts are unable or unwilling to provide a remedy. For many the ECHR is not only a pathway to justice but their only hope of it.

Seen this way, effectiveness is not only about ensuring that there is no widespread totalitarianism in Europe, which evidently the ECHR has not been able to achieve, but also about ensuring that people can and do rely on the Convention (in domestic law, in their everyday interactions with the state, and ultimately in litigation in Strasbourg) to help them to challenge and, ultimately, repress these forms of abusive state power.

Debate 2

Has the Court Entered into the Age of Subsidiarity?

We have already suggested that responsibility for protecting ECHR rights is shared between national and European institutions. The relationship between those institutions is a source of significant tension, and the Court has developed ways of managing it that stress the principle of subsidiarity and attempt to maintain legitimacy in the eyes of states. Former President of the ECtHR, Robert Spano, famously claimed that the Court is now in the 'age of subsidiarity',[25]

[25] Robert Spano, 'Universality or Diversity of Human Rights? Strasbourg in the Age of Subsidiarity' (2014) 14(3) *Human Rights Law Review* 487.

sparking significant debate[26] about the role and place of the Court vis-à-vis states.

The ECtHR has always been a subsidiary international court. This means that disputes about compliance with the Convention should first be dealt with in national courts, and only come to Strasbourg once domestic remedies have been exhausted. This is an important principle in the Convention: the Court is not an appellate court and it is not a substitute for national legal systems. Such understanding of subsidiarity is purely procedural. This rule, contained in Article 35, means that national institutions have the opportunity to resolve a Convention incompatibility without the need for international supervision, and that the Convention is applied domestically and thus becomes embedded in domestic law through practice. Controversy sometimes arises when the Court allows an applicant to bypass this rule because it establishes that there are no effective remedies to protect the applicant's rights in the domestic system.[27] This rare exception cannot undermine the fact that, as a general rule, the ECHR's approach to admissibility gives effect to procedural expectations of subsidiarity.

Understood as a substantive concept, subsidiarity might be said to mean that the Court should not only follow the national system in procedural and chronological terms, but also take into account the substance and process of decisions made at the national level in reaching its own judgment. Although this does not mean that the Court must blindly follow the national decision makers, what it likely does mean is that the Court is expected to recognise national decision makers as having a high level of knowledge of the domestic situation, law, politics and risks, and thus to grant at least some deference to those national decisions.

As already noted, subsidiarity was added to the Preamble to the Convention by means of Protocol 15, and it is obvious that the drafters of this Protocol meant substantive subsidiarity, as procedural subsidiarity has already been enshrined in Article 35. There are disagreements on many aspects of substantive subsidiarity starting from what it actually means in practical terms. The principle of subsidiarity can be used to underpin claims that the Court should leave states to do as they wish; that it should apply less scrutiny to states' human rights protection than it sometimes does. This same concern has been expressed by the former President of the ECtHR, Dean Spielmann, who said

[26] See, among many others, Michal Bobek's speech on the occasion of opening of the judicial year in 2024, 'Revisiting subsidiarity in the age of shared responsibility' at https://prd-echr.coe.int/documents/d/echr/speech-20240126-bobek-jy-eng.

[27] See, for example, *O'Keeffe v Ireland* App no 35810/09 (ECtHR, 28 January 2014). For discussion of exhaustion of domestic remedies in this case, see Conor O'Mahony, 'Subsidiarity of ECHR in O'Keeffe v. Ireland: A Response to Mr Justice Hardiman' in Laura Cahillane, James Gallen and Tom Hickey (eds), *Judges, Politics, and the Irish Constitution* (Manchester Scholarship Online, 2017) available at https://academic.oup.com/manchester-scholarship-online/book/35780/chapter-abstract/311650282?redirectedFrom=fulltext.

'I sometimes detect, a sense that subsidiarity is code for something else, for less scrutiny from Strasbourg. That it means taking the "self" out of judicial self-restraint'.[28] This points to the concern of some that states' expectations of 'subsidiarity' might be that the Court would simply 'stay out' of sensitive domestic matters; a position that is, of course, quite at odds with the basic idea of the Court's applying the Convention, and the Convention's being an effective protection of individual rights. This indicates some of the difficulties with pointing to subsidiarity as a source of legitimacy: it means different things, and creates different expectations, for different stakeholders.

Spano's approach to subsidiarity was somewhat different. He understood subsidiarity in terms of process-based review or procedural review.[29] This focuses not on *what* has been decided but on *how* it has been decided. Reviewing processes is less controversial than reviewing (or 'questioning') the substantive decisions made by national authorities, and in theory empowers states to make choices in hard cases. There are a few practical consequences of process-based review. First, the Court considers the quality of parliamentary debates. If a national parliament made a decision 'properly' and with due regard to human rights, the perception is that it will be less likely to be found in violation of the Convention. This does not mean that the substance of the decision is totally irrelevant, but the threshold to find a violation increases significantly. In other words, the decision made properly will be reversed only if it is clearly in violation of the Convention. A similar approach is employed in assessing the output of other decision-makers, such as national executive authorities, courts, and other bodies.

The turn to process-based review has led the Court to develop several tests to shape national courts' approaches. For instance, in *Murtazaliyeva v Russia*, the ECtHR considered how national courts should decide whether a defence witness must be questioned to satisfy the requirements of Article 6 (right to a fair trial). The Court formulated a three-pronged test to ensure Article 6 compliance, requiring national courts to consider:

1. Whether the request to examine a witness was sufficiently reasoned and relevant to the subject matter of the accusation?

[28] Dean Spielmann, 'Whither Judicial Dialogue?' (2015) at www.echr.coe.int/Documents/Speech_20151012_Spielmann_Sir_Thomas_More_Lecture.pdf, 10.

[29] See, for example, Janneke Gerards and Eva Brems (eds), *Procedural Review in European Fundamental Rights Cases* (Cambridge University Press, 2017); Patricia Popelier, 'The Court as Regulatory Watchdog: The Procedural Approach in the Case Law of the European Court of Human Rights' in Patricia Popelier et al (eds), *The Role of the Constitutional Courts in Multilevel Governance* (Cambridge University Press, 2013) 249; Oddny Mjoll Arnardóttir, 'The "Procedural Turn" under the European Convention on Human Rights and Presumptions of Convention Compliance' (2017) 15(1) *International Journal of Constitutional Law* 9. For a discussion beyond the ECtHR, see, for example, Leonie M Huijbers, *Process-based Fundamental Rights Review: Practice, Concept and Theory* (Intersentia, 2019).

2. Whether the domestic courts considered the relevance of that testimony and provided sufficient reasons for their decision not to examine a witness at trial?
3. Whether the domestic courts' decision not to examine a witness undermined the overall fairness of the proceedings?[30]

The major part of this test does not deal with what has been decided but with whether it was considered and reasoned. To use this specific test as an illustration: it will be less likely that the Court will find a violation of the Convention if the national court considered the relevance of the testimony, rather than in a case where this has not been done. The ECtHR will allow a wide margin of appreciation to the decisions of national courts, but if these decisions are missing completely then the likelihood of the violation is significantly increased.

This turn to process-based review is not without controversy. For some, the ECtHR has abdicated its function as human rights guardian. For others, it has shown self-restraint and developed a way to avoid second-guessing national authorities' judgement in complex cases, thus honouring its nature as a subsidiary court and enabling meaningfully shared responsibility for human rights protection across European and national authorities.

Debate 3

Should the Court be Further Reformed?

Before the ECtHR was established, individuals could not bring a complaint to an international body and demand that state authorities provide justifications for interfering with their human rights. This presented both opportunities and challenges to the Court. When states agreed to the jurisdiction of the Court, it was clear that they were consenting to some external judicial oversight with a resultant reduction in their right to simply rebut any criticisms of their treatment of their own people with claims of 'sovereignty', but the extent to which the Court would develop its jurisprudence, and the reach of the Convention into states' internal affairs, could not have been predicted with certainty. The ECtHR has become an incredibly important judicial institution, not only for the Council of Europe's member states but also internationally. Its judgments have major repercussions in domestic law and politics quite beyond what appears to have been contemplated at the time of its establishment.[31] Perhaps unsurprisingly, the Court has more or less always been in the midst of a reform

---

[30] *Murtazaliyeva v Russia* [2018] ECHR 1047, para 158.

[31] Helen Keller and Alec Stone Sweet, *A Europe of Rights: The Impact of the ECHR on National Legal Systems* (Oxford University Press, 2008); Iulia Motoc and Ineta Ziemele, *The Impact of the ECHR on Democratic Change in Central and Eastern Europe: Judicial Perspectives* (Cambridge University Press, 2016).

process. Some of these processes of reform were initiated by the state parties and formalised through the protocols, which can be substantive or procedural. Substantive protocols add human rights (for example, Protocol 1 included the right to private property (Article 1), the right to education (Article 2) and the right to free elections (Article 3) into the Convention) or substantive guarantees (for example, Protocol 6 prohibited the death penalty). Procedural protocols amend the structure and the working methods of the Court. These reforms are long and complex, and require formal agreement from the states. Other processes of reform were enacted by the Court through changes to its working methods and practice.

Reforms of the Court by Means of Protocols

As first designed, the ECHR system comprised three main organs supervising compliance with the ECHR in Strasbourg. First, there was the European Commission of Human Rights. When an applicant wanted to lodge a complaint, they would first submit it to the Commission, which would consider it and lodge it before the Court if it deemed it to be well founded. It outlined its reasons for these decisions in written opinions. Where that happened, the case would be considered by the ECtHR, which at that time was not a permanent body but met several times a year in Strasbourg. Then as now, the judgments of the Court were legally binding on the respondent party or parties to the case. The third institution was the Committee of Ministers, made up of representatives of each of the member states of the Council of Europe. The Committee of Ministers had some competence to resolve cases politically, but its main role was to supervise the implementation of decisions of the ECtHR.[32]

a. Protocols 11 and 14

The most significant institutional reform was introduced by Protocol 11, which came into force in 1998. It created the Strasbourg system of human rights protection as we know it today, and was introduced in response to the dramatic geopolitical changes in Europe and the expansion in members of the Council of Europe.

The key change introduced in Protocol 11 was abolition of the Commission. This meant that applicants could bring their complaints directly to the Court, rather than going through this 'filtering' system. Accordingly, the Court became a permanent institution[33] with full-time judges.[34] The right of individual petition and the jurisdiction of the Court became mandatory, meaning that, from that point on, all states ratifying the Convention had to accept the jurisdiction of the ECtHR, and all those within the jurisdiction of those states

[32] Protocol 11, Article 46, ECHR.
[33] ibid, Article 19.
[34] ibid, Article 21(3).

could make individual petitions to the ECtHR. The jurisdiction of the Court and the right of individual petition had to be specifically agreed to by the states before Protocol 11 came into force.

Following this institutional reform and the expansion of the membership of the Council of Europe, the number of individual petitions to the Court sky-rocketed. By 2011–2012 there were more than 150,000 pending applications to the Court,[35] and in 2013, 65,900[36] new applications were lodged. The Court was suffocating under this workload. For some, the Court was simply a victim of its own success: since its establishment it had become well known to people across Europe and was seen as the route to justice by people whose domestic legal system had, in their view, failed them.[37] Others were of the opinion that the number of pending applications reflected the failure of Contracting Parties to give proper effect to the Convention and the Court's judgments in their domestic legal systems, particularly given the high number of repetitive (or 'clone') cases coming before the Court.[38] These were cases relating to a question of legal interpretation that had already been established in the Court's jurisprudence, but either the state in question had failed to resolve the issue or other Contracting Parties had not adjusted their legal systems to take account of the Convention principles laid down in judgments of the Court in respect of which they were not respondents.

Whatever the cause (and failure to give effect to the Convention in domestic law is something we return to in chapter 2), all of this meant that the Court was in crisis: it simply did not have the capacity to deal with this volume of applications. The response was Protocol 14, which was opened for ratification in 2004. This allowed for procedural changes, including single-judge adjudication[39] for the speedy rejection of clearly inadmissible applications.[40] Although the drafters of this Protocol asked the Contracting Parties to ratify it urgently, it required ratification by all Contracting Parties before it could come into effect, and Russia, in particular, dragged its heels.[41] Indeed, the final

---

[35] 'The ECHR in Facts and Figures' (2011) at www.echr.coe.int/Documents/Facts_Figures_2011_ENG.pdf.

[36] 'The ECHR in Facts and Figures' (2013) at www.echr.coe.int/Documents/Facts_Figures_2013_ENG.pdf.

[37] See, for example, Phillip Leach, *Taking a Case to the European Court of Human Rights* (3rd edn, Oxford University Press, 2011); and Antoine Buyse and Michael Hamilton (eds), *Transitional Jurisprudence and the ECHR: Justice, Politics and Rights* (Cambridge University Press, 2011).

[38] See, for example, Fiona de Londras, 'Dual Functionality and the Persistent Frailty of the European Court of Human Rights' [2013] 1 *European Human Rights Law Review* 38; and Kanstantsin Dzehtsiarou and Alan Greene, 'Restructuring the European Court of Human Rights: Preserving the Right of Individual Petition and Promoting Constitutionalism' [2013] *Public Law* 710.

[39] Protocol 14, Article 26, ECHR.

[40] ibid, Article 12.

[41] See, for example, Bill Bowring, 'Russia and Human Rights: Incompatible Opposites?' (2009) 1(2) *Gottingen Journal of International Law* 257.

ratification (from Russia) did not come until 2010, at which point Protocol 14 came into force.

The changes introduced in 2010 were far less radical than had been brought about by Protocol 11. It allowed single judges to reject clearly inadmissible applications, whereas previously that required a committee of three judges.[42] Three-judge committees were then given a new competence to decide on repetitive or 'clone cases' on the basis of well-established case law.[43] Overall, then, Protocol 14 was primarily concerned with streamlining, whereas Protocol 11 had effectively retooled the entire Strasbourg machinery.

b. Protocols 15 and 16

Protocols 15 and 16 originate from the Brighton Conference on the future of the European Court of Human Rights.[44] The Declaration adopted as a result of this high-level meeting of the state parties to the Convention included many of the changes that these two Protocols introduced. Protocol 15 was more technical and procedural in nature, and apart from adding references to subsidiarity and the margin of appreciation to the preamble to the Convention, which was mentioned above, it introduced a few practical changes simplifying the Court's procedure or potentially reducing the number of applications. For instance, Protocol 15 reduced the time allowed for the submission of the application after the final decision at the national level from six to four months; it also simplified rejection of those applications that failed to demonstrate significant disadvantage as a result of a violation. This Protocol entered into force on 1 August 2021, with limited controversy.

In contrast, Protocol 16 continues to generate significant academic debate.[45] Unlike Protocol 15, which required ratification by all state parties, Protocol 16 required only 10 ratifications[46] and entered into force on 1 August 2018. This means that the mechanism established by this Protocol is available to only some of the state parties. The UK, Germany, Switzerland and Poland, among others, have not agreed to this Protocol. Pursuant to Article 1 of Protocol 16,

---

[42] Protocol 14, Article 27, ECHR.

[43] ibid, Article 28.

[44] For a detailed discussion of the drafting history of these protocols, see David Milner, 'Protocols no 15 and 16 to the European Convention on Human Rights in the context of the perennial process of reform: a long and winding road' (2014) 17(1) *ZEuS Zeitschrift für Europarechtliche Studien* 19.

[45] See, for example, Toon Moonen and Laurens Lavrysen, 'Abstract but Concrete, or Concrete but Abstact? A Guide to the Nature of Advisory Opinions under Procol No 16 to the ECHR' (2021) 21(3) *Human Rights Law Review* 752; Ada Paprocka and Michal Ziolkowski, 'Advisory Opinions under Protocol No. 16 to the European Convention on Human Rights' (2015) 11(2) *European Constitutional Law Review* 274; Gerards Janneke, 'Advisory Opinions, Preliminary Rulings and the New Protocol No 16 to the European Convention of Human Rights: A Comparative and Critical Appraisal' (2014) 21(4) *Maastricht Journal of European and Comparative Law* 630; Kanstantsin Dzehtsiarou and Noreen O'Meara, 'Advisory jurisdiction and the European Court of Human Rights: a magic bullet for dialogue and docket-control?' (2014) 34(3) *Legal Studies* 444.

[46] At the time of writing in September 2024, 22 states parties had ratified Protocol 16.

the highest courts and tribunals of a Contracting Party to the Convention may request the Court to give advisory opinions on questions of principle relating to the interpretation or application of the rights and freedoms defined in the Convention. This changed the type of advisory opinions that the Court could provide. Article 47 of the ECHR provided that the Court could give advisory opinions at the request of the Committee of Ministers on questions of interpretation of the Convention, provided those questions were not connected to the content and scope of the Convention rights and freedoms. The rationale for this restrictive regime was to avoid duplication of the Court's competencies across contentious cases and in advisory opinions. Given the restrictive nature of Article 47, there had been only three requests to deliver advisory opinions, and only two opinions were actually delivered by the ECtHR (both about election of ECtHR judges)[47] before Protocol 16 came into force.

Advisory opinions under Protocol 16 are different in two key ways. The requesting agents of these advisory opinions are national courts, as opposed to the Committee of Ministers, and the Court may not give advisory opinions on substantive questions of interpretation of the Convention rights.

Protocol 16 was deemed a 'protocol of dialogue'.[48] The idea was to establish an institutionalised way of cooperation between the ECtHR and national courts.[49] However, questions arise as to whether this can be achieved in practice. Under Protocol 16, all advisory opinions have to be adopted by the Grand Chamber of the ECtHR. Given that the Grand Chamber has a very limited capacity,[50] and that advisory opinions will have to be delivered promptly, one of two solutions will have to be adopted here: either the Grand Chamber will have to prioritise advisory opinions and delay decision-making in contentious cases, or the Court will have to start rejecting many requests to give advisory opinions. Both solutions are sub-optimal: the former may distract the Court from important contentious cases; and the latter may reduce the willingness of national courts to submit their requests. Since Protocol 16 entered into force, the Court has rejected three requests for advisory opinions and delivered

[47] The Court declared inadmissible the request to give an advisory opinion in Decision on the competence of the Court, 2 June 2004 at http://hudoc.echr.coe.int/eng?i=003-1339293-1397515. The Court delivered two advisory opinions: Advisory opinion on certain legal questions concerning the lists of candidates submitted with a view to the election of judges to the European Court of Human Rights [GC], 12 February 2008; Advisory opinion on certain legal questions concerning the lists of candidates submitted with a view to the election of judges to the European Court of Human Rights (no 2) [GC], 22 January 2010.

[48] Dean Spielmann, 'Opening Speech' in *Dialogue between Judges* (Strasbourg, 2014) 31; see also Noreen O'Meara, 'Reforming the European Court of Human Rights through Dialogue? Progress on Protocols 15 and 16 ECHR' at https://ukconstitutionallaw.org/2013/05/31/noreen-omeara-reforming-the-european-court-of-human-rights-through-dialogue-progress-on-protocols-15-and-16-echr/.

[49] Voland Thomas and Schiebel Britta, 'Advisory Opinions of the European Court of Human Rights: Unbalancing the System of Human Rights Protection in Europe?' (2016) 17(1) *Human Rights Law Review* 73, 74.

[50] It consists of 17 judges and delivers about up to 30 judgments per year.

seven opinions. The numbers are still fairly low and they do not overwhelm the Court. There are, however, other challenging issues related to Protocol 16 procedure: the legal force of advisory opinions, their ability to cause significant delay in the national cases and their utility for the decision-makers. It is hoped that these issues will be clarified when more opinions are produced by the Court.

Reforms of the Court by Means of Amendments to the Working Methods

Although Protocols are the means of formal treaty change within the Convention system, they are not the only way in which the working methods of the Strasbourg institutions can be reformed. Often the Court itself spearheads important reforms through changing its working methods and, particularly, its Rules of Court. The Rules of Court lay down the procedural workings of the Court and are not ratified by the Contracting Parties. Whilst the fact that these Rules come from the Court itself might be said to endow them with somewhat less legitimacy than the Convention and its Protocols, they have a considerable advantage over formal treaty change because they can be both flexibly applied and speedily amended. They can also assist the Court in developing and applying methods for the prompt handling of cases and, indeed, the reduction of the Court's backlog. Stricter or looser application of the Rules can reduce or increase the number of pending applications, as illustrated by the working of Rule 47.

Rule 47 simply lays down the format in which an application to the Court is to be made and makes clear what pieces of information must be included. However, for a very long time the Rule was not strictly applied, so that applications that did not conform with Rule 47 were still registered with the Court. Since 2014 this has changed. Now the Court has begun to apply this Rule more rigorously and has stopped registering applications that do not comply with it.[51] This has had a dramatic effect on the number of applications registered by the Court. Non-registration very often means that the Court will never have to deal with that application again, as the applicant sometimes cannot re-send the application in the correct format within the time limit of four months. Although one cannot prove an exact link between the strict application of Rule 47 and the number of registered applications to the Court, the statistics do show a temporal correlation between the two. In 2013, 65,800 applications were registered with the Court. In 2014, the figure was 56,200 (a reduction of 15 per cent) and in 2015 it was 40,650. More recently, the

---

[51] See, for example, Adam Wagner, 'Don't Mess Up Your European Court of Human Rights Application … A New Rule' (*UK Human Rights Law Blog*, 11 December 2013) at https://ukhumanrightsblog.com/2013/12/11/dont-mess-up-your-european-court-of-human-rights-application-a-new-rule; and Antoine Buyse, 'Stricter Rules for Lodging Complaints at the European Court' (*ECHR Blog*, 12 December 2013) at http://echrblog.blogspot.co.uk/2013/12/stricter-rules-for-lodging-complaints.html.

number of registered applications has remained fairly stable. In 2021, 44,250 applications were registered, in 2022 there were 45,500 and in 2023 there were 34,650. The lower number of applications in 2023 can be linked to Russia's expulsion from the Council of Europe in 2022, meaning that the Court can no longer accept complaints against Russia.

Several of the Court's innovations have stimulated debate over the years. The introduction of the pilot judgment procedure was perhaps among the most significant of such innovations. It was developed by the Court and was not initially reflected even in the Rules of Court,[52] although Rule 61 was later introduced. The pilot judgment procedure received a mixed reception from academics: some argued that it was damaging to human rights protection in certain cases,[53] while others called it 'the most creative tool the Court has developed in its first fifty years of its existence'.[54] Another commentator pointed out that 'the Court's judicial elaboration of the so-called "pilot judgment procedure" is an innovative response to the problem of repetitive cases'.[55]

Rule 61 explains that a pilot judgment should be used where 'the facts of an application reveal in the Contracting Party concerned the existence of a structural or systemic problem or other similar dysfunction which has given rise or may give rise to similar applications'.[56] In pilot judgments, the Court goes beyond the scope of an individual case and seeks to instigate wider change in the respondent state, often by requiring that it undertake specified reforms. In terms of effectiveness, the picture relating to the pilot procedure is mixed: in some cases it has led to substantial changes in national law and practice; in others, not suggesting these procedures might not be accompanied by sufficient enforcement mechanisms.

Reform of working methods is carried out within the Court's own internal structures – the Plenary Court, the Bureau and the Presidency – as are decisions about the strategic direction of the Court. The Plenary Court consists of all current Judges of the Court. It elects the President and other senior judges from its membership.[57] It also elects the Registrar and Deputy Registrar of

[52] See David T Björgvinsson, 'The "Pilot-Judgment" Procedure of the European Court Of Human Rights' in Gudmundur Alfredsson et al (eds), *International Human Rights Monitoring Mechanisms. Essays in Honour of Jakob Th Möller* (Brill | Nijhoff, 2009) 537.

[53] It was argued, for example, that pilot judgment procedure should not be applied 'where the underlying "systemic" problem is not a particular law or policy, but discriminatory state ideologies rooted in national history'. See Dilek Kurban, 'Forsaking Individual Justice: The Implications of the European Court of Human Rights' Pilot Judgment Procedure for Victims of Gross and Systematic Violations' (2016) 16 *Human Rights Law Review* 731, 733.

[54] Antoine Buyse, 'The Pilot Judgment Procedure at the European Court of Human Rights: Possibilities and Challenges' (2013) 3 *Law of Ukraine: Legal Journal* 303, 303.

[55] Markus Fyrnys, 'Expanding Competences by Judicial Lawmaking: The Pilot Judgment Procedure of the European Court of Human Rights' (2011) 12 *German Law Journal* 1231, 1232.

[56] Rule 61, 'Rules of Court', ECHR.

[57] Rule 8, 'Rules of Court', ECHR.

the Court,[58] and it adopts the Rules of Court and other significant changes in the Court's procedure. The Bureau consists of the most senior Judges of the Court[59] and seems to be one of the most important institutions of the Court, determining its everyday administration. According to the Rules of Court, the President directs the work and administration of the Court. The President also represents the Court and is responsible for its relations with the authorities of the Council of Europe. These internal structures play a vital role in the operation of the Court and the conduct of its judges. For example, voted on by the Plenary Court, the Resolution on Judicial Ethics allows the President to determine its application in individual cases, and he or she can consult the Bureau.

Debate 4

Who Are the Judges of the Court?

The judiciary of the ECtHR comprises 46 judges (one from each Contracting Party) who are resident in Strasbourg and work full-time in the Court. Since Protocol 14 entered into force, the Court can sit in four different formations: single judge; Committees of three judges; Chambers of seven judges; and a Grand Chamber of 17 judges. The formation of the Court that considers an application depends largely on (i) whether it is admissible and how complex the admissibility decision is, and (ii) the complexity of the merits of the case. The admissibility decision is essentially a question of whether the case complies with a formal set of criteria established by the Convention. Some of these criteria are quite technical (for example, every applicant should be a 'victim' of the alleged rights violation[60]), whereas others seem more substantive (for example, that an application is not manifestly ill-founded[61]). In contrast with judgments on the merits, decisions of inadmissibility are rarely published and often scarcely reasoned. The question remains, however, who those people who decide human rights cases in Strasbourg are and how they are appointed to the Court.

It is sometimes said that the judges of the ECtHR are nothing more than unelected bureaucrats. However, the reality is quite different. These judges are all experienced lawyers (some as practitioners, some as judges in their home jurisdictions, some as academics) who are nominated by their home state and then voted into office by the Parliamentary Assembly of the Council of Europe (PACE). The Contracting Party is required to draw up a shortlist of three nominees following a rigorous national procedure. After that the list is submitted

[58] Rules 15–16, 'Rules of Court', ECHR.

[59] Rule 9A, 'Rules of Court', ECHR.

[60] Article 35(3)(b), ECHR. See also Nikos Vogiatzis, 'The Admissibility Criteria under Article 35(3)(b) ECHR: A "Significant Disadvantage" to Human Rights Protection?' (2016) 65(1) *International and Comparative Law Quarterly* 185.

[61] Article 35(3)(a), ECHR. See also Janneke Gerards, 'Inadmissibility Decisions of the European Court of Human Rights: A Critique of the Lack of Reasoning' (2014) 14(1) *Human Rights Law Review* 148.

to the Advisory Panel of Experts on Candidates for Election as Judge to the European Court of Human Rights, which was created by the Committee of Ministers. The Panel checks whether the credentials of the candidates satisfy the requirements of Article 21 of the Convention. This Article specifies that the candidates must be of high moral character and must either possess the qualification required for appointment to high judicial office in their respective state or be Jurisconsults of recognised competence. The Committee of Ministers specified these criteria in their decisions, and these detailed criteria are also considered by the Panel. Finally, the Panel checks whether the selection process was fair, transparent and inclusive.[62] This procedure before the Panel is paper-based and confidential: in other words, the Panel does not interview candidates but only checks their CVs. Moreover, the outcome of the Panel's consideration is not published. If the Panel is of the opinion that replacing one or more candidates is necessary, it requests the state authorities to do so. If they do not comply, the report of the Panel is transferred to the Committee on the Election of Judges to the ECtHR.

The interview by this Committee is the next stage in the selection process. The members of this Committee are members of PACE, who ideally have a background in law or some legal experience, and are geographically spread across different states of the Council of Europe. After interviewing the candidates, this Committee prepares a report on each candidate and recommendations for the full PACE. The Committee can also return the list to the nominating government if it finds that one or more candidates do not satisfy the criteria enshrined in Article 21. Although this sounds like a somewhat drastic measure, it is not entirely unusual as, for example, interviews can reveal that a candidate's spoken French or English is not sufficiently developed for them to serve effectively on the Court. On the other hand, once the Committee is satisfied with the list of three candidates, it communicates its views to PACE, including an indication of the Committee's preferred choice. This information is made publicly available (as are the candidates' CVs) and PACE usually votes according to the recommendations of the Committee. The Article 21 criteria are, of course, somewhat vague, and there is no guarantee that their inclusion in the Convention will ensure that only highly qualified lawyers with expertise in human rights will actually end up serving as judges of the ECtHR. Nevertheless, they are not remarkably different from the kinds of qualifications for appointment as a judge that are found in many domestic jurisdictions, including the United Kingdom.[63]

That is not to say that the methods and processes for appointing judges to the Court are not worthy of review and consideration. Indeed, over the past decades, judicial appointment and independence have been prominent

[62] See Paul Mahoney, 'The Advisory Panel of Experts on Candidates for Election to the European Court of Human Rights' (2023) 4 *European Convention on Human Rights Law Review* 231.

[63] Constitutional Reform Act 2005.

concerns in debates surrounding the Court, even to the extent that election of judges was the subject of a special report from the PACE in 2011.[64] In 2023, the Steering Committee for Human Rights (CDDH), a body entrusted with designing reforms of the Strasbourg system and consisting of state parties' representatives, published another report on the issues related to judges of the ECtHR.[65] As is the case in many judicial systems, the process by which judges are selected is key to ensuring quality (including diversity) and independence on the bench.

The judges of the Court must be highly qualified lawyers. Their reputation and weight at the national level can increase the effectiveness and legitimacy of the Court. That said, the concept of qualification here requires some nuancing: there are some elements of the role that are not usually required in national judges. In many ways these are practical: the candidates should be able and willing to move to Strasbourg for the duration of their time on the Court, and they should be able to speak and work in both French and English. This is in addition to being substantively qualified and meeting the criteria of Article 21, as already mentioned. In addition, single-sex lists of nominees from states will be considered by the PACE only if the sex in question currently accounts for less than 40 per cent of the judges on the Court or if there are exceptional circumstances that justify derogating from the general rule, which is that single-sex lists are prohibited.[66] As well as these basic rules, a further check on the list of nominees that goes to the PACE is the fact that the candidates are required to present their qualifications in a standard CV format (to facilitate comparison between them).

The Convention states that PACE – the deliberative organ of the Council of Europe made up of members of the national parliaments of each member state – should elect a judge from a list of three candidates nominated by the Contracting Party.[67] It was previously the case that the states would send a list of three candidates in the order of their preference (rather than alphabetically), and the preferred candidate would normally be elected. In this system, the combination of politically motivated nominee selection at national level and lack of rigour at PACE level meant that judges of the Court were not always as well qualified or competent as they ought to have been.[68] However, the Council of Europe institutions now take a much more active role in screening candidates and assessing their suitability and qualification for the Court,

[64] 'Ad hoc judges at the European Court of Human Rights: an overview', Committee on Legal Affairs and Human Rights, AS/Jur (2011) at https://goo.gl/rs4gM7, 36.

[65] Available at https://rm.coe.int/issues-relating-to-judges-of-the-ecthr/1680aef54b.

[66] Resolution 1366 (2004) of the PACE, as amended by Resolution 1426 (2005) and Resolution 1627 (2008).

[67] Article 22, ECHR.

[68] See, for example, Loukis G Louciades, 'Reflections of a Former European Court of Human Rights Judge on his Experiences as a Judge' (2010) at http://www.errc.org/article/roma-rights-1-2010-implementation-of-judgments/3613/8.

including demanding more rigorous national processes. There are cases where the process of election of judges continued for years because the government kept failing to submit a satisfactory list. In the meantime, the previously elected national judge continues to work in Strasbourg, and although they cannot occupy administrative positions such as the President of the Court or the section president, they continue adjudicating cases.

This multi-layered process of selection makes for a sometimes slow and somewhat cumbersome process of judicial appointment to the ECtHR, but it is designed to increase the likelihood that only qualified candidates will end up serving in the Court. It cannot, of course, entirely guard against governments' nomination of, and the PACE's election of, 'governmental agents', but it does reduce the likelihood that bad-faith nominations will result in under-qualified judges who act in a partisan manner in favour of their own states.

The Principle of National Representation

Every Contracting Party has a judge on the Court through the so-called principle of national representation. This is intended to ensure that in every case there is always someone with expertise in the national legal systems that are being examined, and as a result the judge from the respondent state is always a member of the Chamber or Grand Chamber in which a case is being considered.[69] Thus, if a case is brought against Iceland, the Icelandic judge will be a member of the Chamber; and if the case is referred to the Grand Chamber, she can sit in the Grand Chamber again in the same case. While the rationale is that this national judge will be able to inform their colleagues about the particularities of the national system, this does not necessarily require a sitting judge from that country. For example, this (admittedly important) task could be done by a non-voting judge in the case, or even by a qualified Registry lawyer preparing briefs in respect of the system in question. We make this point because the principle of national representation has some potentially undesirable implications for judicial independence, whether actual or perceived, in the Court.

First, the knowledge that the national judge will always sit in a case against the Contracting Party may create some perverse incentives for the state in question to nominate 'loyal' judges to the Strasbourg Court. The processes described above are designed to guard against that, but they cannot absolutely prevent it. Second, the national judge can hear the same case twice where, as in our example above, it is heard in the Chamber and then successfully referred to the Grand Chamber, which would not usually be permitted in a national judicial system. As a result, some judges prefer to recuse themselves from sitting in the Grand Chamber and an ad hoc judge is nominated from the Contracting Party to sit as the 'national' judge in the case in question. Where this happens,

[69] Article 26(4), ECHR.

it can effectively resolve the potential conflict identified here, but judges are under no obligation to take this route. This brings us to the third concern with the principle of national representation: it has resulted in a system of ad hoc judges who serve where the national judge cannot sit on the case. This might be for reasons of principle, as noted above, or, for example, because the case is one in which the judge was involved (as advocate or judge) in the national system before being appointed to Strasbourg. Whilst on the face of it the system of ad hoc judges is perfectly reasonable, if not sensible, it was the cause of considerable controversy for some time. It has been argued that governments would sometimes appoint a particular judge for a particular case; the pool was not stable and instead a government would be asked for an ad hoc judge for a specific case. Often this ad hoc judge would be drawn from sitting judges in the national system, and it is not unusual that a government would be aware of the personal views of its more senior judges in relation to particular issues or controversial areas of law. The concern was that this kind of informal knowledge influenced the selection of ad hoc judges, in relation to whom the procedural safeguards in PACE that apply to the appointment of permanent judges to Strasbourg do not operate. Now, however, some precautions have been taken against this. Contracting Parties must submit a list of three potential ad hoc judges, one of whom is to be selected by the President of the Section to sit on the case in question (or, in the case of the Grand Chamber, by the President of the Court).[70] Whilst this addresses concerns, it does not, of course, resolve them, as there are no required procedures for selection of the shortlist of three that goes to the Court. Some states have gone further than this and choose to invite an existing judge of the Court, who was nominated by another state, to act as its ad hoc judge when the situation arises. This has been done by Luxembourg, Lithuania, North Macedonia and Hungary, for example, but the practice is not at all widespread. Moreover, some countries, like Serbia or Montenegro, have not submitted the list at all.

Length and Conditions of Tenure

In the Strasbourg system, as elsewhere, conditions of tenure are key to helping maintain and guarantee judicial independence. Article 23 of the Convention lays down that judges can be appointed for one, non-renewable nine-year term only (previously, renewable six-year terms[71]). Previously, a judge had to retire after they reached the age of 70. Protocol 15 changed this approach and now the candidates cannot be nominated by the state if they are over 65 years of age; but if nominated, they can serve their full tenure. This was done to avoid

[70] Rule 29, 'Rules of Court', ECHR.

[71] Alastair Mowbray, 'Protocol 14 to the European Convention on Human Rights and Recent Strasbourg Cases' (2004) 4(2) *Human Rights Law Review* 331, 335–36.

very short tenures when judges could sit for only four to five years on the bench. This also pushed the retirement age to 74, or even more in some cases.

It was not always the case that the judges on the Court had particularly well-developed conditions of tenure. There is no clear and guaranteed pathway back to work following a term of office in Strasbourg. The judges cannot normally keep their positions at the national level during their time in Strasbourg, meaning that when it is time to retire from the ECtHR, some judges have no further career at the national level. There is no guarantee of employment for the judges, and it is possible that they might be more prone to influence at the end of their tenure in the Court to secure some chances of getting into the highest judicial offices back home. Although there is general concern about the post-tenure career path of ECtHR judges, the issue has not yet been effectively addressed.

Debate 5

What Is the Role of the Registry within the Structure of the Court?

Although the judges are the primary decision makers, the Registry of the Court contains its institutional memory, and much of its intellectual and organisational capacity. Whilst judges are in Strasbourg for nine years only, some members of the Registry spend their whole careers working at the ECtHR. The Registry also exercises considerable influence over the Court, even making prima facie decisions about whether cases are clearly inadmissible or not. In spite of this, the Convention itself describes the Registry very briefly. Article 24 provides that the Court shall have a Registry, the functions and organisation of which shall be laid down in the Rules of Court. However, the Rules are also not comprehensive in this respect. The Registry consists of lawyers from across the Contracting Parties. Ordinarily these would be drawn from most, if not all, Contracting Parties and would normally deal with the applications coming from their countries of origin. The Registrar and Deputy Registrar are the heads of the Registry, and they are responsible for its organisation and activities.

Although the Registry is somewhat in the shadows, its work is crucial. Given the very large workload of the Court, a number of tasks that we tend to associate with judges are actually carried out by members of the Registry. In this the ECtHR is hardly alone, but it is nevertheless noteworthy. For example, it is not unusual for a Registry lawyer to prepare a first draft of a judgment. Of course, the last word belongs to the judges, who can suggest amendments and redraft certain parts, but very often the Registry first proposes the reasoning. The specific details of the drafting process depend, however, on whether the case is dealt with by the single judge, Committee, Chamber or Grand Chamber of the Court.[72]

In practice, a Registry lawyer usually decides the formation of the Court to which a case is initially assigned. So, where the preliminary Registry decision is that the application is clearly inadmissible, it is assigned to a single-judge formation. A judge should not receive any such application from the state of which they are a member, and so judges who are sitting in single-judge formations are assigned particular states. The obligations of a single judge rotate among the members of the Court. This points to an important issue, and one which we return to in chapter 3: in practice, it is a Registry lawyer who is deciding on admissibility in these cases, with the formal decision then taken by the Court sitting in a single-judge formation. Certainly, if that single judge does not agree with the Registry determination, they can refer it to a larger formation of the Court, but this does not happen very often in practice. This shows that seemingly administrative decisions in the Registry can carry serious weight in the Court per se and effectively determine the fate of an application. More complex questions as to admissibility are decided by a Committee, Chamber or Grand Chamber. Admissibility decisions are final and cannot be reviewed. While single judge cannot decide cases on merits, Committees, Chambers and Grand Chamber can. The allocation of the case depends on its complexity. Repetitive cases that can be decided on the basis of the well-established case law by the three-judge Committees. The Committees' judgments are final.

Administratively the Court is further divided into five Sections, one with 10 judges and four with nine. Sections are established for three-year periods, should be balanced in terms of gender and geographic representation, and should reflect the different legal systems among the Contracting Parties.[73] Each Section has a President who is one of the judges from the state allocated to the Section. Sections do not decide any cases themselves, but usually the judges for Chambers are drawn from the judges allocated to a single Section.

For a variety of reasons, some cases end up in the Grand Chamber, which with its 17 judges is the most authoritative formation of the Court. Not only is the Grand Chamber the largest formation, but it also always contains its most senior judges: the President, the Vice-Presidents of the Court and the Presidents of the Sections. The Grand Chamber hears a very small number of cases per year when one considers the workload of the Court overall. Ordinarily, it only hands down no more than 30 judgments every year, although there is

[72] For more details on how cases are deliberated and drafted, see Helen Keller and Corina Heri, 'Deliberation and Drafting: European Court of Human Rights (ECtHR)' in *Max Planck Encyclopaedia of International Law* (Oxford University Press, 2019) at https://opil.ouplaw.com/display/10.1093/law-mpeipro/e3210.013.3210/law-mpeipro-e3210.

[73] Rule 25(2), 'Rules of Court', ECHR.

no strict limit on the number of cases it can hear. There are only two routes, though, by which an individual complaint can end up in the Grand Chamber.

The first is that a party to the case makes an application (known as a referral) under Article 43 of the Convention within three months of a Chamber judgment. A panel of five judges will then decide whether the case raises a serious question as to the interpretation or application of the Convention, or a serious issue of general importance; if so, it refers the case to the Grand Chamber for new consideration. Very few referral applications under Article 43 are successful. The second route to the Grand Chamber is by 'relinquishment' under Article 30. This happens when the Chamber dealing with the case decides that the Grand Chamber should determine it instead of the Chamber itself. According to Article 30, this should happen where the case raises a serious question of interpretation of the Convention, or where the resolution of a question might be inconsistent with a judgment previously decided by the Court.

Registry lawyers play a crucial role in determining the destiny of applications to the Court. This is demonstrated by just three examples. First, they decide whether the application complies with the formalities for application so that it is processed at all. Second, they decide whether it is clearly inadmissible, in which case it goes to a single judge. Third, there may be cases in which the deciding judge(s) does not have competence in the language in which the application is submitted, in which case they must rely on the note summarising the application that has been submitted by the member of the Registry.[74] Although Registry lawyers have a significant role in the operation of the Court, much of what the Registry does is not subject to public accountability mechanisms such as the media scrutiny to which the judges on the Court are subjected. Thus, it is crucial for the operation of the entire Convention system that the integrity and independence of the Registry is checked and guaranteed. Registry lawyers maintain significant discretion in deciding the fate of an application.[75] Strangely, however, the Registry is rarely considered in depth in other academic treatments of the Court.

Protecting and guaranteeing the independence of the Registry means, as a first step, ensuring the independence of the lawyers who work there; and that, in turn, requires some understanding of the institutional structure in question. The Registry has a hierarchal structure, with the Registrar and Deputy Registrar at the top and mostly temporarily employed lawyers at the bottom of the pyramid. The Registrar is appointed by the Plenary of the Court, usually from within the Court's Registry itself. The Registrar is elected for the period of five years and can be re-elected. Marialena Tsirli, who is the current Registrar of the Court, began working in Strasbourg in 1994 and was appointed a Registrar in 2020. The Registry is divided into five Sections, which are equivalent to

[74] Rule 18A, 'Rules of Court', ECHR.

[75] See Cosette Creamer and Zuzanna Godzimirska, 'Trust in the Court: The Role of the Registry of the European Court of Human Rights' (2019) 30(2) *European Journal of International Law* 665.

the Sections of the Court. Each of the Sections has a Section Registrar and a Deputy Section Registrar. They organise the work of lawyers allocated to each Section. All lawyers working in the Registry can be roughly divided into three categories: the permanent lawyers, who have either permanent or permanent in practice contracts; seconded lawyers; and those with temporary contracts. While permanent lawyers are protected from external influences by the longevity of their contracts, seconded and temporary lawyers are more vulnerable from this perspective.

Seconded lawyers are lawyers who are usually employed by the member states, and they are sent to the Court for a period of a few years to help the Court to deal with the cases usually brought against their state. They keep their domestic position while in the Strasbourg and they are paid directly by the state in question. The concerns about the appropriateness of access of such lawyers to the Court were highlighted in scholarship.[76] However, the agreement to recruit such lawyers remains with the ECtHR; moreover, the multiple levels of supervision ('quality checks') might minimise but not remove the potential challenges associated with these lawyers.

The Court has a questionable employment strategy for the third category of lawyers: temporary lawyers (so-called B-lawyers). They are employed on four-year contracts that cannot be extended and which do not have any pathways for internal promotion.[77] As with any short-term contractual employment, this is sub-optimal.[78] Fixed-term employees have fewer incentives to develop institutional loyalty than permanent employees, and perhaps this is even more the case since they cannot, by the terms of their contract, be promoted in that institution.[79] Furthermore, four years is a relatively short cycle in circumstances in which one is learning the (somewhat idiosyncratic) ropes of the institution at the start and seeking new employment (by necessity) at the end.[80] In spite of this, however, it is B-lawyers who are often entrusted with the crucial task of first screening and filtering the incoming applications. Clearly, ensuring the independence and job security of B-lawyers is vital, but it is to date not taken seriously enough by the Court.

Within the Registry there are a number of departments. The Directorate of Jurisconsult is of particular interest here. Rule 18B of the Rules of Court provides that the Court shall be assisted by a Jurisconsult for the purposes of ensuring the quality and consistency of its case law. The Jurisconsult provides

---

[76] Kanstantsin Dzehtsiarou and Donal K Coffey, 'Legitimacy and Independence of International Tribunals: An Analysis of the European Court of Human Rights' (2014) 37 *Hastings International and Comparative Law Review* 271, 310–13.

[77] Kanstantsin Dzehtsiarou, 'One of the Keys to the ECHR Problems' (*Human Rights in Ireland*, 11 September 2012).

[78] ibid.

[79] ibid.

[80] ibid.

opinions and information to the judicial formations and members of the Court. This is a significant task; for example, a Jurisconsult on a regular basis draws the attention of judicial formations to those draft decisions and judgments in pending cases that may create potential conflicts with the case law. Although the judges are free to disagree with the opinions of the Jurisconsult, they are usually taken seriously. As might be expected, however, the Jurisconsult's notes on pending cases are confidential, so it is difficult to assess the impact of this office in real terms. The Jurisconsult is chosen by the Bureau of the Court after a public competition. The Secretary General of the Council of Europe makes the formal appointment.

Apart from highlighting possible tensions in the case law of the Court, the Directorate of Jurisconsult is entrusted with other important tasks, such as facilitating some external relations of the Court and managing the Court's library and the Court's case-law database (HUDOC). Lawyers of the office of Jurisconsult are entrusted with the important task of preparing comparative research reports for some Chamber and nearly all Grand Chamber cases. These reports are requested where a Judge Rapporteur determines that the case is complex and that it is important to know how the matter at hand is dealt with in the other member states to the Convention. Some of these reports also provide information about the Court's own case law, international legal norms, EU law and other comparative jurisdictions on the issue under consideration. Information on national legislation and practice for the comparative research reports is provided by the liaison officers working in the supreme and/or constitutional courts of member states, which form the Superior Courts Network created by the ECtHR. National lawyers working in the Registry also contribute to such reports by providing clarifications on their respective national legal orders. Where they are prepared, these comparative law reports are available to the judges sitting in the case but they are not open to the general public. Arguably, these reports make the reasoning and judgments of the Court more informed and enhance the legitimacy and persuasiveness of the Court's rulings, and they can be influential when the Court is determining the presence or absence of European consensus (which we discuss further in chapter 4).

Another important recent development for which the Directorate of Jurisconsult was responsible was the creation of the Knowledge Sharing platform of the Court.[81] This platform contains the most recent updates on the case law, as well as guides on various Articles of the Convention that summarise key standards of the Court. In effect, the Jurisconsult plays a central role in determining which cases are to be highlighted and which provide the most authoritative standards.

[81] Available at https://ks.echr.coe.int/web/echr-ks.

What this short overview of the Registry illustrates is that this important part of the Court is critical to its operation and has the capacity to exert significant influence over its work. This makes it all the more surprising that it is so infrequently considered in the literature: it is not particularly transparent about its operations, and quite inattentive to the independence and job security of many of its members.

Debate 6

What Are the Consequences of Expulsion from the Council of Europe?

On 16 March 2022, Russia became the first member state of the Council of Europe to be expelled from the organisation, reducing the membership from 47 to 46 states. Anticipating its expulsion, Russia gave notice of its intention to withdraw from the Convention and the Council of Europe on 15 March 2022.[82] The reason for Russia's expulsion was of course violations of international law and the full-scale military attack on another member state of the Council of Europe: Ukraine. Although the process of expulsion, as well as a broader question of the utility of expulsion from an international organisation, is a matter of academic debate,[83] we will concentrate here only on the issues that the Council of Europe organs had to deal with in relation to jurisdiction of the Court vis-à-vis Russia.

The European Convention is a closed treaty, which means that only members of the Council of Europe can be parties to the Convention. Thus, when Russia was expelled from the Council on 16 March 2022, the key issue was whether the expelled state should stop being party to the Convention on the day of the expulsion (ie when it ceased to be a member of the Council of Europe) or six months later (ie mirroring what happens when a state voluntarily withdraws from the Council of Europe). Article 58 of the Convention is not clear on this point,[84] and the only other instance when a state left the Council of Europe (Greece in the 1960s) was not instructive, as that was a case of withdrawal rather than expulsion. There were clear advantages to treating the Court as continuing to have jurisdiction over Russia for

---

[82] Russian Federation, Foreign Ministry Statement on Initiating the Process for Withdrawing from the Council of Europe (15 March 2022) (Russian Withdrawal).

[83] See, for example, Frederick Cowell, 'Council of Europe Expulsion and the European Convention on Human Rights: The Foundations of Involuntary Treaty Withdrawal' (2025) 74 *International and Comparative Law Quarterly* 1.

[84] Kanstantsin Dzehtsiarou and Laurence Helfer, 'Russia and the European human rights system: Doing the right thing … but for the right legal reason?' (*EJIL:Talk!*, 29 March 2022) at www.ejiltalk.org/russia-and-the-european-human-rights-system-doing-the-right-thing-but-for-the-right-legal-reason/.

another six months, given the ongoing hostilities in Ukraine and escalating repression within Russia. Given this, and as it was not clearly prohibited by the wording of the Convention to do so, the Committee of Ministers and the Court declared that the Convention would apply to Russia for a further six months, until 16 September 2022.

It was also quite clear that the Russian authorities would not comply with any the judgments coming from the Court after being expelled from the organisation. The Court thus needed to consider how to treat the thousands of unresolved applications against Russia that were before it at the point of expulsion. Suggestions ranged from complete dismissal of such applications, to 'freezing' them on the one end of the spectrum or continuing as if nothing had happened.[85] For pragmatic reasons, and bearing in mind the Court's continuing jurisdiction for a further six months after expulsion, pending applications were neither frozen nor dismissed. Rather, the Court continued to deal with such cases, though, we can assume, with an eye to which cases to prioritise. This offered an important opportunity for the Court to develop its case law in certain sensitive areas without being unduly worried about the respondent state's response, as, patently, Russia was not going to comply with post-expulsion judgments in any case. Thus in *Fadeyeva v Russia*, the Court effectively required the respondent state to implement legal recognition of same-sex unions;[86] and in the inter-state case of *Ukraine v Russia (re Crimea)*, the Court significantly developed its understanding of the law of occupation and found multiple violations of the Convention by Russia.[87]

Conclusion

This chapter set out and debated critical matters that underpin the whole structure of the ECtHR. We will refer to the debates in this chapter throughout the book. The Strasbourg system of human-rights protection needs to be well balanced and effectively structured in order to work, and in order to be able to make reasonable claims to legitimacy. The Court and its judges should be independent and competent to ensure input legitimacy; other bodies of the Council of Europe must work with the Contracting Parties to enhance the effectiveness of the ECtHR's judgments to improve their output legitimacy. Combined with the perceived moral legitimacy of pursuing rights protection, these structures contribute to the perceived legitimacy of the Court, and thus to the workings of the Convention system for the protection of human rights.

---

[85] Ed Bates, Kanstantsin Dzehtsiarou and Andrew Forde, *Russia, the Council of Europe and the European Convention on Human Rights* (Bristol University Press, 2025).

[86] *Fadeyeva and Others v Russia* App no 50345/18 (ECtHR, 16 January 2025).

[87] *Ukraine v Russia (re Crimea)* App nos 20958/14 and 38334/18 (ECtHR, 25 June 2024).

Further Reading

Ed Bates, *The Evolution of the European Convention on Human Rights: From Its Inception to the Creation of a Permanent Court of Human Rights* (Oxford University Press, 2010).

Robert Spano, 'Universality or Diversity of Human Rights? Strasbourg in the Age of Subsidiarity' (2014) 14(3) *Human Rights Law Review* 487.

Oddny Mjoll Arnardóttir, 'The "Procedural Turn" under the European Convention on Human Rights and Presumptions of Convention Compliance' (2017) 15(1) *International Journal of Constitutional Law* 9.

George Letsas, *A Theory of Interpretation of the European Convention on Human Rights* (Oxford University Press, 2007).

Ed Bates, Kanstantsin Dzehtsiarou and Andrew Forde, *Russia, the Council of Europe and the European Convention on Human Rights* (Bristol University Press, 2025).

Toon Moonen and Laurens Lavrysen, 'Abstract but Concrete, or Concrete but Abstact? A Guide to the Nature of Advisory Opinions under Protocol No 16 to the ECHR' (2021) 21(3) *Human Rights Law Review* 752.

2

Sovereignty and Authority

The European Convention on Human Rights (the Convention or ECHR) does not operate in a vacuum: it is only one of a number of legally binding international instruments with which states must comply at any given time, and which must somehow be harmonised if states are to meet all of their legal obligations. This raises challenging questions that arise in different ways in different circumstances: first, a 'contest' can emerge between the Convention as interpreted and applied by the European Court of Human Rights (the Court or ECtHR) and domestic law, including often domestic constitutional law. In these situations, concerns and claims as to national sovereignty add a particular dimension to the debates about authority, which we consider in Debate 1. A second set of questions arises when it comes to the relationship between the Convention and other bodies of international law, such as European Union (EU) law and the UN Security Council. States need to comply with multiple legal obligations at the same time. For reasons of practicality, these obligations must be reconcilable. In these circumstances, the ECtHR may be required to determine how all of these obligations can apply in harmony, and in a manner that effectively protects human rights. We consider the relationship between the EU and the ECHR in Debates 2 and 3, and between the Convention and other sources of international law in Debate 4.

Debate 1

Who Has the Final Word in Human Rights Cases: The Court or the Contracting Parties?

This part of this chapter is about the distribution of power between the Contracting Parties and the ECtHR: who is the ultimate policy maker in the area of human rights standards? This is a question that leads to major tensions. It is almost inevitable that at some point a respondent party to a case will be unhappy with the judgment of the Court. As we saw in chapter 1, the Court was created to supervise Contracting Parties' compliance with the Convention, and can thus make legally binding findings[1] that a state has violated the Convention, limiting the sovereign privilege of the Contracting States to set their own human rights agendas without reference to international standards.

It is entirely to be expected that Contracting Parties may sometimes be unhappy with and criticise judgments of the Court, but in some extreme cases this criticism can lead to a 'stand-off'. It is such a stand-off we are primarily concerned with here. When constructively put, states' negative reactions to the Court's decisions may encourage the Court to find a more nuanced position, engage in judicial dialogue, create feedback loops[2] and carefully navigate the boundaries of its competence. However, few such benefits flow where there is a stand-off between the Court and a member state.

The exchange of rulings between the ECtHR and the UK Supreme Court in the *Al-Khawaja/Horncastle* cases is a good illustration of an effective feedback loop between the Court and Contracting Parties.[3] These cases concerned the rule that allowed hearsay evidence (any statement of fact other than the one made, of his own knowledge, by a witness in the course of oral testimony)[4] to be admitted in certain circumstances. It was claimed that this violated the Court's 'sole and decisive test', which means that if the testimony of an absent witness is the sole and decisive reason for conviction, a violation of Article 6 of the ECHR will be almost automatically established.[5] There is thus a tension between the hearsay rule of evidence in the domestic law of evidence and the ECtHR-established case law on the right to a fair trial. This tension was surfaced by *Al-Khawaja and Tahery v the United Kingdom*.[6]

Al-Khawaja had been convicted of indecent assault on the basis of statements from a victim who died before she could be cross-examined in court. These statements were the only direct evidence in the case. The Chamber of the ECtHR found a violation of the Convention, because the judgment of the national court relied solely on the hearsay evidence. Given the extent to which such a finding would disrupt the settled laws of evidence in the UK, it was referred to the Grand Chamber.

However, before the Grand Chamber case could be heard, the UK Supreme Court had an opportunity to present its legal position on the same issue in the case of *R v Horncastle*.[7] The Supreme Court expressed the view that the 'sole and decisive test' that was developed by the ECtHR was too rigid and inflexible to be practicable and did not take into account various safeguards provided

---

[1] Article 46, ECHR.

[2] Kanstantsin Dzehtsiarou, 'Keep Me in the Loop: Feedback Exchange between the European Court of Human Rights and State' (2023) 22(3) *Law and Practice of International Courts and Tribunals* 591.

[3] *Al-Khawaja and Tahery v the United Kingdom* [2011] ECHR 2127; and *R v Horncastle* [2009] UKSC 14.

[4] *Horncastle* (n 3).

[5] *Al-Khawaja and Tahery v United Kingdom* (n 3).

[6] ibid.

[7] *Horncastle* (n 3).

by national law in the common law criminal justice system. In other words, the Supreme Court expressed the view that the ECtHR had misunderstood the safeguards related to the hearsay rule and thus had acted in error in finding that it violated Article 6. The Supreme Court's disagreement with ECtHR jurisprudence was thus underpinned by detailed and careful comparison between English law and the law of the ECHR.

The Supreme Court's reaction to *Al-Khawaja and Tahery* turned out to be influential in the Grand Chamber's later consideration of the case. Building on the Supreme Court's judgment, the Grand Chamber found no violation of Article 6 in relation to Mr Al-Khawaja. In doing so, it reassessed the 'sole and decisive test' and made it more flexible to account for the safeguards provided in domestic law. Judge Bratza, in his concurring opinion, called this exchange of legal opinions 'a good example of the judicial dialogue'.[8] In reality, it is rather unusual for a national court to have the opportunity to intervene more or less directly in this way: the period of time between the Chamber and Grand Chamber decisions is usually relatively short, and an appropriate case does not always arise in the domestic courts. That does not mean, however, that no other opportunities for feedback loops arise. The judges of the ECtHR and national authorities have multiple opportunities for engaging in informal feedback loops, through conferences, personal interactions, extra-curial speeches and writings, and quasi-social events such as the opening of the judicial year in the ECtHR. More formally, a national court can request an advisory opinion from the ECtHR and then give feedback on this ruling in its own judgment. National judges also play a crucial role in implementation of the ECtHR judgments and can offer their feedback by fine-tuning the ECHR case law rule to the scenarios in their practice. Although there are obvious benefits in engaging in feedback loops with the Court, they are not without costs. The ECtHR has to invest resources in analysing various types of feedback and react to them. More importantly, feedback from the states may result in a downward calibration of the human rights standards developed by the Court. To some extent, one might argue this is what happened in *Al-Khawaja and Tahery*: the ECtHR's more stringent and demanding rule was relaxed to accommodate existing domestic standards and practices. However, the (in)famous prisoner-voting case law of the Court is perhaps the clearest illustration. Here, the feedback exchange lasted for years, and states expressed fairly damaging criticism of the position of the Court.[9]

In the 2005 case of *Hirst v the United Kingdom (No 2)*, the ECtHR found that the UK law prohibiting prisoners from voting violated the right to free

---

[8] See *Al-Khawaja and Tahery v United Kingdom* (n 3), concurring opinion of Judge Bratza.

[9] See generally Alessandra Osti, 'Prisoners' voting rights and the long-lasting political resistance to the implementation of the European Court of Human Rights' judgments' in Gabriella Citroni, Irene Spigno and Palmina Tanzarella (eds), *The Right to Political Participation: A Study of the Judgments of the European and Inter-American Courts of Human Rights* (Routledge, 2022), 233.

elections as protected by Article 3 of Protocol 1.[10] Whilst a state could impose a ban on some prisoners voting, the UK's blanket ban breached the Convention and thus, in the view of the Court, required reform. The political reaction in the UK was negative: an overwhelming majority in Parliament voted to maintain the law as it was, with many claiming that it was Parliament, not the ECtHR, that should take this decision. The Government expressed a similar sentiment, and so the judgment went unexecuted.

Popular reaction was largely in agreement with this, perhaps to some extent because Mr Hirst himself was an 'unsympathetic character'. Not only had he been convicted of manslaughter, but in winning this case he had, it was sometimes said, opened the door for 'murderers and rapists' to vote, against the will of the sovereign Parliament. The fact that the Court had not held that Mr Hirst had to be allowed to vote,[11] but rather that a *blanket* ban could not be maintained, did not seem to lessen this criticism. Quite the contrary, to some extent. The Court claimed that the right to free elections requires that whether or not someone can vote in any given election must be determined by reference to a Convention-compatible rule or law according to which any exclusions are proportionate and limited. On this reading, the finding in *Hirst (No 2)* simply required that such a rule or law be introduced. However, for others, *Hirst (No 2)* effectively created a right to vote for prisoners.

Interestingly and quite contrary to the latter suggestion, the ECtHR has more recently ruled that even when the blanket ban exists, there might be no violation of the Convention if the applicability of this ban is analysed by the national court. In *Kalda v Estonia (No 2)*, the national court applied the proportionality rule and agreed that the gravity of the crimes committed by the applicant would in any event justify disenfranchisement.[12] The challenging aspect of this judgment is that if the national court decided that the limitation was disproportionate, it would not arguably be able to lift the voting ban as it was clearly provided for in the law. Despite that, and relying on the fact that the national court carefully considered the personal circumstances of the applicant, the Court did not find a violation in this case.

Article 3 of Protocol 1 is unusual for the Convention system: it does not explicitly provide for an individual right. Rather, it clearly creates an obligation to hold elections at reasonable intervals by secret ballot to ensure the free expression of the will of the people. In *its case law* the Court has interpreted this as including a right to vote. Whilst the importance of voting rights is undeniable, the variety of forms in which these rights can be provided is notable. As the Court acknowledged, at the time a number of European states had a blanket ban on prisoner voting, and there was no common practice across the

[10] *Hirst v the United Kingdom (No 2)* [2005] ECHR 681.
[11] ibid, para 84.
[12] *Kalda v Estonia (No 2)* [2022] ECHR 1052.

Council of Europe. Thus, one might have expected states to be given a wide margin of appreciation in deciding on voting rights.[13] Instead, the Court both developed a right to vote *and* prohibited blanket bans on prisoner votes, thus giving states a limited margin of appreciation on this matter. For many who opposed *Hirst (No 2)*, the problem was not only with prisoner voting, but also with how the Court went about reaching its decision.

Hirst (No 2) was just the beginning of a long saga. In a number of judgments following *Hirst (No 2)*, the Court started to specify which restrictions on prisoner voting would comply with the Convention. As has already been pointed out, the Court in *Hirst (No 2)* did not require all prisoners in a given country to have a right to vote, but it also did not explain precisely what would be Convention-compliant.[14] In *Frodl v Austria*, the Chamber of the Court held that the decision to disenfranchise a prisoner should be taken by the judge and only when the nature of the offence justifies restricting the political participation of the offender.[15] Austria requested referral of the judgment to the Grand Chamber but this was rejected. The Chamber judgment became final and was implemented by Austria.[16] In 2008, the Court delivered a judgment in the case of *Calmanovici v Romania*, condemning a blanket ban on prisoner voting, but again did not specify which system of prisoner disenfranchisement would conform to the ECHR.[17] This judgment was implemented and most prisoners can now vote in Romania.

In 2010, five years after *Hirst (No 2)* became final, the Court delivered a pilot judgment in the case of *Greens and MT v United Kingdom*.[18] This did not add much clarity as to what exactly should be done by the Contracting Party in order to satisfy the standard developed in *Hirst (No 2)*. The Court merely reiterated its decision from that case and gave the United Kingdom six months to comply.

In 2012, the Grand Chamber decided another case concerning prisoner voting rights – *Scoppola v Italy (No 3)*.[19] The UK Government submitted a third-party intervention arguing that the Court had misinterpreted the Convention in *Hirst (No 2)*,[20] but in spite of this the Court reiterated the principle laid down in that case, although it was more precise as to what this actually means. Whilst not overruling *Hirst (No 2)*, the Court nevertheless overruled *Frodl* by stating that '[w]hile the intervention of a judge is in principle likely to guarantee the proportionality of restrictions on prisoners' voting rights,

---

[13] The Court acknowledged that there was no uniform practice on prisoner voting across the Contracting Parties.

[14] *Hirst v United Kingdom (No 2)* (n 10), para 84.

[15] *Frodl v Austria* [2010] ECHR 508, para 34.

[16] Ed Bates 'Analysing the Prisoner Voting Saga and the British Challenge to Strasbourg' (2014) 14(3) *Human Rights Law Review* 503, 509–10.

[17] *Calmanovici v Romania* [2008] ECHR 1907.

[18] *Greens and MT v the United Kingdom* [2010] ECHR 1826.

[19] *Scoppola v Italy (No 3)* [2012] ECHR 868.

[20] ibid, para 78.

such restrictions will not necessarily be automatic, general and indiscriminate simply because they were not ordered by a judge'.[21] The Court established that in Italy, disenfranchisement applies only to those prisoners who are convicted for crimes that can be punished by imprisonment for longer than three years.[22] This system was sufficient for the Court to declare that the ban was not automatic or blanket, and it consequently found no violation of the Convention.

The next stage of the prisoner voting saga occurred in Russia before its expulsion in 2022. In 2013, the Court delivered a judgment in *Anchugov and Gladkov v Russia*.[23] The facts of the case are nearly identical to those in *Hirst (No 2)*, with the only significant difference being that automatic disenfranchisement is enshrined in the Constitution of Russia, and located in a provision that can only be amended by adoption of a new Constitution.[24] The Russian Government argued that this was a significant consideration, which should affect the scope of the margin of appreciation afforded to the Government,[25] a claim to which the Court did not accede, finding the Russian law in violation of the Convention.

In Russia, the judgment in *Anchugov* led to a significant backlash against the ECtHR. The Court suggested that the Russian Constitutional Court should interpret the Constitution in a way that would comply with the reading of the Convention adopted by the ECtHR. This has not happened. In its judgment of 14 July 2015, the Russian Constitutional Court declared that Russia could depart from its international obligations if compliance with them would violate the Russian Constitution.[26] When ruling on this issue, one of the judgments that the Russian Constitutional Court clearly had in mind was *Anchugov and Gladkov v Russia*. Furthermore, the Russian Parliament – the State Duma – adopted amendments to the law of the Constitutional Court, allowing it to declare judgments of the ECtHR to be unenforceable in so far as they contradict

[21] ibid, para 99.

[22] ibid, para 106.

[23] *Anchugov and Gladkov v Russia* [2013] ECHR 638.

[24] Article 135 of the Constitution of the Russian Federation, available at http://www.constitution.ru/en/10003000-10.htm.

[25] *Anchugov and Gladkov v Russia* (n 23), paras 85–87.

[26] Decision of the Constitutional Court of the Russian Federation from 14 July 2015 N 21-П 'in the case of verification of constitutionality of Article 1 of the Federal Law "On Ratification of the Convention for the Protection of Human Rights and Fundamental Freedoms and Its Protocols", sections 1 and 2 of Article 32 of the Federal Law "On International Treaties of the Russian Federation", sections 1 and 4 of Article 11, subsection 4 of section 4 of Article 392 of the Civil Procedural Code of the Russian Federation, sections 1 and 4 of Article 13, subsection 4 of section 3 of Article 311 of the Arbitration Procedural Code of the Russian Federation, sections 1 and 4 of Article 15, subsection 4 of section 1 of Article 350 of the Administrative Court Proceedings Code of the Russian Federation, and subsection 2 of Section 4 of Article 413 of the Criminal Procedural Code of the Russian Federation in relation to the request of the group of the members of state Duma (parliament)', available at http://rg.ru/2015/07/27/ks-dok.html (in Russian).

the foundational norms of the Constitution.[27] Unsurprisingly, the first case that the Constitutional Court was asked to consider under this new procedure was the case of *Anchugov and Gladkov*, and it ruled that the Russian Constitution does not allow prisoners to vote and that this determined the matter, rather than the Convention.[28] After *Anchugov and Gladkov*, the ECtHR decided another prisoner voting case, *Söyler v Turkey*. In Turkey, the voting ban is applicable only to those who committed intentional crimes.[29] Starting from 2001, prisoners who were convicted for involuntary offences have been allowed to vote.[30] The Court was not satisfied with this regime, however, because in relation to intentional crimes the Turkish system was even harsher than those in Russia, Italy or the United Kingdom. For instance, even those former prisoners who were conditionally released could not recover their voting rights until their sentence was over.[31] In addition, the Court pointed out that the ban in Turkey was indiscriminate in nature as it did not take into account the gravity of the crime committed or the length of imprisonment.[32] This judgment, therefore, adds some confusion as to the standard that the Contracting Parties should apply in this field: avoiding an absolute and indiscriminate ban is no longer the only requirement. Some other requirements are relevant too. The ban in Turkey was clearly not absolute – those in prison for involuntary crimes could continue enjoying their right to vote – but the measures against those who were imprisoned for intentional crimes appeared to be disproportionately harsh. Although this uncertainty leaves the Court with some flexibility when deciding future cases, it still coveys an impression of ad hoc decision-making, especially comparing it with the judgment in *Kalda v Estonia (No 2)* considered above. For some observers, the meaning of 'absolute and indiscriminate' seems to change over time, depending on the circumstances.

Almost all prisoner voting cases led to difficulties in execution. In 2018, the Committee of Ministers, which supervises execution of ECtHR judgments, closed *Hirst (No 2)*. This means that the Committee was satisfied that the (relatively minor) changes to administrative rules allowing prisoners released on temporary licence to vote were sufficient. In 2019, the Committee closed the execution in the cases of *Anchugov and Gladkov v Russia and Söyler v Turkey*, with the Russian and Turkish authorities making the minimal possible changes in their laws and practice to accommodate the changes.

[27] The Amendments to the Federal Constitutional Law on the Constitutional Court of the Russian Federation of 14 December 2015 N 7-ФКЗ, available at http://docs.cntd.ru/document/420322320.

[28] The Judgment of the Russian Constitutional Court as to the Possibility of Execution of the Judgment of the ECtHR in the case of *Anchugov and Gladkov v Russia*. Press release of the judgment is available at www.ksrf.ru/ru/News/Pages/ViewItem.aspx?ParamId=3281b (in Russian).

[29] *Söyler v Turkey* App no 29411/07 (ECtHR, 17 September 2013), para 26.

[30] ibid, para 30.

[31] ibid, para 38.

[32] ibid, para 41.

Thus, the prisoner-voting debate is a good illustration of a vexed dialogue between the Court and the Contracting Parties, rooted in questions of sovereignty and authority. It raises questions such as 'Why should the Court have the last word in this debate?' and 'Why should judges have the authority to determine the policy question of whether prisoners should vote or not?'

One might wonder why disenfranchisement of prisoners has generated so much controversy. As already noted, one can criticise the reasoning of the Court in these cases, but there is more to it than that. Three key conditions were present for this to generate a stand-off. First, because voting rights are usually determined by legislation, the Court's judgments created direct conflict with parliamentary preferences. In pretty much in all prisoner-voting cases, Strasbourg bodies found themselves accepting minimal changes to administrative rules as sufficient for the purposes of execution. Second, prisoner voting concerns the civic entitlements of an unpopular minority, easily vilified in the media and among the voting public. Third, national authorities may perceive this to be a question in which the ECtHR should not get involved either because the question is perceived as 'political', or because it has become a focal point for wider dynamics of anti-internationalism or Euroscepticism, or, indeed, a mixture of both, as in Turkey and the UK.[33]

The accumulation of these three conditions may explain why decisions as to prisoner voting cause stand-off in some countries but not in others: in Austria, the judgment in *Frodl v Austria*[34] was executed without any major issues,[35] and in Ireland the national parliament initiated appropriate reforms without there having been any specific ECtHR judgment against them.[36] Yet in Turkey and the UK the prisoner-voting issue was a major bone of contention.

Clearly, the Court should not avoid dealing with important social issues, even if they concern a challenging topic on which the national parliament might have something to say. To do so would undermine the *raison d'être* of the Court, namely the protection of minorities and other unpopular groups who cannot be protected through normal democratic processes. But the ECtHR still needs to take account of the possible backlash to its decisions and be prepared to confront it. The stand-off related to prisoner voting was arguably costly for the Court's reputation. Finally, the real effect of this case law was relatively minor. The standard was significantly watered down through

[33] Backbenchers' debate on the question of prisoner voting ban 2011: Hansard Report, available at www.publications.parliament.uk/pa/cm201011/cmhansrd/cm110210/debtext/110210-0002.htm.

[34] *Frodl v Austria* (n 16).

[35] Federal law amending the Federal Constitutional Law, the National Elections Regulation 1992, the Federal President Election Law 1971, the European Elections Act, the Voter Evidence Law 1973, the European Voter Evidence Law, the Law on Referendums 1972, the Law on Popular Petitions 1989, the Law on National Surveys 1973 and the Code of Criminal Procedure 1975, available at www.ris.bka.gv.at/Dokumente/BgblAuth/BGBLA_2011_I_43/BGBLA_2011_I_43.pdf (in German).

[36] Electoral (Amendment) Act 2006, Number 33 of 2006.

the execution, which represents another important feedback loop between the states and the ECtHR.

The Court needs to navigate a very narrow corridor between doing too much and not doing enough, between ensuring its authority and respecting sovereignty of the Contracting Parties. The Court needs to have the Contracting Parties on board, because implementation of the judgments is almost entirely voluntary despite some diplomatic pressure from the Committee of Ministers. If states systematically ignore the judgments of the Court, the system will lose its authority and influence. At the same time, if the Court is too deferential to the Contracting Parties it will also gradually lose its authority, because it will be ineffective in its key mission of protecting human rights.

Debate 2

What Is the Relationship between the EU and the ECHR?

Twenty-seven of the 46 Contracting Parties to the Convention are also Member States of the EU and, thus, under obligations to comply with both the ECHR and EU law. On the face of it, this might be a difficult task. At least in the earlier decades of its operation, the Union (as it now is) was not a human rights organisation. Rather, its primary purpose was to pursue its four freedoms: free movement of goods; free movement of workers; free movement of capital; and freedom to provide services. All of these were fundamental to the effective establishment of the common market and its smooth operation, so that they were the key focus for the authorities and institutions in Brussels and Luxembourg.

However, as EU law developed, EU citizens began to challenge it on the grounds, among other things, that it violated their human rights. The difficulty for these applicants in earlier cases was that human rights were not explicitly protected in EU law. Of course, these people had rights under the ECHR, but the EU was (and still is) not a party to the Convention (and so one could not make a complaint directly against the EU in Strasbourg). Therefore, the application had to be directed to the individual Contracting Parties to the ECHR, which were legally bound to implement EU laws. Some of these laws (particularly Regulations) have direct effect, that is they become domestic law by virtue of becoming EU law and without the intervention of the national state in the meantime.[37] Others (such as Directives) do require implementing measures by the state, so that there is a piece of domestic law that might be challenged rather than needing to directly challenge the EU law itself.

Thus, figuring out the ways in which a person who resided in a Member State of the EU could enjoy their rights under the ECHR, even when the laws of the EU are being implemented, was a difficult task. Interestingly, it was the

[37] *Costa v Ente Nazionale Energia Elettrica (ENEL)* [1964] ECR 585.

European Court of Justice (as it was then called), rather than the ECtHR, that took the first major steps in ensuring that EU law does not breach human rights standards. In *Internationale Handelsgesellschaft*, decided in 1979,[38] the Court made the following important finding:

> [R]espect for fundamental rights forms an integral part of the general principles of law protected by the Court of Justice. The protection of such rights, whilst inspired by the constitutional traditions common to the Member States, must be ensured within the framework of the structure and objectives of the [Union].[39]

Of course, it is one thing to find that rights must be protected within EU law, but identifying which rights those are is a great challenge, especially when, as was then the case, the law of the EU itself did not include express fundamental rights protections. The European Court of Justice in *Internationale Handelsgesellschaft* mentioned 'the constitutional traditions common to the Member States' when referring to the rights that might be protected in EU law; but having in mind the diversity in constitutional traditions, it is almost impossible to list the rights that EU law should comply with from that simple statement alone. In the later case of *Nold*,[40] the European Court of Justice moved a step further. Again, it mentioned common constitutional traditions across the EU, but it also referred to international human rights treaties.[41] The Preamble to the ECHR refers to 'common values' of the original signatory states – a phrase that bears some similarity to that used by the European Court of Justice. Indeed, in the case of *Rutili*, the ECHR received specific mention.[42] All of this means that, through its case law, the European Court of Justice effectively established (i) that protection and enjoyment of fundamental rights is a general principle of EU law, (ii) that these rights are those that are shared between the Member States' common constitutional traditions, and (iii) that they are broadly reflected in the rights protected by the ECHR.

Whilst these were important developments for EU law in particular, they did not address the question of how the ECHR conceived of the relationship between EU law and the Convention. This was most extensively addressed by the Court in the case of *Bosphorus Hava Yolları Turizm ve Ticaret Anonim S,irketi v Ireland* (*Bosphorus*).[43] This case neatly illustrates how states may be required to comply with competing international obligations at the same time. The case concerned an aircraft, leased by *Bosphorus Airways* from a Yugoslavian owner, which had been impounded by Ireland. In impounding the aircraft, Ireland had

[38] *Internationale Handelsgesellschaft mbH v Einfuhr- und Vorratsstelle für Getreide und Futtermittel* [1970] ECR 1125.

[39] ibid, para 4.

[40] *Nold v Commission* ECLI:EU:C:1974:51.

[41] ibid, para. 13.

[42] *Rutili v Ministre de l'Interieur* [1975] ECR 1219.

[43] *Bosphorus Hava Yolları Turizm ve Ticaret Anonim Sirketi v Ireland* [2005] ECHR 440.

been implementing a piece of EU law (Council Regulation 990/93), which in turn had been introduced to give effect to sanctions against what was then the Federal Republic of Yugoslavia, imposed by the UN Security Council as part of its reaction to the Yugoslav war. *Bosphorus* claimed that this interfered with its right to property under Article 1 of Protocol 1 of the ECHR. Interestingly, it had first claimed a breach of rights in the European Court of Justice, but failed in that case because the Court held that interference was proportionate.[44] Thus, having failed in the European Court of Justice, Bosphorus attempted to establish a violation of the ECHR in Strasbourg.

In rejecting this claim, the ECtHR reflected on the relationship between international law (including EU law) and the Convention. In so doing, it laid down what has become known as the *Bosphorus* presumption:

> In the Court's view, State action taken in compliance with such legal obligations is justified as long as the relevant organisation is considered to protect fundamental rights, as regards both the substantive guarantees offered and the mechanisms controlling their observance, in a manner which can be considered at least equivalent to that for which the Convention provides ... By 'equivalent' the Court means 'comparable'; any requirement that the organisation's protection be 'identical' could run counter to the interest of international cooperation pursued ... However, any such finding of equivalence could not be final and would be susceptible to review in the light of any relevant change in fundamental rights protection.
>
> If such equivalent protection is considered to be provided by the organisation, the presumption will be that a State has not departed from the requirements of the Convention when it does no more than implement legal obligations flowing from its membership of the organisation.
>
> However, any such presumption can be rebutted if, in the circumstances of a particular case, it is considered that the protection of Convention rights was manifestly deficient.[45]

Following on from this, and given that the protection of rights is a general principle of EU law (as outlined above), the EU was identified as an international organisation that enjoyed this presumption. What this means, in effect, is that where a state is implementing EU law, it is assumed that the EU law itself respects the ECHR, unless a manifest deficiency in rights protection is established in respect of the particular law in question. The ECtHR was prepared to be more deferential to legal rules that originated in the EU than those emanating from national legal orders.

[44] *Bosphorus Hava Yollari Turizm ve Ticaretas v Minister for Transport, Energy and Communications and Others* ECLI:EU:C:1996:312.

[45] ibid, paras 155–156.

This presumption is not without controversy. There are at least two bases upon which one might be sceptical of it. The first is the additional burden that it might be said to place on anyone who is trying to assert their Convention rights in respect of the implementation of EU law. For these applicants, there is a starting assumption that the law in question is Convention-compliant *simply because* it comes from the EU, an organisation that is not itself a Contracting Party to the Convention (something we consider further below). Although the burden of establishing a violation *always* falls on the person asserting a breach of rights, in these cases that burden seems somewhat heavier, simply because the state is implementing EU law. In other words, the standard of scrutiny is effectively lowered because the state is implementing an international obligation. The second question that arises here is why the EU should enjoy such a presumption in the first place. On balance, it seems likely that it should: fundamental rights are legally protected within the EU, EU measures can be annulled for failure to respect rights, and the Court of Justice of the European Union has repeatedly shown itself to be willing to do this. On the other hand, there is no shortage of examples of EU measures that have been found to not comply with human rights (for example on mass surveillance[46] or terrorist blacklisting[47]). In other words, just as states can sometimes take a misstep and introduce law that violates human rights, so too can the EU. Bearing this in mind, one might question whether it is justifiable that the EU is endowed with this presumption of compliance with a human rights treaty to which it is not a signatory.

In spite of these questions, however, the *Bosphorus* presumption continues to apply. This was made clear in the case of *Avotiņš v Latvia*.[48] The facts of this case are complex, but for our purposes we need only note that there was a debt-related judgment against Avotiņš from a Cypriot court, which his creditors attempted to enforce in Latvia, where he resided. Avotiņš challenged the Latvian court's order, which had been issued under a piece of EU law known as the Brussels I Regulation. This allows for mutual recognition of civil judgments across the domestic courts of the Member States of the EU. This Regulation provides that in enforcing such a judgment, domestic courts in the country where enforcement is sought 'may under no circumstances [review] its substance' but must accept it. This is in line with the EU's principle of mutual recognition: that all states in the EU have rights protections and are parties to the ECHR, and thus it can be assumed that their procedures and processes are human rights-compliant. Here the applicant claimed that the Cypriot judgment had been given in violation of his right to defence, and thus that Latvia breached his right to due process under Article 6 of the Convention by enforcing it.

[46] Joined Cases C293/12 and C594/12 *Digital Rights Ireland* ECLI:EU:C:2014:238.

[47] Joined Cases C402/05 and C415/05P *Kadi and another v European Union Council* ECLI:EU:C:2008:461.

[48] *Avotiņš v Latvia* App no 17502/07 (ECtHR, 23 May 2016).

The ECtHR held that the *Bosphorus* presumption could be applied here: in the field of mutual recognition, EU law required rights compliance in a manner that could be considered at least equivalent to that demanded by the ECHR. But of course, this is not the end of the story: a violation of the Convention could still be found if Avotiņš established that the protection of rights in the EU in the field of mutual recognition was 'manifestly deficient'. This judgment made clear that 'manifestly deficient' is a difficult standard to meet. The ECtHR was highly critical of the fact that EU law requires courts to recognise and enforce the judgments of other courts without being able to enquire as to their substance. However, it seems that this was still not enough to rebut the *Bosphorus* presumption. The Court held:

> [T]he Court must satisfy itself … that the mutual recognition mechanisms do not leave any gap or particular situation which would render the protection of the human rights guaranteed by the Convention manifestly deficient … [W]here the courts of a State which is both a Contracting Party to the Convention and a Member State of the European Union are called upon to apply a mutual recognition mechanism established by EU law, they must give full effect to that mechanism where the protection of Convention rights cannot be considered manifestly deficient. However, if a serious and substantiated complaint is raised before them to the effect that the protection of a Convention right has been manifestly deficient and that this situation cannot be remedied by European Union law, they cannot refrain from examining that complaint on the sole ground that they are applying EU law.[49]

Note the final sentence here: not only must someone raise a 'serious and substantiated' claim that EU law was 'manifestly deficient' in protecting his Convention rights, but so too must he establish 'that this situation cannot be remedied by European Union law'. Only if all of these conditions are fulfilled will the *Bosphorus* presumption be rebutted.[50]

Another possible way of getting around the *Bosphorus* presumption is establishing that the national authorities had sufficient discretion in implementing EU rules and could enforce them without violating ECHR rights. In *Ilias and Ahmed v Hungary*, the ECtHR established that treatment of asylum seekers contrary to the Convention was not prescribed by EU law and therefore the *Bosphorus* presumption was not applicable.[51]

The upshot of all of this is that EU and ECHR law have both developed to build a 'mosaic' of rights protection in Europe.[52] On the one hand, the EU has developed fundamental rights as a general principle of EU law, and indeed,

---

[49] ibid, para 116.

[50] See also *Michaud v France* [2012] ECHR 2030.

[51] *Ilias and Ahmed v Hungary* App no 47287/15 (ECtHR, 21 November 2019), para 97.

[52] See Sionaidh Douglas-Scott, 'Europe's Constitutional Mosaic: Human Rights in the European Legal Space' in Jo Shaw, Stephen Tierney and Neil Walker (eds), *Europe's Constitutional Mosaic* (Hart Publishing, 2011) 97; See also Sionaidh Douglas-Scott, 'A Tale of Two Courts: Luxembourg,

following the Treaty of Lisbon, there is now a Charter of Fundamental Rights of the European Union, which has constitutional status in the EU and uses the ECHR as a key interpretive guide.[53] Meanwhile, the ECtHR has developed a legal presumption in *Bosphorus* that is designed to ensure that ECHR Contracting Parties can implement EU law in a practicable and effective way, but which may have sacrificed effective rights protection on the altar of efficiency by making it very difficult to rebut that presumption. Undoubtedly, this is at least partially because the EU itself cannot be directly challenged in the ECtHR. This leads us to the next debate: should the EU accede to the ECHR?

Debate 3

Should the EU Accede to the ECHR?

The EU has not yet acceded to the ECHR.[54] This is in some ways curious, as EU accession to the Convention has long been contemplated and the Lisbon Treaty introduced the commitment that the EU 'shall' accede to the ECHR.[55] Moreover, Protocol 14, which entered into force in 2010, amended the Convention to allow the EU to accede. However, at the time of writing in early 2025, accession has still not occurred.

The 'first' draft accession agreement was finalised in 2013.[56] This agreement was sent to the Court of Justice of the European Union for assessment of its legality from the point of view of EU law, and quite to the surprise of many, it found that as designed the draft agreement was not lawful.[57] While full accounts of the reasons for this are provided elsewhere,[58] the role of the autonomy of EU law in the Court's reasoning is particularly significant for our purposes.

As Douglas-Scott has noted, '[t]he autonomy of EU law, and its specific, *sui generis* nature, has been a running theme throughout its legal

---

Strasbourg and the Growing European Human Rights Acquis' (2006) 43(3) *Common Market Law Review* 629.

[53] Article 6, Treaty on European Union (TEU).

[54] For some time, it was thought that the EU did not have the legal competence to accede to the Convention: *Opinion 2/94* [1996] ECR I-1759.

[55] Article 6(3), TEU.

[56] Draft revised agreement on the accession of the European Union to the Convention for the Protection of Human Rights and Fundamental Freedoms (47+1(2013)008rev2).

[57] Opinion 2/13 *Accession of the European Union to the European Convention for the Protection of Human Rights and Fundamental Freedoms* ECLI:EU:C:2014:2454.

[58] See, for example, Joris Larik, 'The Accession of the European Union to the European Convention on Human Rights' (2014) 51(5) *Common Market Law Review* 1542; Tobias Lock, 'The Future of EU Accession to the ECHR after Opinion 2/13: Is It Still Possible and Is It Still Desirable?' (2015) 11(2) *European Constitutional Law Review* 239.

history'.[59] Among other things, this principle means that the Court of Justice – and *only* the Court of Justice – determines the meaning of EU law. Whilst this was originally designed to ensure that national courts could not propagate alternative interpretations of EU law and thus undermine the unity of EU law, here it was also presented as a key reason to reject an arrangement in which the ECtHR has the capacity to call into question the Court of Justice's findings as to EU law. This has been heavily criticised by EU lawyers,[60] and raises important broader questions about the role and identity of the Court of Justice, but for our purposes it highlights a key tension that might arise should the EU accede to the Convention.

It is one thing to say that the two courts might develop a system of mutual respect and presumed compliance, and even that together they have developed an impressive system of European public law, but it is quite another to suggest that the EU might be ***bound*** by the Convention as interpreted and applied by the ECtHR. The latter was, it seems, beyond the pale for the Court of Justice, suggesting that future clashes of authority could be foreseen between the courts.

In late 2023, a further draft of an accession agreement was completed. The Council of Europe's continuing commitment to accession is indicated by the final declaration of the Reykjavík Summit of Heads of State and Government of the Council of Europe, which welcomed the revised draft accession agreement and 'express[ed] … commitment to its timely adoption'.[61] Although one cannot predict whether this draft agreement will be considered to have found a satisfactory way through the challenges that befell the first, Gragl has argued that the revised draft reflects

> the effort and diligence that the negotiators of the revised [draft accession agreement] put into their work over the last couple of years in order to accommodate the CJEU's demands enumerated in Opinion 2/13 – and I think that they have likely succeeded in doing so and thus in paving a way for the Union to become a High Contracting Party to the European Convention of Human Rights.[62]

Even if the accession is formally concluded, a question of its desirability remains. Certainly, EU accession to the Convention would allow for further

[59] Sionaidh Douglas-Scott, 'Autonomy and Fundamental Rights: The ECJ's Opinion 2/13 on Accession of the EU to the ECHR' (2016) *Europarättslig Tidskrift*, special edition, 31.

[60] Lock (n 58).

[61] Council of Europe, *Reykjavík Declaration. United Around Our Values* (2023), 7 at https://rm.coe.int/4th-summit-of-heads-of-state-and-government-of-the-council-of-europe/1680ab40c1.

[62] Paul Gragl, 'The New Draft Agreement on the EU Accession to the ECHR: Overcoming Luxembourg's Threshold' (2025) 6(1) *European Convention on Human Rights Law Review* 39.

harmonisation of the ECHR and EU fundamental rights law, thus further developing what we may term 'European public law', as well as ensuring that all areas of EU activity are subject to judicial review of some kind in some court. These are not insignificant or undesirable aims. However, on the other hand there is a strong argument that accession to the ECHR is simply unnecessary. This is worth exploring further. We have already seen that as early as 1970, the Court of Justice made it clear that fundamental rights were protected by EU law, and it soon became established that a violation of rights could be the basis for annulling a piece of EU law. Now there is a Charter of Fundamental Rights that gives further effect to that principle. The Charter's Preamble states that it aims 'to strengthen the protection of fundamental rights in the light of changes in society, social progress and scientific and technological developments by making those rights more visible in a Charter', and it applies to the EU at all times and to member states when they are applying EU law. Indeed, the Charter arguably goes beyond the ECHR by protecting various social rights, including the right to work (Article 15), rights of the elderly (Article 25), right of access to a free placement service for job seekers (Article 29) and a right of access to healthcare (Article 35). Where a right in the Charter is also in the Convention, the Charter right is to be understood by reference to how the corresponding Convention right is understood, so that the ECHR acts as a 'floor' of protection, with the Court of Justice free to interpret the Charter as giving more protection to rights than the Convention but never as giving less.[63]

Given all of this, it is not entirely clear what 'added value *for rights protection*' would come from accession, particularly given the complexity and difficulty of accession. Lock acknowledges that so many concessions would have to be made to satisfy the requirements laid down in *Opinion 2/13* that accession may have the effect of reducing, rather than increasing, rights protection in real terms.[64] For Lock the accession will 'likely result in an overall strengthening of the ECHR system', but it will also lead to some considerable practical changes in how the Strasbourg Court operates. Moreover, the EU will be a unique Contracting Party with significant influence over the procedures. This will also likely lead to a 'starker differentiation between EU and non-EU Member States, which will be particularly evident where a non-EU Member State is applying EU law'.[65]

However, there are at least three creditable arguments that accession should still be pursued. First, having two regional courts, both of which are developing a human rights jurisprudence, might create multiple and perhaps conflicting standards of human rights protection. Even though, as already noted,

[63] Article 52(3), Charter of Fundamental Rights of the European Union.

[64] Lock (n 58).

[65] Tobias Lock, 'Implications of the Revised Draft EU Accession Agreement for the ECHR' (2025) 6(1) *European Convention on Human Rights Law Review* 65.

rights protected in the EU's Charter of Fundamental Rights and the ECHR must be interpreted by the Court of Justice using the Convention as a 'floor', this does not entirely preclude the possibility that European human rights law will become (further) fragmented. Whilst fragmentation can lead to higher standards of rights protection, this is not inevitably the case, meaning that for some – including the CDDH[66] – the possibility of fragmentation is a cause for concern, so that a failure of accession 'might in the long term cause serious damage to the credibility, authority and long-term future of the Convention mechanism'.[67] Second, if we were to accept that the protection of rights by the Court of Justice of the European Union, referring to the Convention as the Charter requires it to, meant that accession is not necessary, it would be difficult to see why the same argument should not be made by states wishing to leave the ECHR and whose domestic legal systems also protect rights. Nothing about the Court of Justice of the European Union makes it so clearly distinguishable from, for example, domestic constitutional or supreme courts as to say that this argument can be applied *only* to it. Third, accession would mean that the EU would be held accountable for complying with the Convention, thus plugging the accountability gap that arises from the application of the *Bosphorus* presumption to Contracting Parties' application of ever-expanding EU law.[68]

Debate 4

What Is the Relationship between the ECHR and Other Sources of International Law?

While not all Contracting Parties to the ECHR are also member states of the EU, all have a range of international legal obligations that they must abide by. There are thus other potential conflicts between states' international legal obligations. This question arises most sharply when states are implementing Chapter VII resolutions of the UN Security Council. These are resolutions passed for the purposes of international peace and security, and which are binding on all member states of the United Nations (UN) by virtue of the Charter of the UN. Article 103 of that same Charter further provides:

> In the event of a conflict between the obligations of the Members of the United Nations under the present Charter and their obligations under any other international agreement, their obligations under the present Charter shall prevail.

[66] Steering Committee for Human Rights – a Council of Europe body that among other competences can propose further reforms of the ECtHR.

[67] CDDH, *Report on the Longer Term Future of the European Convention on Human Rights CDDH* (2015) R84 Addendum I, 65.

[68] See, for example, Lock (n 58).

This raises a serious question, and a difficult one: if a UN Security Council Resolution requires a Contracting Party to the ECHR to act in a manner that violates Convention rights, can a violation be found, or does Article 103 of the UN Charter effectively compel states to act in such a way? This is by no means an insignificant query. If the answer is that states must comply with the Convention at all times, then they may be placed in an almost impossible situation of irreconcilable international obligations. However, if Article 103 of the UN Charter means that states are required to subordinate their Convention obligations to their other international obligations where they are in conflict, the whole concept of Convention rights as legal protections is called into question, not least because the UN Security Council itself is not obliged to have regard to the ECHR when formulating its Chapter VII resolutions.

In the joined cases of *Behrami v France* and *Saramati v France, Germany and Norway*, the Grand Chamber was asked to consider whether Contracting Parties to the ECHR could be held liable for breaches of the Convention in respect of acts done when they were acting as part of NATO's Kosovo peacekeeping forces (KFOR) and the United Nations Mission in Kosovo (UNMIK).[69] These forces were UN-led, multinational forces acting under Security Council Resolution 1244 (1999). Rather than determine the question put to it per se, the Court held that the actions of member states in these circumstances were attributable to the UN (which is not a Contracting Party to the ECHR) not to the Contracting Parties themselves. Thus, no assessment of Convention-compatibility could be undertaken: these actions simply did not 'count' as actions of the ECHR Contracting Parties.[70]

In many ways, this approach seems like 'avoidance': rather than having to determine the impact of Article 103 of the UN Charter on Convention obligations, the Court simply side-stepped the issue through its attribution decision. What *Behrami* suggests is that *when acting as part of a UN mission* established by resolution of the UN Security Council, Contracting Parties to the ECHR will not be subjected to Convention analysis.[71] From a rights-protection perspective this is deeply problematic, especially as the Court has also found that there is no breach of the right of access to a court under Article 6 where a domestic court affords the UN immunity[72] from claims, even where the actions were done within the Council of Europe and with the involvement of European states.[73]

In sum, this means that where there is a UN mission, *neither* the ECHR Contracting Parties involved in the mission *nor* the UN are likely to be held

---

[69] *Behrami andBehrami v France and Saramati v France, Germany and Norway* App nos 71412/01 and 78166/01 (ECtHR, 2 May 2007).

[70] ibid, para 44.

[71] See also *Bankovic' and Others v Belgium and Others* [2001] ECHR 890, which is discussed in full in chapter 6 (where Contracting Parties operated as part of a NATO mission).

[72] Article 105, Charter of the United Nations.

[73] *Stichting Mothers of Srebrenica and Others v the Netherlands* [2013] ECHR 739.

accountable under the Convention. There is, rather, a substantial accountability gap here, which the ECtHR has not found a way to plug and which has, arguably, been exacerbated by its decision in *Behrami*. This raises serious questions about the effectiveness of the Convention and its system: if Contracting Parties are not accountable for violations of the Convention when they act under the auspices of the UN, and if the UN enjoys immunity that is recognised by the ECHR system, surely there is reason to wonder at the ability of the Convention to properly protect rights. The fact that the operations in question often involve military intervention and high-risk in times of armed conflict adds a further dimension of risk to rights, which is discussed in full in chapter 6 (on the Convention in times of insecurity, including war).

The Court has taken a somewhat more Convention-promoting path in respect of situations where Contracting Parties are ***implementing*** UN Security Council resolutions through their domestic laws or actions. This has been a particularly difficult question for the Court in recent years, as individuals have challenged the ways in which member states have implemented UN Security Council requirements to intervene in the financial affairs of people, organisations and states for the purposes of, for example, disrupting terrorist financing and sanctioning states.[74]

The most recent case in this line is *Al-Dulimi and Montana Management Inc v Switzerland*,[75] decided in June 2016. This case concerned UN Security Council Resolution 1483 (2003), through which all UN member states had been required to freeze all funds and assets of the former Government of Iraq, of Saddam Hussein, and of senior members of the former Iraqi regimes and their immediate family members or legal entities. The frozen and seized assets would then be transferred to the Development Fund for Iraq. The persons and entities to which the sanctions regime would apply were identified by a Sanctions Committee established by the Security Council, and both of the applicants had been placed on the list by this Committee, following which Switzerland had begun proceedings to appropriate their assets in Swiss banks.

The applicants claimed that the methods by which they were put on the list violated their rights under Articles 6 and 13 of the Convention, because there was no channel by which listing could be disputed through judicial review. This posed a quandary for the Court: it cannot directly review the actions of the Sanctions Committee because the UN is not a Contracting Party to the Convention. However, it can – and did – consider whether, in implementing Resolution 1483, Switzerland had complied with its obligations under the ECHR. In this respect it found a breach of the Convention because Switzerland did not allow for judicial review of the applicants' listing in its domestic courts. Switzerland argued that it was obliged to implement Resolution 1483

[74] See especially *Al-Jedda v the United Kingdom* [2011] ECHR 1092; *Nada v Switzerland* [2012] ECHR 1691.

[75] *Al-Dulimi and Montana Management Inc v Switzerland* [2016] ECHR 576.

and that, in any case, Article 103 of the UN Charter made it clear that its obligations under that Charter prevailed over its obligations under the Convention.

The question of whether there was a conflict between the requirements of Resolution 1483 and those under the Convention was key to the decision in the case: after all, Article 103 only applies '[i]n the event of a conflict between the obligations of the Members of the United Nations under the present Charter and their obligations under any other international agreement'. Switzerland argued that there was clearly a norm conflict between Resolution 1483 and the Convention so that it was bound to apply the Resolution and freeze these assets. However, for several judges in the Grand Chamber there was no necessary conflict. In earlier cases on similar sanction regimes the Court had introduced a presumption that Security Council resolutions were intended to comply with human rights law,[76] so that they would be taken to do so unless they explicitly said otherwise.[77] On this reasoning, when a provision in a Resolution is unclear, it is to be interpreted harmoniously with the ECHR and a presumption of compliance (similar to the *Bosphorus* presumption) is to be applied.

The finding that no conflict with the Convention will be found to arise unless it is explicitly constructed by the wording of a Resolution is a deft way to step around the logical implications of Article 103's being engaged (which would be that a Contracting Party is not obliged to comply with the Convention where it conflicts with the Resolution). However, there is a question mark over how helpful this is in real terms. In *Al-Dulimi*, as in similar cases, the state remained obliged to apply the Resolution to those persons and entities listed by the relevant Sanctions Committee of the UN. Domestic courts cannot serve as a forum for review of the UN Security Council: they do not have the authority to overrule a decision of the Security Council, which is not subject to their jurisdiction. Indeed, in *Al-Dulimi* the Court accepted as much, holding:

> Turning to the precise obligations imposed by the Convention on Switzerland in the present case, the Court accepts that the Federal Court was unable to rule on the merits or appropriateness of the measures entailed by the listing of the applicants. ... However, before taking the above-mentioned measures, the Swiss authorities had a duty to ensure that the listing was not arbitrary.[78]

The Court thus required the state in question to obtain sufficient information to allow its courts to be able to scrutinise the listing, but one wonders what kind of order a court that found the listing to have been arbitrary could possibly make. Does the ECtHR seriously contemplate a domestic court's ordering a government to refuse to implement a UN Security Council Resolution in any

[76] *Al-Jedda v the United Kingdom* (n 74); *Nada v Switzerland* (n 74).

[77] In *Nada v Switzerland*, the presumption of compliance was rebutted by the clear wording of the Resolution: *Nada v Switzerland* (n 74).

[78] *Al-Dulimi and Montana Management Inc v Switzerland* (n 75), para 150.

particular case? Might it be ordered to make representations for delisting to the Sanctions Committee? How should a domestic court deal with situations where the information provided to ground the listing is highly sensitive and cannot be revealed to the listed person or entity? Or with situations where the grounding information cannot be shared with the court but is instead summarised in a statement from the government? The Court held that Article 6 would be violated if listed persons and entities could not submit information to the domestic court, or if relevant information was not sought from the Sanctions Committee (even under a confidential procedure), but there is little clarity about how the rights violation could be effectively remedied in such cases.

There is similarly little clarity on how the harmonious interpretation is to be implemented in practice. This likely depends on the extent to which the Court holds that a Contracting Party has a 'scope of discretion' in applying the Resolution in any particular case. Security Council Resolutions are applied by states *within their domestic legal systems*; in other words, the means to achieving the end of compliance can vary across different legal systems. In principle, this suggests that a Contracting Party to the Convention might design a means of implementing a Security Council Resolution in domestic law that complies with the Convention. However, one wonders whether this is realistic in the case of sanctions regimes: states are legally obliged to freeze the assets of persons and entities included on the list drawn up by the Sanctions Committee so that, in practice, there is very little discretion to be exercised. In spite of this, both the ECtHR and, in similar litigation, the Court of Justice of the European Union[79] have held that such discretion *does* exist, and that rights must be respected when exercising this discretion unless the Resolution explicitly provides otherwise.

At first blush, this appears somewhat futile: it does very little in real terms to truly resolve the question of authority that arises for a state when it appears to be bound to comply with two sets of international obligations that are difficult to reconcile. It may well be that the real value of decisions such as *Al-Dulimi* is that they shape how ECHR member states are likely to make representations to the UN Security Council when sanctions and similar regimes are being designed, so that they can try to ensure fair(er) procedures are built into the extensive regimes of financial disruption that have been introduced to deal with terrorism and insecurity.[80] Beyond that, however, it is difficult to see how cases such as *Al-Dulimi* – admirable in principle – are effective in practice. In 2022, the Committee of Ministers closed the execution of *Al-Dulimi*, stating that Swiss law and case law had developed in a way that meant the Federal Court

[79] *Kadi and another v European Union Council* (n 47).

[80] For a similar argument in respect of the *Kadi* decision, see Fiona de Londras and Suzanne Kingston, 'Rights, Security and Conflicting International Obligations: Exploring Inter-Jurisdictional Judicial Dialogues in Europe' (2010) 58 *American Journal of Comparative Law* 359.

could now examine complaints submitted by persons included on sanctions lists on the merits.[81]

Conclusion

The ECtHR operates within a complex system of multiple international obligations that national governments are required to implement. Moreover, national governments also enjoy significant authority in deciding how these obligations are implemented. Since the interrelations between national and international obligations, and between various levels of international obligation themselves, are not clearly hierarchal, obligations can sometimes seem to conflict with one another. When one of those sets of obligations originates in the ECHR, this creates significant challenges for the effectiveness of the Convention and requires delicate handling by the Court. As we have seen in this chapter, in trying to address these difficult questions, the Court has largely attempted to engage productively with both national authorities and international standards, finding ways to make them work together, to integrate them and to respond to the operation of national legal systems. That said, the Court's judgments are binding, and the obligation to execute (ie give effect to) these judgments exists whether the national authorities agree with them or not. We return to this latter point in far more detail in chapter 8.

Further Reading

Alessandra Osti, 'Prisoners' voting rights and the long-lasting political resistance to the implementation of the European Court of Human Rights' judgments' in Gabriella Citroni, Irene Spigno and Palmina Tanzarella (eds), *The Right to Political Participation* (Routledge, 2022).

Sionaidh Douglas-Scott, 'Europe's Constitutional Mosaic: Human Rights in the European Legal Space' in Jo Shaw, Stephen Tierney and Neil Walker (eds), *Europe's Constitutional Mosaic* (Hart Publishing, 2011).

Tobias Lock, 'Implications of the Revised Draft EU Accession Agreement for the ECHR' (2025) 6(1) *European Convention on Human Rights Law Review* 65.

[81] At https://hudoc.exec.coe.int/ENG?i=CM/Notes/1443/H46-33E.

3

Admissibility

Although rarely covered in much detail in the academic literature, admissibility is extremely important. More than 90 per cent of all applications are declared inadmissible,[1] meaning that the substantive claims of rights violation in the vast majority of complaints submitted to the Court are never considered by the judges there. Articles 34 and 35 of the European Convention on Human Rights (ECHR or Convention) outline the criteria for admissibility with which any application submitted to the European Court of Human Rights (ECtHR or Court) must comply in order to be considered on the merits. According to Article 34:

> The Court may receive applications from any person, non-governmental organisation or group of individuals claiming to be the victim of a violation by one of the High Contracting Parties of the rights set forth in the Convention or the Protocols thereto.

Article 35 establishes the admissibility criteria:

> 1. The Court may only deal with the matter after all domestic remedies have been exhausted, according to the generally recognised rules of international law, and within a period of four months from the date on which the final decision was taken.
> 2. The Court shall not deal with any application submitted under Article 34 that:
>   (a) is anonymous; or
>   (b) is substantially the same as a matter that has already been examined by the Court or has already been submitted to another procedure of international investigation or settlement and contains no relevant new information.

[1] That 90% of applications are inadmissible is the Court's own assessment. For instance, the Court's own report on admissibility mentions this figure. See *The Admissibility of an Application* at www.echr.coe.int/Documents/COURtalks_Inad_Talk_ENG.PDF, 1.

3. The Court shall declare inadmissible any individual application submitted under Article 34 if it considers that:
   (a) the application is incompatible with the provisions of the Convention or the Protocols thereto, manifestly ill-founded, or an abuse of the right of individual application; or
   (b) the applicant has not suffered a significant disadvantage, unless respect for human rights as defined in the Convention and the Protocols thereto requires an examination of the application on the merits.

Admissibility rules are a key mechanism for managing the Court's workload and, to some extent, for maintaining its institutional identity as a subsidiary regional court. Admissibility rules are also, however, a barrier to individuals all across the Council of Europe accessing substantive adjudication in Strasbourg. Thus, admissibility-related decision-making in the ECtHR matters greatly not just for the everyday work of the Court, but also for any serious engagement with questions of effectiveness and legitimacy that, as we have already seen in chapter 1, motivate much of our enquiry throughout this book. In Debate 1 of this chapter, we consider the relationship between admissibility and the legitimacy of the ECtHR. In some ways this is linked to the question of who can make an application to the Court – who counts as a 'victim' of an alleged Convention violation? And how serious should an alleged violation be for the ECtHR to consider it? We discuss these issues in Debates 2 and 3.

At first glance, it may appear that admissibility criteria are 'simple' rules, capable of technical and technocratic application. Whilst admissibility decisions do often involve a high degree of technocratic and bureaucratic decision-making, often by the Registry of the Court, it will become clear throughout this chapter that the ECtHR retains much discretion in this area. The rules and their application are such that the Court can often find a way to deem admissible a case that it considers warrants substantive adjudication, even if it seems to sideline the admissibility criteria. This cuts the other way too, of course, so that the criteria can be applied with particular stringency if there is a caseload backlog that needs to be addressed. Thus, admissibility mechanisms available to the Court enable it to choose the most important applications and consider them, even if they are not strictly speaking admissible. This is certainly not an uncontroversial approach to admissibility, and it raises questions about how much discretion the ECtHR should have in deciding on admissibility: we consider this in Debate 4.

In Debate 5 we analyse how the Court can negotiate two competing objectives: being an effective constitutional tribunal that can shape European Public Order; and reviewing each and every application that has been submitted to the Court. The Court's application of the rules of admissibility is crucial here. If admissibility is narrowly defined then few applications will filter through the system and the Court will have more time to deal with 'important' applications.

Having said that, this approach is not without its drawbacks: it can reduce individual applicants' faith in the system.

Debate 1

How Do Admissibility Criteria Affect the Court's Legitimacy?

In chapter 1 we argued that subsidiarity, effectiveness and judicial methodology are important bases of the ECtHR's legitimacy. Two admissibility criteria are directly linked to these: exhaustion of domestic remedies; and the four-month time limit for lodging an application.[2]

Exhaustion of domestic remedies under Article 35 is a reflection of procedural subsidiarity. It requires that domestic mechanisms be 'exhausted' before the ECtHR is asked to consider an alleged violation, so that the national mechanisms have the opportunity first to assess and, where appropriate, redress the violation. The four-month rule ensures that the Court's decisions are predictable and do not disrupt the domestic legal order any more than is necessary, by placing some temporal certainty on whether the domestic resolution of an alleged rights violation is likely to be contested at the European level. Both of these criteria seem fairly straightforward and capable of relatively easy assessment, and of routine and formal application. However, as with any rules, the extent to which they might be rigidly or flexibly applied can have implications for the extent to which the entity applying them (here the ECtHR) is perceived to be acting legitimately in doing so. Thus, should a potentially extremely grave violation be deemed inadmissible, and therefore not be considered, because it was received one hour after the time limit had expired? And if not – if there is a case for a more flexible application of the rule – how can consistency in application be achieved so that the Court does not appear arbitrary or capricious in its admissibility decisions?

Let us consider this first in relation to the four-month rule; perhaps one of the most straightforward and strictly applied admissibility criteria. Thousands of applications are declared inadmissible because they were not submitted on time. The Court does not normally allow extension of the four-month period, although it used to allow for the time limit to be met through a fairly minimal engagement by the applicant with the Court. Around 20 years ago, an applicant or their lawyer could send a letter briefly explaining the facts of the case and, if that letter arrived within the six-month period (as it was then), it would stop the time successfully and the full application could be submitted at a later

[2] On 1 August 2021, Protocol 15 entered into force and changed the ECHR. Prior to this, the application could be submitted no later than six months after exhaustion of domestic remedies. Protocol 15 reduced this term to four months.

date. Sometimes this would be months or even years later, and the Court would reject the subsequent application only if too much time had elapsed between the introduction of the initial letter and the full application form. This system was very beneficial to applicants, but of course raised challenges for the Strasbourg system of human rights protection as so many files remained open, often for years, before any substantive decision on them could be taken. Thus, the ECtHR decided to stop this practice, and now the four-month time limit can be interrupted only by a fully completed application form. Moreover, as was mentioned in chapter 1, application forms that do not comply with Rule 47 of the Rules of Court are not even registered, and as a result do not interrupt the four-month period. Save for some special circumstances (like continuing violations or multiple violations), the Court thus appears to have prioritised legal certainty and predictability in its application of the four-month rule.[3]

The Court has much broader discretionary powers when assessing whether domestic remedies have been exhausted. First, the Court must decide whether the remedy available in domestic law is effective, so that an applicant would be required to exhaust it before going to Strasbourg. Of course, this involves the Court in making substantive decisions as to the quality of remedies provided in domestic law, but it ensures that states cannot evade supervision by the ECtHR simply by introducing formal and ineffective remedies. This leads inevitably to the application of discretion in admissibility decision-making. What does it mean for a remedy to be effective?

The Court normally states that an effective remedy is capable of acknowledging a violation and offering *restitutio in integrum* or adequate compensation if restitution is not possible.[4] Remedies that cannot directly address and rectify alleged violations (like determinations of ombudspersons),[5] or which cannot immediately prevent deterioration of the applicant's situation, are considered ineffective. In extradition cases, for example, applicants are not required to exhaust any domestic remedies that would be incapable of suspending the proposed extradition if granted.[6] The Court reserves considerable discretion in deciding whether a remedy is *in principle* effective or not. If a remedy that is considered effective in principle is not exhausted then the application will be declared inadmissible as premature; but if someone exhausts a remedy that is considered ineffective in principle, they might miss the four-month time period so that their application to Strasbourg would be inadmissible. Just because a remedy is ineffective in principle does not mean that it might not be effective

[3] See, for example, *Idalov v Russia* App no 5826/03 (ECtHR, 22 May 2012), paras 127–133 for multiple violations; *McDaid and Others v the United Kingdom* App nos 34822/97 and five others (European Commission of Human Rights, 9 April 1996) for continuing violations; and Rule 47(6)a, Rules of Court.

[4] See, for example, *Lukenda v Slovenia* [2005] ECHR 682, para 44; *Demopoulos and Others v Turkey* [2010] ECHR 306, para 114.

[5] See *Egmez v Cyprus* [2000] ECHR 681, para 67.

[6] See, for example, *De Souza Ribeiro v France* [2012] ECHR 2066.

in a particular case, but such a case would not change its nature in the eyes of the ECtHR, and future complainants would not be required to exhaust it. To illustrate: a potential applicant might apply to an ombudsperson who might manage to resolve this particular case, so that the applicant would no longer be a 'victim' from the perspective of the ECtHR; but this would not mean that every potential future applicant would have to engage with an ombudsperson, whose powers are considered too limited for this process generally to be deemed an effective remedy under the Convention.

Changes in the means of its application and operation can shift the status of a remedy from 'ineffective in principle' to 'effective in principle', or vice versa. This of course reflects the fact that the effectiveness of a remedy will often very much depend on the context in which it is made and received, and the enforcement infrastructure that surrounds it. Thus, the Court first assesses the effectiveness of the remedy per se when it is introduced at the national level, and then considers its effectiveness in practice, sometimes changing its assessment by reference to how the remedy works 'in the real world'. This can be illustrated by reference to the Italian 'Pinto Law': an attempt to remedy undue delays in criminal proceedings that the Court has frequently found to violate Article 6 of the Convention.[7]

Responding to these repeated findings of violation, the Italian authorities introduced the 'Pinto Law' in 2001. This provided for special judicial review of the length of proceedings and some compensation where undue delay was considered to have occurred. Initially, the Court deemed this remedy effective.[8] However, its optimism about the remedy soon dissipated as Italian national courts began applying the 'Pinto Law' in practice. In *Scordino v Italy*, the ECtHR determined that the amount of compensation that is awarded by Italian courts under the 'Pinto Law' was incompatible with the Court's practice, meaning that the remedy was ineffective and therefore did not need to be exhausted.[9] The remedy was thus, in principle, ineffective.

From the point of view of the state authorities, this approach might be seen as an assault on the principle of procedural subsidiarity, because the 'Pinto Law' may have been effective in at least some cases. However, the legitimacy of the ECtHR would be undermined if an applicant had to wait for a long time at the national level for an ineffective remedy simply because the ECtHR is reluctant to make determinations of 'in principle' ineffectiveness. Here, as in all cases establishing whether a remedy is effective or not, the Court must balance the applicants' interests against the systemic interest in maintaining procedural subsidiarity, and be prepared to intervene if applicants' rights are not properly protected. This allows for the Court to balance its interest in procedural subsidiarity, the Contracting Parties' interest in being subjected to international

[7] See, for example, *Capuano v Italy* [1987] ECHR 10; and *Di Mauro v Italy* [1999] ECHR 63.

[8] See, for example, *Daddi v Italy* App no 15476/09 (ECtHR, 2 June 2009).

[9] *Scordino v Italy* [2004] ECHR 412.

supervision only where the national system has inadequately tried to attend to rights violations, and individuals' interest in the protection of their human rights. The connections between all of these interests, and indeed the difficult task of balancing them, on the one hand, and the development and maintenance of legitimacy, on the other, are clear.

Debate 2

Who Can Apply to the Court?

Article 34 states that the Court can receive applications from any person, non-governmental organisation (NGO) or group of individuals claiming to be the 'victim' of a violation. The concept of 'victim' is thus important here. The Court cannot accept applications that would require it to consider laws *in abstracto* (ie applications asking the Court to undertake an abstract review of the compatibility of a legal provision with the ECHR[10]) but must instead deal with concrete situations of alleged violation. This partly reflects the institutional limitations of the Council of Europe. Where a domestic constitutional court undertakes an abstract review that results in a finding with potentially far-reaching impacts, the other organs of the state (such as the parliament) can attempt to mitigate that, perhaps by proposing a constitutional change in a corrective referendum or similar. In other words, the judicial power is usually counter-weighted within the infrastructure of the state. This is not as clearly the case in the Council of Europe, where no such counterweight can easily be identified. Perhaps even more importantly, abstract review allows for very wide judicial intervention in governance of a scale and nature that is not clearly appropriate to a supranational court. National governments, parliaments and the judiciary have the primary responsibility for the administration of the state; as the ECtHR is subsidiary, its findings should intrude on the domestic sphere only inasmuch as required by the application of the Convention to concrete factual circumstances. This is precisely why the Court needs to be able to identify a victim: so that a concrete scenario can clearly be sketched and the assessment and judgment made in relation to that.

Having said that, there are more complex cases, such as in relation to covert surveillance discussed below, in which the applicant simply cannot prove that they are a direct victim of a violation. On a strict application of the rules, the Court should declare such an application inadmissible, even if it means that apparent violations of the Convention are not addressed by the Court. In reality, the Court exercises some flexibility and discretion here; if there is

---

[10] Some national constitutional courts can review constitutionality of a law disconnected with its application in a particular case. For example, abstract review is allowed in Germany, Italy, Spain, Moldova, Serbia, Montenegro and many other countries. See Wojciech Sadurski, *Rights Before Courts: A Study of Constitutional Courts in Postcommunist States of Central and Eastern Europe* (2nd edn, Springer, 2014).

absolutely no other way to bring the potential violation before it, the ECtHR may deem the application admissible. Otherwise, it will strike it out and await a complaint in which the victim requirement has been fulfilled.

The ECtHR has departed even further from the requirement to avoid *in abstracto* review in recent climate change litigation, where the NGO that was not a direct victim of a violation was declared to have standing in the ECtHR.[11] This novel approach of the Court led to a debate among commentators, with some calling it a revolution in admissibility criteria.

Although the victim requirement seems straightforward on the face of it, of course there are some situations where a direct victim cannot easily be identified. The Court will occasionally elect to allow those applications to be considered on the merits, prioritising the effective protection of rights over the legal certainty that would come with a strict and uncompromising application of this admissibility rule. We identify six areas in which the ECtHR has significantly departed from a strict construction of the victim requirement.

Potential Victims

In the Court's jargon, 'potential victims' means that the applicants have not yet directly suffered any harm from the violation but there is convincing evidence of the likelihood that a violation affecting them personally will occur.[12] This covers a wide array of the situations in which the ECtHR assesses the possibility of the future occurrence of the violation. The term 'potential victims' covers a very broad range of possible applicants, and as a result it is difficult to identify a relatively clear degree of likelihood that some alleged violations would happen.

In some cases, the alleged future violation will almost certainly happen. For instance, in ***Burden v the United Kingdom***, the applicants complained that the inheritance property tax on the surviving cohabiting sister was discriminatory if compared to people living in a same-sex relationship who did not pay such tax. The applicants, elderly ladies, were alive at the moment of submission of the application, but the Government requested this application to be dismissed as the applicants were not victims yet and none of them had actually paid the tax. The ECtHR rejected this argument, stating that

> given the applicants' age, the wills they have made and the value of the property each owns, the applicants have established that there is a real risk that, in the not-too-distant future, one of them will be required to pay substantial inheritance tax on the property inherited from her sister. In these circumstances, the applicants are directly affected by the legislation and can claim to be victims of the alleged discriminatory treatment.[13]

---

[11] *Verein KlimaSeniorinnen Schweiz and Others v Switzerland* [2024] ECHR 304.

[12] Practical Guide on Admissibility Criteria at www.echr.coe.int/documents/d/echr/admissibility_guide_eng, para 46.

[13] *Burden v the United Kingdom* [2008] ECHR 356, para 35.

The lesser degree of certainty is required in the cases of extradition and deportation, the applicants in which would also fall within the definition of potential victims. It is a well-established rule of the Court that extradition of applicants to the states where they may face torture is contrary to Article 3 of the ECHR.[14] Here the applicant has not necessarily suffered any harm yet but needs to prove that they are under threat of expulsion to a state where they may be of risk of torture. Although the threat of expulsion is easy to establish and the respondent state usually would not even contest this point, establishing that the applicant will risk torture in the receiving state in certain cases is tricky, and the test here is lower than virtual certainty.

Even less certainty is required when the Court considers cases where 'a law violates ... [an applicant's] rights, in the absence of an individual measure of implementation, if he is required either to modify his conduct or risk being prosecuted or if he is a member of a class of people who risk being directly affected by the legislation'.[15] The case of *Dudgeon v the United Kingdom* is a good example here.[16] The UK Government argued that the law criminalising consensual same-sex relations had not been used for a long time and the applicant did not suffer any harm as a result of it. The Court rightly rejected this argument, but one might argue that in this case, the ECtHR allowed the application with less certain risk to be admissible. If the Court's standard was to allow applications only with certainty, in *Dudgeon* the ECtHR would have had to reject the application and wait until the law was applied in practice.

Although admissibility on the basis of being a 'potential victim' is necessary for proper adjudication of cases at the ECtHR, the variations in how potentiality is understood across different circumstances makes clear the Court reserves very broad discretion to decide when a risk of future violation justifies declaring such applications admissible.

Victims of Covert Activities

In some cases, the Court will receive an application about covert activities undertaken by the state. Here, the applicant cannot of course strictly establish victim status, as the covert nature of the activities in question means that nobody can tell for certain whether they were subject to them or not, unless this becomes evident in the subsequent criminal proceedings. Here, the Court should, strictly speaking, deem the application inadmissible, but doing so would mean that the covert nature of the activity would be enough to insulate it from the ECtHR's supervision: a clearly undesirable situation. The Court can thus consider the victim requirement to be satisfied in certain circumstances. This approach has a long history in the case law of the Court,[17] but it

[14] See *Soering v the United Kingdom* [1989] ECHR 14.

[15] *Burden* (n 13) para 34.

[16] *Dudgeon v the United Kingdom* [1981] ECHR 5.

[17] See *Klass and Others v Germany* [1978] ECHR 4.

is well illustrated by the more recent Grand Chamber judgment in the case of *Roman Zakharov v Russia*,[18] in which the applicant challenged secret surveillance of telephone communications in Russia under Article 8.

Here, the applicant could not establish that his telephone communications had been subject to surveillance: the surveillance was, after all, *secret*. However, rather than deem the application inadmissible because victim status could not conclusively be established, the Court prioritised the effectiveness of human rights protection and considered the probability that the applicant's phone conversations were actually interfered with, to assess whether the victim requirement was satisfied. The Court stated that it

> accepts that an applicant can claim to be the victim of a violation occasioned by the mere existence of secret surveillance measures, or legislation permitting secret surveillance measures, if the following conditions are satisfied. Firstly, the Court will take into account the scope of the legislation permitting secret surveillance measures by examining whether the applicant can possibly be affected by it, either because he or she belongs to a group of persons targeted by the contested legislation or because the legislation directly affects all users of communication services by instituting a system where any person can have his or her communications intercepted. Secondly, the Court will take into account the availability of remedies at the national level and will adjust the degree of scrutiny depending on the effectiveness of such remedies.[19]

In other words, if the applicant is a member of a group that may be affected and there is no remedy at the national level that would protect his interests then the Court will find this application admissible, even if individual victimhood cannot conclusively be established.

The same dilemma between legal certainty and effectiveness is evident when it is hard to identify a particular victim from a group of potential victims. Here, the ECtHR cannot be sure that each and every applicant is a victim of a violation but nevertheless deems their applications admissible. In *Finogenov and Others v Russia*,[20] the Court was asked to consider whether the use of gas against terrorists during the Moscow theatre siege in October 2002 was compatible with the ECHR. In this case, the Government argued that the deaths of 125 hostages were not caused by the gas deployed during the rescue operation but were due to pre-existing illnesses exacerbated by the siege. The Court was reasonably sceptical that 125 persons of different ages and physical conditions could die simultaneously at the same place from various pre-existing health conditions.[21] At the same time, the Court could not rule out that none of the deaths had been thus caused. The question was whether the likelihood

[18] *Roman Zakharov v Russia* [2015] ECHR 1065.
[19] ibid, para 171.
[20] *Finogenov and Others v Russia* [2010] ECHR 589.
[21] ibid, para 201.

that some of the deceased were not victims should mean that all of the applications were struck out. The Court thought not:

> As transpires from the Government's submissions, and as the events of the case clearly show, the gas was, at best, potentially dangerous for an ordinary person, and potentially fatal for a weakened person. It is possible that some people were affected more than others on account of their physical condition. Moreover, it is even possible that one or two deaths amongst the applicants' relatives were natural accidents and were not related to the gas at all. Nevertheless, it is safe to conclude that the gas remained a primary cause of the death of a large number of the victims.[22]

If legal certainty had been prioritised in this case (so that the possibility that the applicants had not been victims resulted in the case's being deemed inadmissible), the extent to which the Russian Government had violated (or complied with) the Convention in planning and executing this operation could not have been considered at all by the ECtHR.

Deceased Victims

Another context in which the Court prioritises effectiveness over legal certainty is when nobody but a specialised NGO can bring a complaint on behalf of a deceased applicant. For a long time, it has been the Court's practice that if an applicant is dead, their case can be continued only by their relatives. If such relatives are not known, are absent or do not have an interest in the case then it is to be discontinued. This rule was reconsidered by the ECtHR in *Centre for Legal Resources on behalf of Valentin Câmpeanu v Romania*.[23] The victim in this case had severe mental disabilities and was HIV positive. His mother had abandoned him at birth, and he died in grossly inadequate conditions in the care of the state. The Court described these conditions thus:

> On 20 February 2004 a team of monitors … noticed Mr Câmpeanu's condition … Mr Câmpeanu was alone in an isolated room, unheated and locked, which contained only a bed without any bedding. He was dressed only in a pyjama top. At the time he could not eat or use the toilet without assistance. However, the staff at the [hospital] refused to help him, allegedly for fear that they would contract HIV. Consequently, the only nutrition provided to Mr Câmpeanu was glucose, through a drip. The report concluded that the hospital had failed to provide him with the most basic treatment and care services.[24]

In this case, there were no relatives who could bring the case to the Court on behalf of the deceased. The ECtHR had to consider whether an NGO,

---

[22] ibid, para 202.
[23] *Centre for Legal Resources on behalf of Valentin Câmpeanu v Romania* [2014] ECHR 972.
[24] ibid, para 23.

the Centre for Legal Recourses (CLR), could apply on his behalf. The CLR was neither the direct nor indirect victim of this violation, and had no power of attorney from the deceased. A strict approach to the ECHR rules would suggest that the application ought to have been deemed inadmissible. The Court came to a different conclusion, however, stating that

> in the exceptional circumstances of this case and bearing in mind the serious nature of the allegations, it should be open to the CLR to act as a representative of Mr Câmpeanu, notwithstanding the fact that it had no power of attorney to act on his behalf and that he died before the application was lodged under the Convention. To find otherwise would amount to preventing such serious allegations of a violation of the Convention from being examined at an international level, with the risk that the respondent State might escape accountability under the Convention as a result of its own failure to appoint a legal representative to act on his behalf as it was required to do under national law. Allowing the respondent State to escape accountability in this manner would not be consistent with the general spirit of the Convention, nor with the High Contracting Parties' obligation under Article 34 of the Convention not to hinder in any way the effective exercise of the right to bring an application before the Court.[25]

Here, the CLR was clearly not the victim, but the Court decided that in the interest of fairness and effective rights protection the application warranted assessment on its merits. It thus made it clear that in exceptional cases NGOs could continue an application on behalf of a deceased victim. This exception to the victim rule has since been used in other cases: *Kondrulin v Russia*[26] and *Association for the Defence of Human Rights in Romania –Helsinki Committee on behalf of Ionel Garcea v Romania*.[27]

Corporate Victims

As legal persons, corporations can make applications to the ECtHR; the question is who can take the application on their behalf. Normally, that would be the head of the corporate body, such as the CEO or director. However, if the corporation is in the process of liquidation this question becomes more challenging. Whilst a state-appointed liquidator should ordinarily represent the company, in certain circumstances the shareholders might lodge an application with the Court. In the case of *Agrotexim and Others v Greece*, the Court held that this would be permitted only where 'it is clearly established that it is impossible for the company to apply to the Convention institutions through the organs set up under its Articles of incorporation or – in the event of

[25] ibid, 112.

[26] *Kondrulin v Russia* [2016] ECHR 772.

[27] *Association for the Defence of Human Rights in Romania – Helsinki Committee on behalf of Ionel Garcea v Romania* [2015] ECHR 309.

liquidation – through its liquidators'.[28] Whilst this is a very high standard, it does not absolutely preclude a shareholder-initiated application to the Court where it is necessary because the ordinary organs of the company, for whatever reason, cannot act in this way on its behalf. In the case of *Capital Bank AD v Bulgaria*, the ECtHR explained that allowing a state-appointed liquidator to represent a particular company in the ECtHR will in some cases lead to undermining 'the very essence of the right of individual applications by legal persons, as it would encourage governments to deprive such entities of the possibility to pursue an application lodged at a time when they enjoyed legal personality'.[29] That would in turn mean that the rights enjoyed by legal entities under the Convention could became illusory. In *OAO Neftyanaya Kompaniya Yukos v Russia*,[30] the Court once again used its discretion at the admissibility stage. The applicant company was effectively bankrupted and sold by the Russian authorities, meaning that it had ceased to exist before the Court had a chance to consider the case. Strictly speaking, then, no victim existed and the application should have been deemed inadmissible. The ECtHR declared this application admissible, because otherwise it would encourage authorities to liquidate companies in order to avoid international responsibility for violation of their rights.

Climate Change and Admissibility

While climate change is already impacting on everyday life, it is foreseeable that the most severe impacts will be felt in the future. A question thus arises as to whether and, if so, how human rights law can recognise future harmful effects of climate change as giving rise to current violations. Furthermore, climate change has impacts on all of us, raising questions as to whether the prohibition on *actio popularis* can be navigated to enable the Court to consider claims relating to climate change without undermining the general rule requiring 'victim' status. *Verein KlimaSeniorinnen and others v Switzerland* sharply illustrated the challenges of admissibility in relation to climate change.[31] The case was brought by a group called Verein KlimaSeniorinnen ('Senior Women for Climate Protection in Switzerland'), which claimed that the measures taken in Switzerland (including domestic climate targets) were not sufficient to address and limit global warming, and thus violated Articles 2 and 8 of the ECHR. The group specifically argued that older women – such as the applicants – were especially impacted by heatwaves, which could be linked to climate change. While the Court did not consider that the individual women applicants had victim status, it did find the case admissible in part for the organisation they

[28] *Agrotexim and Others v Greece* [1999] ECHR 42, para 66.
[29] *Capital Bank AD v Bulgaria* [2005] ECHR 752, para 80.
[30] *OAO Neftyanaya Kompaniya Yukos v Russia* [2009] ECHR 287.
[31] *Verein KlimaSeniorinnen Schweiz and others* (n 11).

had founded. In doing so, it found that an individual could establish victim status in climate-change cases on satisfaction of two conditions:

(a) the applicant must be subject to a high intensity of exposure to the adverse effects of climate change, that is, the level and severity of (the risk of) adverse consequences of governmental action or inaction affecting the applicant must be significant; and
(b) there must be a pressing need to ensure the applicant's individual protection, owing to the absence or inadequacy of any reasonable measures to reduce harm.[32]

In contrast, the Court found that organisations might have standing to lodge an application to the ECtHR regarding allegations of inadequate climate action by a state where three conditions are fulfilled:

(a) The organisation is lawfully established in the jurisdiction concerned or has standing to act there;
(b) The organisation can demonstrate that it pursues a dedicated purpose in accordance with its statutory objectives in the defence of the human rights of its members or other affected individuals within the jurisdiction concerned, including protecting rights against the impacts of climate change;
(c) The organisation can demonstrate that it can be regarded as genuinely qualified and representative to act on behalf of members or other affected individuals within the jurisdiction who are subject to specific threats or adverse effects of climate change on their lives, health or well-being as protected under the Convention.[33]

While these criteria enable associations to bring claims to the ECtHR in circumstances not anticipated by earlier case law, articulation of these criteria might be considered a novel approach to preventing effectively universal access to the Court in climate litigation[34] while ensuring that some climate-change-related claims can be considered in the Court. While there is some debate as to whether this indicates continuity with the Court's existing approach to NGOs acting on behalf of victims who cannot represent themselves,[35] or whether it is a radical departure from the Court's approach to admissibility, it is reasonable to claim

[32] ibid, para 487.
[33] ibid, para 502.
[34] See Marko Milanovic, 'A Quick Take on the European Court's Climate Change Judgments' (*EJIL: Talk!*, 9 April 2024) at www.ejiltalk.org/a-quick-take-on-the-european-courts-climate-change-judgments/.
[35] George Letsas, 'The European Court's Legitimacy After KlimaSeniorinnen' (2024) 5(4) *European Convention on Human Rights Law Review* 444. See also Corina Heri, 'KlimaSeniorinnen, the prohibition of actio popularis cases, and future generations – a false dilemma?' (*EJIL: Talk!*, 19 December 2024) at www.ejiltalk.org/klimaseniorinnen-the-prohibition-of-actio-popularis-cases-and-future-generations-a-false-dilemma/.

that the Court prioritised effectiveness of human rights protection over strict adherence to existing admissibility criteria in this case. Further elaboration in the ECtHR's case law is awaited, to see how these new criteria for admissibility work in practice.

As we can see, the Court takes the victim requirement seriously, usually applying it strictly to ensure an appropriate level of legal certainty. However, if it is impossible to prove victim status, or if an application cannot be made by the victim directly, the Court may prioritise the effectiveness of human rights protection over strict application of the victim rule and allow the application in order to ensure the complaint can be adjudicated upon. The Court thus attempts to strike a balance between strict application of the rules and effectiveness-oriented discretion, illustrating that even the most straightforward-looking admissibility criteria involve some degree of *judgement* in their application.

Debate 3

How Significant Must Disadvantage Be?

In 2010, Protocol 14 introduced a new admissibility criterion focusing on the significance of the alleged violation, which was subsequently amended by Protocol 15. Article 35(3)(b) now reads:

> The Court shall declare inadmissible any individual application submitted under Article 34 if it considers that:
>
> ...
>
> (b) the applicant has not suffered a significant disadvantage, unless respect for human rights as defined in the Convention and the Protocols thereto requires an examination of the application on the merits.

This criterion adds considerable discretion at the stage of assessing admissibility. It also calls into question the extent to which the Court may have to balance broader, systemic interests (in prioritising the 'most important' cases) and the principle of individual complaint and individual justice in the ECtHR:

> On the face of it, 'no significant disadvantage' appears to be a criterion that is intended to allow the Court to be more selective by filtering out less important cases (with importance being determined by using significance of disadvantage as a proxy), thus allowing the ECtHR to focus on cases that might be said to have more potential for development of the Convention.[36]

[36] Fiona de Londras and Kanstantsin Dzehtsiarou, 'Managing Judicial Innovation in the European Court of Human Rights' (2015) 15(3) *Human Rights Law Review* 523, 531. The history of the introduction of this new criterion points to its attempt to achieve all of these things: Antoine Buyse, 'Significantly Insignificant? The Life in the Margins of the Admissibility Criterion

The former Prime Minister of the United Kingdom, David Cameron, famously called the ECtHR a 'small claims court', and it seems this amendment of the Convention was a response to such criticism.[37] Whenever the question of significant disadvantage is considered by the Court[38] as a matter of admissibility, an underlying claim is being made that reflects the tension between the Court's *adjudicatory function*, namely resolving legal conflicts between a specific applicant and respondent state, and its *meta-function* (sometimes called constitutionalist function), where the Court acts as a standard-setting institution that can impact multiple comparable cases:[39]

> The implicit claim is either (i) that the disadvantage suffered is so significant that a refusal to hear the case when it is otherwise inadmissible would be unjustifiable on constitutionalist grounds, even if its resolution requires judicial innovation and (ii) that the disadvantage suffered is so insignificant (thus the case does not raise 'real' constitutionalist questions) that even compliance with the other admissibility grounds ought not to be sufficient for the Court – overburdened and in need of rationalising its workload as it is – to agree to hear it.[40]

In no circumstances could it be suggested that this analysis is simple or automatic, or that it requires no discretion.

The Court has made it clear that determining whether the disadvantage suffered by the applicant was significant requires consideration of '[t]he applicant's *subjective* feeling about the impact of the alleged violations [and] has to be justifiable on *objective* grounds'.[41] This means that the Court will consider what is at stake (the objective element) and the impact of this potential damage on the applicant (the subjective element). Of course, both require a good deal of judgement in order to assess them, even as a matter of admissibility. The Court considers both financial and non-financial disadvantage: while with the former it is possible to establish some sort of threshold, the latter is open to a wider margin of discretion.

The criterion also raises questions about the extent to which the Convention is beginning to shift from a principle of individual justice and universality of rights protection. It is of the essence of human rights as protected by ECHR law that they are available to all, and that all breaches are subject to

in Article 35 § 3 (b) ECHR' in Brianne McGonigle et al (eds), *The Realization of Human Rights: When Theory Meets Practice. Studies in Honour of Leo Zwaak* (Intersentia, 2013) 107.

[37] Nicholas Watt, 'David Cameron Calls for Reform of European Court of Human Rights' (*The Guardian*, 25 January 2012) at www.theguardian.com/law/2012/jan/25/david-cameron-reform-european-court.

[38] This new admissibility criterion can be raised by a respondent government or by the Court of its own motion, see *Ionescu v Romania* [2010] ECHR 1023.

[39] See Kanstantsin Dzehtsiarou, *Can the European Court of Human Rights Shape European Public Order?* (Cambridge University Press, 2021) chapter 4.

[40] de Londras and Dzehtsiarou (n 36) 531.

[41] *Korolev v Russia* [2010] ECHR 1051 (emphasis added).

mechanisms to ensure that they are remedied. The 'no significant disadvantage' admissibility criterion seems to undermine this claim, suggesting that the ECtHR will step in to ensure protection of human rights only if the alleged violation is significant. This is of course justifiable from a purely instrumental point of view: the Court does not have unlimited resources, it cannot replace national systems of human rights protection, and dealing with minor claims can potentially delay its involvement with larger-scale issues. One might argue that the 'no significant disadvantage' requirement is a proper compromise between the ideal of universality and the reality of limited resources. On the one hand, the Convention allows small claims to be rejected; but on the other hand, the Convention puts an obligation on the Court to consider the consequences for the meta-function of the Court if the case is declared inadmissible due to there being no significant disadvantage. In some instances, even small claims can major consequences, and the ECtHR should ensure that it does not dismiss one of such cases as insignificant. Pursuant to Article 35, the ECtHR should not deploy this admissibility criterion if 'respect for human rights' requires examination of the case. In some cases, the Court ruled that this criterion should not be considered if the case raises a novel issue of principle[42] or when it relates to a systematic problem.[43]

Thus it seems that if the issue is of prima facie importance for the meta-function of the Court, lack of significant disadvantage becomes irrelevant. Since neither 'significant disadvantage' nor 'respect for human rights' can be defined with precision, the ECtHR is free to use wide discretion in applying this criterion.

DEBATE 4

HOW MUCH DISCRETION SHOULD THE COURT HAVE IN DECIDING ADMISSIBILITY?

In Debates 2 and 3 we have already established that admissibility criteria leave the Court with a considerable amount of discretion, even in what seems at first glance to be a 'merely' technical assessment of admissibility. This may seem confounding. As Tickell has observed:

> Determination of the admissibility of applications is conceived as the self-evident administration of clear rules, operating without flexibility and without discretion. Case 'filtering' under the Convention's admissibility criteria is envisaged as a solid 'iron cage' of weary but dogged administration, its clear rules gating the legally, politically and ethically laden work of adjudication which admissible, 'meritorious' cases are subjected to. This distinction is neatly captured by the official terminology. The admissibility of an application is determined by a

[42] See *Daniel Faulkner v. the United Kingdom* [2016] ECHR 823.
[43] See *Finger v Bulgaria* [2011] ECHR 781.

> 'decision', while the merits of a case are assessed in a 'judgment'. Admissibility decision-making is not a 'judgment' in institutional terms, but in the orthodox understanding, it is also assumed to involve no judgment on the part of judges and Registry lawyers.[44]

However, in truth there are *no* admissibility criteria that would exclude discretionary decision-making. Indeed, so extensive is the discretion in practice that what is presented as an admissibility decision can often seem much more like a judgment on the merits. Moreover, even the Court's own Guide on Admissibility refers to two admissibility criteria as being based on merits. These criteria are 'manifestly ill-founded' and 'no significant disadvantage'.[45] Here one can expect a greater level of reasoning by the ECtHR than is usually the case with decisions on admissibility. Most admissibility decisions are not published, but they are final and cannot be reviewed. Moreover, the judges usually decide inadmissibility on the basis of a short note prepared by the lawyers of the Registry who are originally from the respondent state against which the application was brought. These notes explain the basic facts of the case and (very) briefly the reasons for declaring it inadmissible. Lists of putatively inadmissible cases

> transmitted electronically to the single judges contain only one or two-sentence summaries of each matter recommended for dismissal, identifying the right being invoked; the judges do not see the applications and a few have complained of feeling that they are expected to 'rubber-stamp' the decisions of the Registry.[46]

Although these notes from the Registry are checked and rechecked by more experienced lawyers, the original 'filtering' is often done by a relatively inexperienced 'B lawyer'. This initial screening is crucial for the fate of the case. Although this shadow decision-making is very effective and quick in tackling the Court's backlog, it raises questions of procedural legitimacy. In the past, the applicants were not even told on the basis of what criterion the application was declared inadmissible. In 2017, the Court changed its practice and started informing the applicants of the reason for inadmissibility. In practice this means that the Court sends a very short, generic, paragraph-long decision indicating, for example, that the application did not disclose any appearance of a violation of the rights enshrined in the Convention. While this new approach enhances the transparency of admissibility decision-making somewhat, it clearly cannot be compared with full decisions.

[44] Andrew Tickell, 'Dismantling the Iron-Cage: the Discursive Persistence and Legal Failure of a "Bureaucratic Rational" Construction of the Admissibility Decision-Making of the European Court of Human Rights' (2011) 12(10) *German Law Journal* 1786, 1789.

[45] See at www.echr.coe.int/documents/d/echr/admissibility_guide_eng.

[46] Dinah Shelton, 'Significantly Disadvantaged? Shrinking Access to the European Court of Human Rights' (2016) 16(2) *Human Rights Law Review* 303, 309.

The requirements that there would be no abuse of the right of individual petition and that the application ought not to be manifestly ill-founded both allow for very significant discretion. The Court used abuse of petition to reject 'petty' applications even before Protocol 14 introduced the 'no significant disadvantage' admissibility criterion discussed in Debate 3.[47] Abuse of petition can mean anything from providing false documents[48] or identity,[49] to failing to update the Court about important developments in the case at the national level, the use of offensive language[50] or disclosure of the terms of friendly settlements. Undoubtedly, decisions about apparent abuse of the right of petition are complex. They require an understanding of the national legal system and national language, and often call for an assessment of an applicant's aim in making an application. Although some instances declaring an application to be an abuse of right of individual petition can be rather straightforward, complexities do arise.

The decision of the Court to reject as inadmissible the application from a well-known Russian LGBTQI activist Alekseyev on the basis of this criterion led to a debate about the role of admissibility. The reason for that was the insults directed towards the Court and its judges by the applicant. The Court explained it as following:

> The Court … observes that the statements about the Court and its judges published on the accounts in question are virulently and personally offensive and threatening. In particular, Mr Alekseyev published the judges' photographs with such captions as 'alcoholic', 'drug addict', 'corrupt', and 'this crone owes me 100,000 euros … God will punish her'. He also called the judges, among other terms, 'European bastards and degenerates', 'freaks', 'venal scum' and 'idiotic'. He wished that they would 'snuff it as soon as possible like dogs', threatened to 'torture [them] … with litres of vodka' and announced that 'it [was] time to set fire to the European Court of Human Rights'. He also stated: 'We should not have given wenches the right to vote … They should be cooking soup'. These statements clearly exceed the limits of normal, civic and legitimate criticism.[51]

As this shows, the Court has wide discretion in determining what constitutes abuse of rights. The same is true of manifestly ill-founded claims, which are those that treat the ECtHR as a court of fourth instance, applications with a clear absence of a violation, unsubstantiated applications and the like. In these cases, the line between an admissibility decision (manifestly ill-founded) and a merits decision (no violation) seems very thin indeed, and the Court appears to use substantial discretion in categorising the outcome as one or the other.

---

[47] See *Bock v Germany* [2010] ECHR 139; and *Dudek v Germany* [2010] ECHR 1991.

[48] *Poznanski and Others v Germany* App no 25101/05 (ECtHR, 3 July 2007).

[49] *Drijfhout v Netherlands* [2011] ECHR 408.

[50] *Kolosovskiy v Latvia* App no 50183/99 (ECtHR, 29 January 2007).

[51] *Zhdanov and Others v Russia* [2019] ECHR 565, para 83.

Let us illustrate this by reference to situations where there is a clear or apparent lack of violation. In *Mentzen v Latvia* the applicant complained that the Latvian authorities had changed her surname according to Latvian spelling rules.[52] Although the ECtHR had established that there was an interference with the rights protected by the Convention and discussed the proportionality of the interference, the result was that the application was deemed manifestly ill-founded instead of the Court's making a finding of no violation. Although legally speaking the outcome is almost the same, there is a procedural difference (where there is no violation a case can be referred to the Grand Chamber) and a symbolic difference for the applicant.

In some instances, cases that are declared manifestly ill-founded by the ECtHR are not only accepted by other international adjudicators but result in the finding of violations there. In *Singh v France*,[53] the ECtHR considered whether the French requirement to appear bareheaded in official photographs was compatible with the freedom of religion of those followers of the Sikh religion, who have a religious obligation to wear a turban. The ECtHR decided that religious rights can be limited in the interests of public safety, and declared the application manifestly ill-founded. The same applicant brought a complaint about the same matter to the Human Rights Committee (UN HRC) – the UN body that supervises implementation of the International Covenant on Civil and Political Rights. Article 18 of the Covenant protects the freedom to manifest religion in a similar way to Article 9 of the ECHR. The UN HRC declared this application admissible and found a violation of the Covenant in this case. While it is quite normal that different international tribunals weigh different aspects of the proportionality test differently, this reveals a troubling situation as, by finding the case to be manifestly ill-founded, the ECtHR denied the opportunity for the applicants to be heard on the merits, whilst another tribunal considered this case and found a violation.[54]

Steven Greer has written:

> It is naïve … to regard the manifestly ill-founded criterion as an objective test. Determining if an application is, or is not, manifestly ill-founded requires the exercise of judgment and the interpretation of conduct, facts, and norms; it is, therefore, inescapably discretionary. Some commentators maintain that many complaints are rejected on this basis simply because the Court does not have the resources to consider them properly.[55]

While many recognise that the 'manifestly ill-founded' admissibility rule can lead to the rejection of complaints that are not manifestly deficient on their

[52] *Mentzen v Latvia* App no 71074/01 (ECtHR, 7 December 2004).

[53] *Singh v France* [2008] ECHR 1906.

[54] *Singh v France*, HRC, 26/09/2013, CCPR/C/108/D/1928/2010.

[55] Steven Greer, 'What's Wrong with the European Convention on Human Rights' (2008) 30(3) *Human Rights Quarterly* 680, 686.

merits, this is generally recognised as a pragmatic mechanism for freeing up judicial time for cases that are more serious, and to avoid dealing with cases that it is evident will not lead to any change.[56] In other words, it is arguable that 'manifestly ill-founded' decisions help to keep an overburdened and under-resourced court operating effectively. This is yet another illustration of the Court's having to negotiate competing grounds of its legitimacy. On the one hand, the Court has to deliver judgments in a timely manner; on the other, it should avoid allowing procedural simplifications to create so much discretion that equally meritorious cases may have utterly divergent outcomes.

'Manifestly ill-founded' is not the only criterion that gives the Court extensive discretion to decide on admissibility. The same could be said of a decision that a victim has lost their victim status because 'the national authorities have acknowledged, either expressly or in substance, and then afforded redress for, the breach of the Convention'.[57] Even if these conditions are satisfied, the ECtHR might consider whether there are any reasons related to European Public Order that would justify continuation of the proceedings.[58] The Court has also reserved some discretion in deciding whether the redress provided by the Contracting Party is sufficient to justify discontinuation of a case. In *Ciorap v Moldova (No 2)*,[59] for example, the Moldovan Supreme Court explicitly acknowledged that denial of medical treatment combined with the conditions of detention amounted to inhuman treatment of the applicant, and awarded him compensation of €600 for non-pecuniary damage. The ECtHR might have considered the applicant's victim status to have been resolved through this award, but instead declared the case admissible because the compensation was considered to be grossly inadequate.[60]

The ECtHR cannot accept an application if it has been adjudicated by or is pending at another international tribunal. Although rare, deciding on admissibility in such cases involves assessment of the parties in the respective proceedings, the relevant legal provisions relied on by them, the scope of their claims and the types of the redress sought in order to assess whether they are properly regarded as the same complaints. This is not always straightforward. In *Folgerø and Others v Norway*,[61] the Court considered whether the refusal of the Norwegian authorities to grant the applicants a full exemption from religious classes in public schools violated their rights under Article 9 of the ECHR and Article 2 of Protocol 1. A very similar complaint was submitted by another complainant to the UN HRC. Moreover, the complaint was brought to the UN HRC after the same national proceedings to which both groups of

[56] See, eg, David Harris et al, *Harris, O'Boyle and Warbrick Law of the European Convention on Human Rights* (4th edn, Oxford University Press, 2018), 75.

[57] *Amuur v France*, 25 June 1996, Reports of Judgments and Decisions 1996-III, para 36.

[58] *Paez v Sweden*, 30 October 1997, Reports of Judgments and Decisions 1997-VII, para 30.

[59] *Ciorap v Moldova (No 2)* [2010] ECHR 1138.

[60] ibid.

[61] *Folgerø and Others v Norway* [2011] ECHR 2189.

applicants were parties.[62] To all intents and purposes, then, these were very similar if not effectively the same complaint, but the ECtHR declared the application admissible, formally focusing on the fact that the applicants in the UN HRC were not the same people as the applicants in the case before it. In contrast, *POA and Others v the United Kingdom*[63] concerned the blanket ban on industrial action by prison officers. The applicants – the prison officers' trade union and two of its officials – argued that the ban was incompatible with Article 11 of the ECHR. The complaint had been also raised before the International Labour Organisation (ILO) Committee on Freedom of Association, and according to the Court the complaints to the ILO and ECtHR were virtually identical, although not all the applicants were the same.[64] Some of the applicants to the ECtHR were individual persons, not the trade union as such, and they were not and could not be the claimants in the ILO as it only accepts collective applications. However, the Court declared this application inadmissible because 'applicants must be seen as being closely associated with the proceedings and the complaints before the Committee on Freedom of Association, by virtue of their status as officials of the POA'.[65] It is difficult to see what can have made the difference between *Folgerø and Others* and *POA and Others*, but one was deemed inadmissible and the other not, both under the same principle. Here the effects of the Court's discretion were clearly felt.

Even the very narrowest of admissibility criteria allow for some discretion. Take, for example, the rule against anonymous applications. This requires that the applicant be identified in applications, and when a case is communicated to the respondent government the name of the applicant will be revealed. The rationale behind this is fairly simple: the respondent government needs to know who the applicant is if it is to be able to prove that alleged human rights violation did not happen. The Court normally informs the Contracting Parties about the name of the applicant, even if they fear that such disclosure might put them at risk of ill-treatment. Whilst the ECtHR can anonymise the name of the applicant in such a case, this only means that the public at large will not know their name; the respondent state will. Even in respect of this – seemingly unambiguous – rule, however, the Court exercises discretion. In *Shamayev and Others v Georgia and Russia*,[66] the applicants were of Chechen origin and were awaiting extradition from Georgia to Russia. The events complained of took place during the war in Chechnya, and the applicants were wanted in Russia on suspicion of terrorism. Some of the applicants submitted pseudonyms instead of their real names in their initial applications to the Court (they later disclosed their true identities). The Russian Government argued that the application was anonymous and should be declared inadmissible, but the ECtHR disagreed,

[62] ibid.

[63] *POA and Others v the United Kingdom* [2013] ECHR 600.

[64] ibid, para 28.

[65] ibid.

[66] *Shamayev and Others v Georgia and Russia* App no 36378/02, (ECtHR, 16 September 2003).

stating that 'the Court does not question the fact that, behind the tactics of concealing true identities for reasons that can be understood, there are persons who are real, concrete and identifiable by a sufficient number of indicia, other than their names'.[67] This can be contrasted with *'Blonje' v the Netherlands*, in which the applicant also used a pseudonym but the Court declared the case inadmissible.[68] There are very few published decisions of the Court dealing with anonymity, as it seems that there are not too many such applications and the majority of them are dealt with by a single judge and never pronounced publicly. Although the *Shamayev* judgment is exceptional, it underpins the argument that we are making here, namely that admissibility is far from being free from judicial discretion and the process of admissibility needs to be closely scrutinised.

Debate 5

How Does Admissibility Relate to Effectiveness?

It seems that the Court derives at least some of its legitimacy in the eyes of individuals from the fact that it accepts applications from each and every person who is under the jurisdiction of one of 46 Contracting Parties to the Convention. Of course, inadmissible applications can and perhaps should be rejected, and we have already seen that the criteria of admissibility have plenty of discretion built into them. As a result, the outcome of an application is not always easily predictable. This lack of predictability has allowed some commentators to argue that the Court picks and chooses which applications it deems important enough to assess on their merits through admissibility decisions.[69] The suggestion is that the Court is really making decisions about importance, prioritising cases of potential standard-setting significance and continuing to perform the 'dual functions': the adjudicatory one and the meta-function.

This allegation is perhaps fuelled by the fact that admissibility decisions are lacking in transparency; there is not usually a written and well-reasoned text explaining the admissibility decision. The Court justifies this by reference to the limited resources available and the practical difficulties of providing reasons in every inadmissibility decision. The truth is that in most cases unsuccessful applicants do not even know specifically why they failed a particular admissibility criterion. Given this, the argument goes that the Court may well be moving away from a vision of individual justice and instead embracing the framework of 'constitutional' justice, which prioritises its meta-function within which it

[67] ibid.

[68] *'Blondje' v the Netherlands* [2009] ECHR 1495.

[69] See Steven Greer and Luzius Wildhaber, 'Revisiting the Debate about "Constitutionalising" the European Court of Human Rights' (2012) 12(4) *Human Rights Law Review* 655; Fiona de Londras, 'Dual Functionality and the Persistent Frailty of the European Court of Human Rights' (2013) 1 *European Human Rights Law Review* 38.

need only focus on vaguely defined strategic cases that can improve the system of human rights as a whole.

This conclusion can also be corroborated by references to the Court's official priority policy,[70] which was introduced in 2009 to ensure important cases would be dealt with in a timely manner. Before 2009, all cases were dealt with in chronological order, which meant that some crucial issues that needed prompt resolution could be stuck in the Court's docket for years. Pragmatically, the introduction of this priority policy strengthens the meta-function of the ECtHR, meaning that the applications raising questions capable of having an impact on the effectiveness of the Convention system in a general sense have priority even over the applications related to the right to life, the prohibition of torture and the prohibition of slavery. This policy was further updated in 2021, and the direction of travel emphasising the meta-function of the Court became even more obvious. The Court established the category of the so-called 'impact cases' among those that do not fall within the highest three categories of the previous priority policy. The Court identified the following criteria for selecting the 'impact cases': 'the conclusion of the case might lead to a change or clarification of international or domestic legislation or practice; the case touches upon moral or social issues; the case deals with an emerging or otherwise significant human rights issue'.[71] If this is seen together with the mandatory friendly settlement phase of every case through which many applications can be resolved,[72] the Court is prioritising its resources in order to concentrate on its general impact on the development of human rights standards, rather than focusing them on remedying individual human rights violations *for the sake of ensuring they are remedied.*

This has an impact not only on the Court's ability to develop its meta-function, which some consider would increase its overall effectiveness, but also on the likelihood of the Contracting Parties' being the subjects of adverse decisions. Currently, over 80 per cent of admissible cases result in a finding of violation of the ECHR,[73] so that, as Shelton has commented, '[l]imiting admissibility means limiting condemnation'.[74] Of course, the proponents of limited admissibility argue that the Court is simply unable to deal with all applications that are submitted to it, and loses its impact on shaping European Public Order when it tries to do so.[75] However, there are at least two counter-arguments to that.

---

[70] 'The Court's Priority Policy' at www.echr.coe.int/documents/priority_policy_eng.pdf.

[71] At www.echr.coe.int/documents/d/echr/Court_that_matters_ENG.

[72] See Veronika Fikfak, 'Against settlement before the European Court of Human Rights, International Journal of Constitutional Law' (2022) 20(3) *International Journal of Constitutional Law* 942.

[73] In 2016 the Court delivered 993 judgments; in 828 judgments (83%) the Court found at least one violation of the Convention (HUDOC database search).

[74] Dinah Shelton, 'Significantly Disadvantaged? Shrinking Access to the European Court of Human Rights' (2016) 16(2) *Human Rights Law Review* 303, 306.

[75] See de Londras (n 69).

First, the Court derives at least some of its moral legitimacy from the fact that every person under the jurisdiction of the 46 Contracting Parties can bring a complaint and this complaint will be dealt with. This rule is egalitarian and non-arbitrary (at least on the face of it). Here two clear sources of the Court's legitimacy might be in tension with one another: its effectiveness and its moral purpose of universal rights protection. Can the Court sacrifice some less important applications (irrespective of how this might be defined in practice) in order to achieve more impact in particular problematic areas? Of course, the answer to this question will be a matter of degree, depending on how much positive impact the Court can make and how many applications should be sacrificed in order to achieve that. If it takes the Court decades to come to an important application because it has to deal with hundreds of low-importance or inadmissible applications then its effectiveness will be very low. On the other hand, if the Court concentrates on a handful of 'important' cases, ignoring all other potentially meritorious applications, then the ECtHR might lose its role as an effective adjudicator and applications may simply not make their way to the Court at all. Taken from this perspective, the argument goes that the ECtHR needs to strike a very delicate balance between assessing the importance of the issues it deals with and maintaining the right of individual petition. Indeed, this is effectively what the Court already attempts to do.

Second, in order to have a positive impact on rights in at least some Contracting Parties, the Court cannot easily avoid repetitive cases. This is because it has become clear that countries in respect of which repetitive cases are brought are either unwilling or unable to adopt effective solutions to systemic and recurring human rights violations (such as detention conditions or delays in criminal proceedings) and that the Court offers (and should offer) some satisfaction to the aggrieved applicants.[76] One might wonder whether this is the proper role of an international tribunal, but on the other hand it may create sufficient pressure on Contracting Parties to introduce reforms to avoid constant embarrassment at the international level that there would eventually be a positive rights-enhancing outcome.

We must not forget that we still live in a Europe where millions of people cannot receive redress in their domestic legal systems, where human rights abuses occur daily and are serious, and where for many the ECtHR truly is the only hope of protecting rights and effecting change. In these circumstances, it is difficult to avoid the argument that the Court ought to continue to take individual applications, even where they might not seem serious enough for the level of resource that will be applied to addressing them, because people frankly *need* it to do so. However, what we have seen in this chapter is that through application of the admissibility criteria in ways that display significant

[76] Kanstantsin Dzehtsiarou and Alan Greene, 'Restructuring the European Court of Human Rights: Preserving the Right of Individual Petition and Promoting Constitutionalism' [2013] *Public Law* 710.

discretion, this is not necessarily happening, or at least not consistently enough to sustain this argument. Neither is the Court clearly abandoning this approach and embracing a sole focus on its meta-function. For some, it is precisely this that makes the Court effective: its ability to do both, albeit imperfectly. For others, a decision between the two is urgently required. Ultimately, this goes once more to the question of what the ECtHR is for, and how its purpose can be achieved.

Conclusion

Every formation of the Court can declare a judgment inadmissible, including the Grand Chamber.[77] As we have seen in this chapter, many decisions that are formally made by a formation of the Court are effectively pre-determined by Registry lawyers, a part of the Court we have already argued is opaque, under-studied and vitally important to the work of the Court. This is of concern not just because of the lack of transparency, but also because, as we have shown, every criterion of admissibility allows some exceptions, and the Court can adjust these criteria if circumstances require it. Admissibility criteria range between those that allow very broad discretion and are akin to judgments on merits (such as manifestly ill-founded complaints or abuse of the right to individual petition), and those that are less open to interpretation but still leave some space for decision-making to the Court (such as the four-month rule or the rule against anonymous applications). Not only that, but admissibility is a key stage in the management of the work of the Court, which must sometimes decide between its adjudicatory and meta-function.

Further Reading

Kanstantsin Dzehtsiarou and Alan Greene, 'Restructuring the European Court of Human Rights: Preserving the Right of Individual Petition and Promoting Constitutionalism' [2013] *Public Law* 710.

George Letsas, 'The European Court's Legitimacy After KlimaSeniorinnen' (2024) 5(4) *European Convention on Human Rights Law Review* 444.

Dinah Shelton, 'Significantly Disadvantaged? Shrinking Access to the European Court of Human Rights' (2016) 16(2) *Human Rights Law Review* 303.

Andrew Tickell, 'Dismantling the Iron-Cage: the Discursive Persistence and Legal Failure of a "Bureaucratic Rational" Construction of the Admissibility Decision-Making of the European Court of Human Rights' (2011) 12(10) *German Law Journal* 1786.

[77] *Bankovic and Others v Belgium and Others*, ECHR 890ECHR 2001-XII; *Behrami and Behrami v France and Saramati v France, Germany and Norway* App nos 71412/01 and 78166/01 (ECtHR, 2 May 2007).

4

Evolution or Revolution?

Interpretation of the Convention by the European Court of Human Rights

The European Court of Human Rights (ECtHR or the Court) has long held that the European Convention on Human Rights (ECHR or the Convention) is a living instrument to be interpreted in light of present-day conditions. What this means, in essence, is that the Convention is subject to evolutive interpretation, that is its meaning can 'evolve' over time. As one might imagine, this is hardly without controversy. It raises questions not only about the appropriate role of judges in 'making' law (as it is sometimes put), but also about whether what the Convention is now said to mean (having been subject to evolutive interpretation) is what the states actually signed up to. In other words, to return to chapter 1, is it *legitimate* when we consider what states consented to when they ratified the Convention? Does evolutive interpretation mean that states are being held to international standards to which they have never truly consented? Or should states be presumed to consent to a human rights instrument and its associated system of application and enforcement (such as the ECHR and its infrastructure) *as interpreted and applied* by its assigned adjudicator (in this case, the Court and, before that, the Commission and the Court)? If so, how can this presumption be justified and when can it be rebutted?

Even if it is the case that states should be seen as consenting broadly to the *system* as it develops and is applied, it is clear that evolutive interpretation has the potential to create tensions between the Court and the Contracting Parties. At the very least, states may raise a metaphorical eyebrow when the Court finds them to have obligations under the Convention that were not and could not have been foreseen when they signed up to it. At its peak, this can underpin damaging claims that the Court is illegitimate. Given this context, we might wonder why the Court engages in evolutive interpretation at all. Why does it open itself up to claims of illegitimacy? What is the value that evolutive interpretation brings to the Strasbourg system of human rights protection? This is the first debate that we will consider here. Even if evolution might be said to be valuable in a system designed to protect rights, determination of a 'tipping point' for such evolution can be hotly contested; the 'tipping moment' is the moment at which the law is ripe for evolution and the Court acts accordingly. The second debate we will consider relates to precisely this question: when does the Court decide it is time for evolution, and how does it come to that decision? It is often assumed that evolutive interpretation broadens the scope of human rights protection and improves human rights standards, but is evolutive interpretation necessarily progressive, or can rights protection be lowered by the application of the 'living instrument' doctrine? This is the third debate that we will look at in this chapter.

Debate 1

Is Evolutive Interpretation of the Convention Necessary?

The argument against evolutive interpretation is, in essence, an originalist one: it is the claim that the document means what it meant when it was signed.[1] Any development beyond that is illegitimate because it involves the Court (perceived as undemocratic) in 'making law'. This is a common argument in relation to written domestic constitutions, for example, but it is one to which there is a compelling response in that context. Let us, for these purposes, analogise the Convention to a constitution for a moment. Constitutions should have a certain chrononomy: they should be able to account for the past, govern the present and accommodate the future.[2]

As society evolves, and as new governance challenges emerge, it is unlikely that a strictly originalist approach to any text would allow for it to meet that standard of chrononomy, meaning that one of three things must happen: the Constitution must be formally changed to account for social change and new governance challenges; the Constitution must evolve (through judicial interpretation and everyday constitutional practice) to govern contemporary society; or the Constitution must be left to be unfit for purpose, governing only the phenomena that can be squeezed into the text as it was at the time that it was written, and therefore failing to deal properly with social and legal phenomena that develop subsequently. Each of these positions has its value and its drawbacks. The first allows for popular rejuvenation of the constitutional landscape, although it also brings a certain degree of instability. It can also be manifestly late and ineffective in dealing with complex current legal issues, as formal legal change is often time consuming and (for good reasons) difficult to achieve. The second position allows for constitutions to evolve in order to ensure that all areas of government activity are effectively governed by the constitutional *acquis*. Having said that, judicial interpretation resembles law-making and opens the courts to criticism. The third option brings the

[1] The arguments of originalism are widely used in debates regarding the meaning of the US Constitution. See, for example, John McGinnis and Michael Rappaport, *Originalism and the Good Constitution* (Harvard University Press, 2013).

[2] Richard Kay, 'Constitutional Chrononomy' (2000) 13(1) *Ratio Juris* 31.

virtue of legal stability and certainty whilst also limiting the possibility of what some (derisorily) term 'judicial activism'. The effectiveness of such an approach is, however, limited by the difficulties of applying concepts that are over 70 years old to the current events.

Of course, the ECHR is not a constitution per se, but some of these same arguments might be said to arise in respect of it. The Convention emerged in a very particular set of circumstances: when the continent of Europe (and beyond) had just emerged from the Second World War and the Holocaust, when Europe (and the world) was dividing into 'the West' and 'the Rest' in political terms, and when political stability and peace were far from guaranteed. The Convention, then, had a certain context and was intended to achieve a particular outcome: to protect us from the re-emergence of totalitarianism and to firmly identify human rights as having the capacity to *limit* states' desired actions. An originalist view of the Convention would say that this is what the Convention was designed to do, and that this is *all* the Convention is designed to do, so that using it to prevent the state from deporting a suspected terrorist, or to require the state to recognise someone's true gender, is taking it too far. It is arguably not what the states consented to.

Of course, whether this is right or not depends on one's perspective on what the Convention was for. Was the Convention designed simply to protect the rights specified therein in the manner understood at the time? Or was the Convention drafted to ensure that human rights would be an effective limitation on state power? If the latter, then evolution of our understanding of the rights therein is not only legitimate but also, arguably, *necessary*. Without it, we might wonder whether, for example, rights implications arising from developments in technology (eg, AI-assisted government decision-making, advances in genetics, and assisted human reproduction) could be effectively addressed by application of the Convention. A literal originalist approach to the meaning of the Convention would suggest that the Court should not deal with any of those issues, at least inasmuch as they give rise to novel questions of rights that did not arise and would not have been contemplated in 1950; that the text of the Convention has a clear and 'true' meaning, to which judges should limit themselves.[3] Even some enthusiasts of a restrained judiciary accept that the shortcomings that would flow from such propositions show evolution in some senses is necessary.[4]

It is worth noting, also, that the Convention's status as an international treaty makes it ripe for evolutive interpretation. Given the role of consent in creating intentional obligations, this may at first seem counter-intuitive, but

[3] For a powerful critique in the ECHR context, see Sandra Fredman, 'Living Trees or Deadwood: The Interpretive Challenge of the European Convention on Human Rights' in NW Barber, Richard Ekins and Paul Yowell (eds), *Lord Sumption and the Limits of the Law* (Hart Publishing, 2016) 45.

[4] See, for example, Lord Hoffmann, 'Judges, Interpretation, and Self-Government' in Barber, Ekins and Yowell (eds) (n 3) 67.

international law does not require a strict adherence to the idea of *original* consent as the *sole* basis for obligation. Article 31(1) of the Vienna Convention on the Law of Treaties (VCLT) provides that '[a] treaty shall be interpreted in good faith in accordance with the ordinary meaning to be given to the terms of the treaty in their context and in the light of its object and purpose'. The context is expressly said to include '[a]ny subsequent practice in the application of the treaty which establishes the agreement of the parties regarding its interpretation'.[5] Based on this, the established practice of Contracting Parties in executing judgments of the Court (*including those featuring evolutive interpretation*) and in not enacting Protocols to reverse or undo evolutive understandings of the Convention at least suggests that states were consenting not only to what the Convention might be said to have meant in 1950 but also to its being developed, understood and interpreted in a manner that allowed for evolution. This is not entirely unusual in international law; indeed, it might be said to be a common approach to human rights treaties, which are generally considered to be dynamic in nature.[6] Wessel argued that one could arrange all treaties across a spectrum ranging from, at the one extreme, 'dynamic' treaties and, at the other extreme, 'end of game' treaties.[7] The former treaties are concluded between cooperating parties in order to promote common values; the latter are concluded to freeze a given set of relations in existence at a certain moment in time. For Wessel, '[d]ynamic treaties ... should be interpreted using relational contract principles, such as the parties' current practice'.[8] The ECHR is clearly a dynamic treaty, created to spread common values among the Contracting Parties.[9] The Preamble points out that it was concluded to further realise cooperation of the Contracting Parties in the area of human rights protection. Therefore, their subsequent practice in this area should be reflected in the judgments of the ECtHR, and the argument of 'consent' cannot, alone, sustain a claim of illegitimacy.

That said, the extent to which one might question the legitimacy of evolutive interpretation can differ depending on the kind of originalism being adopted.[10] Put relatively simply, one form of originalism demands that the

[5] Article 31(3)(b) VCLT.

[6] In connection with the practice of interpretation under the American Convention on Human Rights, see Lucas Lixinski, 'Treaty Interpretation by the Inter-American Court of Human Rights: Expansionism at the Service of the Unity of International Law' (2010) 21(3) *European Journal of International Law* 585.

[7] Jared Wessel, 'Relational Contract Theory and Treaty Interpretation: End-Game Treaties v Dynamic Interpretation' (2004) 60 *Annual Survey of American Law* 149, 149.

[8] ibid, 150.

[9] Malgosia Fitzmaurice, 'Dynamic (Evolutive) Interpretation of Treaties (Part II)' in Johan Lammers (ed), *Hague Yearbook of International Law* (Martinus Nijhoff Publishers, 2009) 3.

[10] There is a voluminous literature on originalism, but the key competing accounts are well presented in Lawrence Solum, 'What is Originalism? The Evolution of Contemporary Originalist Theory' in Grant Huscroft and Bradley Miller (eds), *The Challenge of Originalism: Theories of Constitutional Interpretation* (Cambridge University Press, 2011) 12.

text in question (here, the Convention) remain cryogenically frozen as at the time it was written so that it means *only* what it meant then. It necessarily flows that such a claim is underpinned by an understanding of terms that are used in human rights treaties, such as 'torture' or 'arbitrary detention', as having a clear and objectively determinable meaning – a claim that is strongly disputed.[11] In truth, a literal approach to originalism is somewhat uncommon. Taken to its logical end point, it would require the Convention to either be unfit for purpose or constantly subjected to formal amendment, which, as we saw in chapter 1, takes place by means of protocols and is a long and difficult process that states can try to hold up for reasons that are not always entirely bona fide.

A looser, and more common, approach to originalism holds that the meaning of a text can be developed but only inasmuch as that reflects the original intent of the founders/original drafters. This kind of originalism will be familiar to those who have studied US constitutional law, in particular, although it is not limited to that jurisdiction. It accepts that texts of a constitutional or quasi-constitutional nature do need to have some capacity for evolution and interpretation, but limits that to what was originally intended by the text and thus, in an international law setting in particular, to what might be said to have been reasonably within the contemplation of the state at the point at which consent was given. This type of originalism is also problematic, as it is often unclear what the intention of the drafters of the Convention (or similar text) might have been.

In the earlier days of the Court, it used evolutive interpretation to extend protection under Article 8 to 'illegitimate' children, in a case that illustrates how thin the line between 'interpreting in line with original intent' and 'evolving the Convention' can be: *Marckx v Belgium*.[12] At that time, Belgium treated children of unmarried biological parents less favourably than children whose biological parents were married. The Court had to consider whether this violated the Convention, but of course the Convention said nothing about it directly (although it does protect the right to respect for private and family life in Article 8). The Belgian Government argued that when the Convention was ratified, such differences were considered appropriate and thus acceptable by the Convention standards. The Court disagreed:

> It is true that, at the time when the Convention of 4 November 1950 was drafted, it was regarded as permissible and normal in many European countries to draw a distinction in this area between the 'illegitimate' and the 'legitimate' family. However, the Court recalls that this Convention must be interpreted in the light of present-day conditions. In the instant case, the Court cannot but be struck by the fact that the domestic law of the great majority of the member

[11] Fredman (n 3).

[12] *Marckx v Belgium* [1979] ECHR 2.

> States of the Council of Europe has evolved and is continuing to evolve, in company with the relevant international instruments.[13]

There was, thus, a violation of the Convention. One might argue that this is in line with the original intent of the Convention (to protect family and private life, including the family life of people whose families were not based on marriage), whilst another might say that it represented evolution because the states accepted that 'illegitimate' children could be treated less favourably at the time that the Convention was drafted. This kind of case – one that can arguably be defended by reference to relatively plausible claims of original intent – is not the type most commonly singled out for criticism. Rather, it is cases where the Court applies an evolutive approach in order either to depart from its earlier decisions or to find Convention protection in respect of 'emerging' areas or claims not clearly contemplated by the Convention text that tend to be critics' focus.

It is not entirely unusual for the Court to hold that its interpretation of the Convention in an earlier case should be set aside in favour of a new interpretation that has 'evolved' by reference to, for example, changing practice across states or changing social and scientific understandings. Later in this chapter, we will expressly consider the role of 'European consensus' in such cases, but for now we can focus on the principled issue of evolution per se, without necessarily considering *how* the evolution is justified. The Court's understanding of what the Convention requires may develop over time. The best example is, perhaps, the Court's jurisprudence on whether one has a right to have one's true gender recognised by the state when one has a transgender identity.

In a line of cases, largely against the UK, that started in the 1980s,[14] the Court was asked to consider whether the UK's failure to fully recognise a preferred gender identity for post-operative applicants violated the Convention. Under national law, some legal documents such as birth certificates could not be changed even after gender reassignment surgery, and even though such surgery could be provided on the National Health Service (ie by the state). For more than a decade, the Court repeatedly found that the Convention did not *require* full documentary recognition of reassigned gender; instead, whether to recognise reassigned gender was within the UK's margin of appreciation and was not required by Article 8. However, in these cases the Court hinted that this would not always be the case; as law, science and society developed, this would not always remain within states' discretion. This point was reached in *Christine Goodwin v the United Kingdom*, when the Court held:

> [T]he very essence of the Convention is respect for human dignity and human freedom. Under Article 8 of the Convention in particular, where the notion of personal autonomy is an important principle underlying the interpretation of its

[13] ibid, para 41.

[14] *Rees v the United Kingdom* [1986] ECHR 11; *Cossey v the United Kingdom* [1990] ECHR 21.

> guarantees, protection is given to the personal sphere of each individual, including the right to establish details of their identity as individual human beings … In the twenty first century the right of transsexuals to personal development and to physical and moral security in the full sense enjoyed by others in society cannot be regarded as a matter of controversy requiring the lapse of time to cast clearer light on the issues involved. In short, the unsatisfactory situation in which post-operative transsexuals live in an intermediate zone as not quite one gender or the other is no longer sustainable.[15]

Thus, the Convention's Article 8 protection of private life finally evolved to positively protect the right to officially be recognised in one's preferred gender.

All types of evolutive interpretation attract criticisms. One key objection is that evolution creates instability in the law: a legal standard may change, even though Contracting Parties have taken steps to ensure that its previous understanding has been effectively incorporated into domestic legal standards. In this telling, states cannot be sure what legal standard to apply for fear that it may change as a result of judicial interpretation. There are at least three responses to this pragmatic claim against evolutive interpretation.

First, it is not certain that such practical considerations should be determinative for the Court. Letsas has argued that the judges of the Court should not enter into a cost–benefit calculation in deciding their approach to interpretation; for him, problems associated with the lack of predictability must be trumped by the moral value of human rights.[16] However, one does not need to endorse such a strong position in order to accept that pragmatic considerations need not be determinative; this is not to say that they should never be accounted for at all (after all, legal certainty *is* one of the key aspects of the rule of law, and maintaining legitimacy through consistency has positive implications for the Court's overall capacity to protect rights) but simply that they should not be given such weight as to always prevent evolution where it seems normatively acceptable to undertake it. So, a concern with legal certainty might ground the claim that the Court should engage in evolution *carefully* and in a *reasoned* manner, but it should not stop the Court from applying evolutive interpretation when that is necessary to ensure effective rights protection. The principle of effectiveness, namely that rights enshrined in the ECHR should be 'practical and effective', is a well-established principle of interpretation of the Convention.[17] Ensuring this effectiveness is hardly possible without occasionally resorting to evolution.

---

[15] *Christine Goodwin v the United Kingdom* [2002] ECHR 588, para 90.

[16] George Letsas, *A Theory of Interpretation of the European Convention on Human Rights* (Oxford University Press, 2007) 74.

[17] *Marckx* (n 12), para 31. See also Daniel Rietiker 'The Principle of "Effectiveness" in the Recent Jurisprudence of the European Court of Human Rights: Its Different Dimensions and Its Consistency with Public International Law – No Need for the Concept of Treaty Sui Generis' (2010) 79(2) *Nordic Journal of International Law* 245.

Second, the fact that evolutive interpretation is used does not mean the Convention is volatile. Sometimes the possibility of evolution is signposted to Contracting Parties in earlier cases. For example in the case of *SH and Others v Austria*, the Court considered whether the Austrian ban on using sperm and ova donation for in vitro fertilisation violated the Convention.[18] The Grand Chamber of the Court decided that it did not, but informed the respondent party that it needed to keep under review the developments in science and law in this area,[19] clearly signalling a potential evolution on this question in the future. Thus, although the Court did not evolve the Convention in this case, it made it clear that states must be prepared for this in the future, thus giving 'fair warning' of future potential change and dampening claims of volatility at the time when that change comes. Austria listened and amended its law in 2015,[20] and by doing so spared the Court from delivering another judgment in this area. The Court used a similar approach in *Dániel Karsai v Hungary*, in which the Court considered whether the access to physician-assisted dying should be guaranteed under the Convention. The Court did not find a violation but made clear that this area will be kept under review.[21]

In giving those signals, it is important that the Court maintains consistency across its case law so that states know what the Court might be looking out for in deciding whether the tipping point has been reached. It does not always succeed in doing so. Let us return to the cases on gender identity to illustrate this. In *Sheffield and Horsham v the United Kingdom*, the Court found that the failure to recognise preferred gender on state documents did not violate the Convention, pointing to the lack of European consensus on the matter.[22] However, it signalled to the UK that it would monitor the situation, indicating that should a European consensus develop, this would feed into a change in the Court's consideration of whether the Convention had been violated. Only four years later, in *Christine Goodwin v the United Kingdom*, the Court did find a violation,[23] but on the basis of an international trend and *not* a European consensus, thus opening itself up to criticism for seeming to vary the benchmarks between cases on the same issue.[24]

Third, even where the legal standard evolves with little advance warning, the Contracting Party will in reality have some time to adjust its practices in order to accommodate it: execution of a judgment is not expected overnight. Indeed, quite unlike many national constitutional systems where a finding of

---

[18] *SH and Others v Austria* App no 57813/00 (ECtHR, 3 November 2011).

[19] ibid, para 118.

[20] For a discussion of the policy change in this area in Austria, see Erich Griessler and Mariella Hager, 'Changing Direction: The Struggle of Regulating Assisted Reproductive Technology in Austria' (2016) 22(3) *Reproductive Biomedicine and Society Online* 68.

[21] *Dániel Karsai v Hungary* App no 32312/23 (ECtHR, 2 September 2024), para 167.

[22] *Sheffield and Horsham v the United Kingdom* [1998] ECHR 69.

[23] *Christine Goodwin v United Kingdom* (n 15).

[24] For a more in-depth discussion, see Kanstantsin Dzehtsiarou, *European Consensus and the Legitimacy of the European Court of Human Rights* (Cambridge University Press, 2015) 65–71.

rights violation can result in the immediate strike down of a statute and a resultant legal 'gap' that often needs to be filled quickly, a finding of violation does not automatically disturb the national legal system, which must, instead, be expressly adjusted to execute the judgment. The claims as to certainty, then, seem insufficient to ground a strong case against evolution.

On all bases, it is difficult to sustain an argument of simple illegitimacy for evolution per se, but this does not mean that there are no real concerns here, particularly on the question of *when* the tipping point has been reached and how the Court determines that. It is to this that we now turn.

Debate 2

How Does the Court Determine the Moment of Evolution?

As indicated above, the Court generally claims to be reflecting societal and technological developments when it applies an evolutive approach to interpretation, but of course this does not mean that the exercise is simply technocratic. Instead, the Court must assess whether there is sufficient development to justify evolutive interpretation, and as a result the Court clearly has significant discretion on this matter. Depending on how it interprets the prevailing conditions, the Court can speed up, slow down or even veto certain developments in rights protection that could only be achieved through evolutive interpretation.

Finding the right moment for evolution is crucially important for the effectiveness and legitimacy of the Court: push for evolution too early and the judgment might never be executed and the reputation of the ECtHR will suffer; do it too late and the Court might be perceived as irrelevant and unwilling to address real-life rights violations. Whilst, as outlined below, the Court applies different methods in order to try to identify whether the moment for evolution is ripe, the truth is that this is ultimately a matter of *judgement*: it cannot be 'scientifically' determined.

In exercising its judgement on this matter, then, the Court is open to allegations of illegitimacy, both from Contracting Parties (along the lines outlined in Debate 1) and from applicants and other interested parties who may complain that the Court is going too fast, too slow or in the wrong direction. The clearest way to address these kinds of criticisms is to apply rigour, method and clarity of reasoning in the decision to take an evolutive approach (or not). The key technique that the Court uses in this respect is 'consensus'.[25] Although this does not prevent the Court from applying discretion, it does provide the ECtHR with some indicia through which its assessment might be said to be grounded in reality, and thus its reasoning becomes more persuasive. In other words, using consensus reasoning can help to ensure that the Court is

[25] Kanstantsin Dzehtsiarou, 'European Consensus and the Evolutive Interpretation of the European Convention on Human Rights' (2011) 12(10) *German Law Journal* 1730.

reflecting reality, rather than *creating* law; that is, to show judicial self-restraint in resorting only to necessary and acceptable evolution.[26]

The Court uses four different kinds of consensus in doing this: European consensus; international consensus; internal (ie domestic) consensus; and consensus among experts. Let us consider each in turn.

European Consensus

European consensus is a method of interpreting the ECHR that relies on comparative analysis of the law and practice of the Contracting Parties to the Convention, which may then justify evolutive interpretation. If the Court concludes that there is no European consensus on the rights-protection claim that is before it, it usually decides that this is an issue on which Contracting Parties enjoy a broad margin of appreciation. We will consider the margin of appreciation in chapter 5, but for now it is sufficient to say that where something falls within the state's margin of appreciation, it will have considerable discretion to decide on its domestic legal and policy position in respect of it: a range of different approaches will be permissible under the Convention, provided they comply with the basic requirements of the Article in question (eg, are limited by reference to what is 'necessary in a democratic society', etc).

The case of *Bayatyan v Armenia* is a good illustration of how European consensus can work.[27] Here, the Court considered whether Article 9 was violated where someone was punished for refusal to perform military service in contravention of his beliefs as a Jehovah's Witness. Accommodation of conscientious objection had not previously been considered by the Court as a requirement of the freedom of religious belief under Article 9.[28] In *Bayatyan*, the Court found that a large number of Contracting Parties allowed for an alternative to military service in order to respect conscientious objections. Thus, failure to do so violated the Convention:

> [T]he Convention is a living instrument which must be interpreted in the light of present-day conditions and of the ideas prevailing in democratic States today. Since it is first and foremost a system for the protection of human rights, the Court must have regard to the changing conditions in Contracting States and respond, for example, to any emerging consensus as to the standards to be achieved.[29]

[26] Fiona de Londras and Kanstantsin Dzehtsiarou, 'Managing Judicial Innovation in the European Court of Human Rights' (2015) 15(3) *Human Rights Law Review* 523.

[27] *Bayatyan v Armenia* [2011] ECHR 1095.

[28] *Grandrath v Germany* App no 5591/72 (European Commission of Human Rights, 2 April 1973) 161; and *GZ v Austria* App no 5591/72 (European Commission of Human Rights, 2 April 1973) 161.

[29] *Bayatyan v Armenia* (n 27), para 102.

The Court noted that in the late 1980s and the 1990s there was an obvious trend among European countries, both existing Council of Europe member states and those that joined the organisation later, to recognise the right to conscientious objection. All in all, 19 of those states that had not yet recognised the right to conscientious objection introduced such a right into their domestic legal systems around the time when the Commission took its last decisions on the matter. Hence, at the time when the alleged interference with the applicant's rights under Article 9 occurred, namely in 2002–03, only four other member states, in addition to Armenia, did not provide for the possibility of claiming conscientious-objector status. Furthermore, three of those had already incorporated that right into their Constitutions but had not yet implemented that by law. Thus, already at the material time there was nearly a unanimous consensus among all Council of Europe member states, the overwhelming majority of which had already recognised in their law and practice the right to conscientious objection.

The growth in the legal recognition of conscientious objections within the Contracting Parties allowed the Court to justify departing from its previous case law and establishing this standard of rights protection. This illustrates the fact that European consensus can help to rebut the argument that evolution means uncertainty, as developing trends across the Contracting Parties can alert states to the possibility that the Court will evolve in jurisprudence in this fashion. In this case, the developing tendency to recognise conscientious objection was manifest: Armenia was one of only a handful of Contracting Parties that failed to accommodate such objections. Attention to the developing European consensus here would have mitigated any putative 'surprise' element. Similarly, and more recently, European consensus was used in justifying evolutive interpretation in relation to legal recognition of same-sex couples.[30]

This is not to suggest that European consensus is without criticism. It is, for example, quite a conservative way to approach evolution: rather than lead the way in developing human-rights protection, the Court 'follows' trends in the Contracting Parties. Whilst this may be considered appropriate given the fact that the Court is subsidiary, and the perceived limitations of appropriate judicial activity, for some this approach is problematic. For these commentators, human rights are standards that should be developed by reference to something more normatively rich than the sum of approaches that are taken by the Contracting Parties. European consensus, or the 'counting of states', does not seem to allow the Court to develop rights per se; rather, it lets national trends determine supra-national standards.[31] In the words of Jens Theilen:

> European consensus constitutes, one might say, *too much* of a compromise … it provides a way in which principled and strategic considerations can be brought together in a way which disguises the tensions between them. By providing this

[30] *Fedotova v Russia* [2023] ECHR 55, para 178.

[31] For analysis of criticism of European consensus, see Dzehtsiarou (n 25) 115–42.

> kind of compromise and distracting from the tensions inherent in the argumentative structures of regional human rights law, a strong focus on consensus orients the ECtHR away from potentially more transformative results and forms of reasoning.[32]

This relates to a further critique of European consensus: that it is effectively a majoritarian approach to human rights that should not, by their nature, be determined by such an approach.[33] This argument rests on the fact that one of the roles of human rights law is to protect those persons and groups who are under-represented in democracy. Marginalised and under-represented people such as convicted criminals, children or national, religious or sexual minorities do not always have the 'clout' to establish protection through national political or, indeed, judicial processes, and part of the role of institutions such as the ECtHR is to address that deficit and protect their rights, even if that is unpopular within the relevant polity. European consensus cuts across this by seeming to acquire its legitimacy from reflecting domestic trends. There are three possible counter-arguments to this. First, the Court has in fact used European consensus to protect the rights of these very marginalities: religious minorities,[34] lifelong prisoners,[35] 'illegitimate' children[36] and homosexual men,[37] for example, have succeeded before the Court through leveraging a European consensus approach. Second, consensus identifies a minimal standard of human-rights protection, and the Contracting Parties are free to set a higher standard. Finally, European consensus is not a strictly binding concept; the Court can set it aside if there are convincing reasons to do so. Perhaps, in cases of protection of some vulnerable minorities, the Court might decide that in spite of consensus, the state may divert from the standard of consensus because, for example, the state is in a situation of transition,[38] or the Court is satisfied that the people of the state in question hold a particular moral position on an issue of profound moral disagreement.[39] Furthermore, the inquiry into whether or not a consensus exists is not necessarily the end of the Court's assessment; it has been known to question *why* an apparent European consensus either does or does not exist *as a matter of fact*, and whether Contracting Parties are considering introducing similar laws, to determine whether

[32] Jens T Theilen, *European Consensus between Strategy and Principle: The Uses of Vertically Comparative Legal Reasoning in Regional Human Rights Adjudication* (Nomos, 2021) 19.

[33] See Eyal Benvenisti, 'Margin of Appreciation, Consensus, and Universal Standards' (1999) 31 *Journal of International Law and Politics* 843.

[34] *Bayatyan v Armenia* (n 27).

[35] *Vinter and Others v the United Kingdom* [2013] ECHR 645.

[36] *Fretté v France* App no 36515/97 (ECtHR, 26 May 2002).

[37] *Dudgeon v the United Kingdom* [1981] ECHR 5.

[38] *Tańase v Moldova* App no 7/08 (ECtHR, 27 April 2010).

[39] See, for example, *A, B and C v Ireland* [2010] ECHR 2032.

a European consensus exists *as a matter of judicial reasoning*. This is well illustrated by the Court's judgment in the controversial case of *SAS v France*.[40]

In this case, the Court had to decide whether the French ban on wearing full-face veils in public places violated Article 8 of the ECHR. The Court's consideration of comparative law in this case is particularly curious. It established that '[t]o date, only Belgium has passed a law that is comparable to the French Law of 11 October 2010, and the Belgian Constitutional Court has found it compatible with the right to freedom of thought, conscience and religion'.[41] In other words, there was manifestly *no* consensus across the Council of Europe in support of such a ban. In the past, the Court had stated that when only two states deviate from the commonly accepted standard, this indicates a very strong consensus *against* the respondent state's position.[42] In *SAS*, however, the Court observed that the issue of religious dress (especially full-face coverings) is more pressing in some states than in others, and that this has to be taken into account when analysing the results of comparative legal research,[43] so that the lack of consensus in favour of allowing such a law did not stand against a finding that such a law was compatible with the Convention. This was notwithstanding the fact that there are clearly more than only two countries in Europe with a substantial Muslim population, and these other states have not determined that such a ban is required. The Court concluded that the lack of such a law in other states did *not* indicate a European consensus *against* the ban of public display of religious headscarves:

> [C]ontrary to the submission of one of the third-party interveners, there is no European consensus against a ban. Admittedly, from a strictly normative standpoint, France is very much in a minority position in Europe: except for Belgium, no other member State of the Council of Europe has, to date, opted for such a measure. It must be observed, however, that the question of the wearing of the full-face veil in public is or has been a subject of debate in a number of European States. In some it has been decided not to opt for a blanket ban. In others, such a ban is still being considered.[44]

Although the Court's reasoning in *SAS v France* is open to significant criticism, it does illustrate that consensus is not binding. Rather, it acts as a rebuttable presumption in favour of the 'consensus compliant interpretation' of the Convention; namely, if there is consensus or an identifiable trend then the Court will solidify the rule supported by consensus, even if this means that the Convention should be interpreted evolutively. This presumption can be rebutted if there are reasons for the respondent state justifiably to deviate from the established trend.

---

[40] *SAS v France* [2014] ECHR 695.

[41] ibid, para 40.

[42] *A, B and C v Ireland* (n 39), para 235.

[43] *SAS v France* (n 40), para 156.

[44] ibid, para 156.

International Consensus

The second type of consensus is consensus based on international law (international consensus), determined by analysis of international treaties mostly signed and ratified by the Contracting Parties to the ECHR and the law and practice of other international tribunals. Clearly, this is quite different from the European consensus approach: rather than consider legal and policy positions across individual states, the Court looks to international law per se.

The Court has used developments in international law to justify evolutive interpretation on many occasions, including in its earlier cases. In *Marckx v Belgium*, for example, the Court referred to two international conventions (the Brussels Convention of 12 September 1962 on the Establishment of Maternal Affiliation of Natural Children, and the European Convention of 15 October 1975 on the Legal Status of Children born out of Wedlock) in determining that differential treatment of 'illegitimate' children was prohibited by the Convention.[45] Interestingly, neither of these was yet in force at the time; rather, they showed an emerging understanding and consensus across international law that children whose parents were not married should not be treated differently in law.

In *Mamatkulov and Askarov v Turkey*, the Court has also relied on developments in international law to justify evolutive interpretation of the Convention.[46] The key issue in this case was the legal force of interim measures issued by the Court, that is

> urgent measures which, according to the Court's well-established practice, apply only where there is an imminent risk of irreparable harm. Such measures are decided in connection with proceedings before the Court without prejudging any subsequent decisions on the admissibility or merits of the case in question.[47]

The vast majority of interim measures are of negative character; they oblige the respondent state not to worsen the situation of the applicant. The most common example is when the applicant is about to be removed to a country in which she may be the subject of ill-treatment contrary to Article 3 of the Convention; the Court can request the respondent state not to remove her before the Court's judgment in this case. More rarely, Contracting Parties are asked

[45] *Marckx v Belgium* (n 12).

[46] *Mamatkulov and Askarov v Turkey* [2005] ECHR 64.

[47] Press Unit, *Factsheet: Interim Measures* (2016), Rule 39, Rules of Court. See also Helen Keller and Cedric Marti, 'Interim Relief Compared: Use of Interim Measures by the UN Human Rights Committee and the European Court of Human Rights' (2013) 73 *Zeitschrift für ausländisches öffentliches Recht und Völkerrecht (Heidelberg Journal of International Law)* 325; Yves Haeck, Clara Burbano Herrera and Leo Zwaak, 'Strasbourg's Interim Measures under Fire: Does the Rising Number of State Incompliances with Interim Measures Pose a Threat to the European Court of Human Rights?' (2011) 11 *European Yearbook of Human Rights* 375.

to fulfil certain duties under interim measures. For example, the Court can request the respondent party to transfer a sick inmate to a civil hospital.

In its earlier case law, the Court held that interim measures were not legally binding;[48] however, it changed this position in *Mamatkulov and Askarov*.[49] Having regard 'to general principles of international law and the view expressed on this subject by other international bodies since *Cruz Varas and Others* [in which the Court stated that violation of interim measures does not violate the Convention]',[50] the Court decided its interim measures should have legally binding character. In reaching this decision, the Court expressly relied on the practice of international tribunals, such as the Inter-American Court of Human Rights, the UN Human Rights Committee and the International Court of Justice.

The use of international consensus to underpin evolutive interpretation has several benefits. The Court itself has emphasised the importance of external sources by pointing out that '[t]he Convention and its Protocols cannot be interpreted in a vacuum but must be interpreted in harmony with the general principles of international law of which they form part'.[51] In *Demir and Baykara v Turkey*, the Court stated that it has 'never considered the provisions of the Convention as the sole framework of reference for the interpretation of the rights and freedoms enshrined therein'.[52] The ECHR is a part of international law, and some provisions of the Convention explicitly refer to it.[53] Thus, it is quite sensible for the Court to attempt to ensure that the Convention is developed in a manner that is consistent with international law.

This has the additional benefit of attempting to ensure 'systemic integration' between international instruments and principles of international law, rather than creating or exacerbating potential conflicts between them.[54] We saw in chapter 2 that states have multiple international obligations at any given time, and that these may appear to be in conflict with one another, so that bearing international law and practice in mind when developing the Convention helps to create harmony between these obligations. This is of benefit not only to the Contracting Parties, but also to international law itself of which, of course, the Convention is a part; it is a way in which the Court can contribute to the

---

[48] *Cruz Varas and Others v Sweden*, 20 March 1991, Series A no 201.

[49] *Mamatkulov and Askarov v Turkey* (n 46).

[50] ibid, para 110.

[51] *Marguš v Croatia* [2014] ECHR 523, para 129.

[52] *Demir and Baykara v Turkey* [2008] ECHR 1345, para 67.

[53] Articles 7, 15 and 35 of the Convention. The CDDH has discussed a proposal to include 'the general principle that the Convention as a whole should be interpreted in harmony with other principles of international law' in the Preamble to the Convention. It has rejected this proposal, however, because it would be time-consuming, whilst added value would be limited. Report of the Steering Committee for Human Rights (CDDH), 101.

[54] On the general importance of this, see Martti Koskenniemi, ILC, 'Fragmentation of International Law: Difficulties Arising from the Diversification and Expansion of International Law' (2006) UN Doc A/CN.4/L.682.

difficult but important task of trying to avoid the unnecessary and/or unproductive 'fragmentation' of international law – a major concern in that field.[55]

This is not to suggest that there are no potential criticisms of the Court's reliance on international consensus in its decision-making. Why should, for example, an international treaty to which the respondent state is not a party be taken into account in determining the nature and scope of its Convention obligations? What about customary international law to which the state has consistently objected? And how does the Court decide which international treaties, or principles of international law or (quasi-) judicial decisions it will take into account from the vast field that is 'international law'? In the words of Dzehtsiarou:

> The Court's legitimacy is narrated in terms of subsidiarity and substantive dialogue with the Contracting Parties. Consequently, the key challenges to the Court's legitimacy are defined in terms of its remoteness from the matter at hand and lack of democratic input … [If] the external sources [the ones emanating from outside of the Council of Europe] clash with the interpretation accepted by the majority of the Contracting Parties, the Court's reliance on the former can arguably be challenged as illegitimate.[56]

All of this, combined with the fact that the role of the Court is to develop, apply and interpret the *Convention* and not to contribute to the development of international law per se, suggests that the Court ought to tread softly in the field of international consensus, applying it in conjunction with a European consensus analysis.

Internal Consensus

The third type of consensus is internal consensus. In this type of consensus, which is very rarely deployed, the Court attempts to establish a prevailing position within the respondent state's population, which may then justify the state's approach being found compatible with the Convention *even if* it is in contrast with European and/or international consensus. Even establishing such an internal consensus is fundamentally challenging. In some cases, the national position may have been determined by popular referendum, so that the referendum results are used to argue that the internal consensus exists. However, even then the meaning of referendum results is not always straightforward. Where a populace is given a choice between, for example, Option A and Option B in a referendum, all the result tells us is which of these options the majority of those who voted preferred, not whether the 'real world' consensus is really in

[55] ibid.

[56] Kanstantsin Dzehtsiarou, 'What Is Law for the European Court of Human Rights?' (2017) 49(1) *Georgetown Journal of International Law* 89, 93–94.

line with a putative Option C on which they never had the opportunity to vote. This is well illustrated by *A, B and C v Ireland*.[57]

In this case, the Court considered whether the extremely restrictive abortion regime then in place in Ireland (where abortion was available only where there was a 'real and substantial risk' to the life of a pregnant woman) was compatible with the Convention.[58] Only three countries in Europe at the time had a more restrictive abortion law than Ireland: Andorra, Malta and San Marino. In contrast, 40 Contracting Parties allowed abortion if there was a risk to the mother's health, suggesting that there was European consensus towards allowing abortion on broader grounds than available in Ireland. However, Ireland's restrictive approach to abortion at the time was entrenched in the Irish Constitution, into which it had been inserted following a referendum in 1983.[59] In subsequent referenda (in 1992 and 2002), the electorate had voted on whether to restrict access to abortion further by expressly prohibiting it in cases where the risk to the pregnant woman's life emanated from the risk of suicide, but this had twice been rejected. At the time of *A, B and C v Ireland*, the Irish electorate had never been given an opportunity to vote to liberalise Ireland's abortion law.[60] Furthermore, when negotiating both the Maastricht and Lisbon Treaties at EU level, Ireland had secured protocols to allow for the maintenance of the status quo regarding abortion, seemingly in response to popular demand.

Based on this, the Irish Government argued that the law in Ireland represented the profound moral position of the Irish people, and that this internal consensus should mean that Ireland could maintain its particular stance on abortion, in spite of the fact that it was out of line with the apparent European consensus. Rather than focusing on the alignment in legal provision of abortion across the 40 Contracting Parties that allow for abortion in cases where the pregnant woman's health is at risk, the Court noted that there was no consensus (of any kind) on the question of when life begins. As this is central to the question of whether and to what extent abortion might be made available in law, states enjoy a wide margin of appreciation; and where, as the Irish Government claimed was the case in Ireland, there was an internal consensus, that could justify a restrictive abortion law regime that would be compatible with the Convention.

We have previously argued that this case illustrates the Court's identification of a 'trumping internal consensus' for the first time in its jurisprudence, that is an internal consensus that could trump the established European *legal*

[57] *A, B and C v Ireland* (n 39).

[58] The law on abortion has since been changed in Ireland. See The Health (Regulation of Termination of Pregnancy) Act 2018.

[59] Article 40.3.3, Constitution of Ireland. See Fiona de Londras and Mairead Enright, *Repealing the 8th: Reforming Irish Abortion Law* (Policy Press, 2018).

[60] This changed in 2018, when a large majority voted to remove the constitutional prohibition on abortion. See, eg, Katherine Browne and Sydney Calkin (eds), *Post Repeal: Reflections and Futures* (Zed Books, 2019).

consensus.[61] Here the Court avoided evolving the Convention to protect a right to access abortion, even though a European consensus appeared to exist. Clearly, the concept of 'trumping internal consensus' is a dangerous one. On the one hand, it allows the Court to avoid 'forcing the hand' of a state on a matter of particular sensitivity, such as abortion. On the other hand, the idea that a national sentiment could override an international standard found in the Convention seems to fly in the face of supra-national rights protection per se. Unquestionably, the fact that this case related to abortion was relevant: this remains a topic on which the Court is reluctant significantly to develop its jurisprudence.

Given the clear difficulties with using 'trumping internal consensus', it is perhaps unsurprising that *A, B and C* is the only case in which it has been deployed by the Court, although it is certainly not the only time a Contracting Party has made such an argument. In the very first case in which the Court deployed evolutive interpretation – *Tyrer v the United Kingdom* – the UK attempted to rely on internal consensus. In this case, the Court considered whether corporal punishment ('birching') of an under-age offender in the Isle of Man violated Article 3 of the ECHR.[62] The Government argued that 'the judicial corporal punishment at issue in this case was not in breach of the Convention since it did not outrage public opinion in the Island';[63] in other words, birching was an accepted form of punishment there and, if the populace was not outraged, should not be considered to violate Article 3. The Court disagreed:

> [E]ven assuming that local public opinion can have an incidence on the interpretation of the concept of 'degrading punishment' appearing in Article 3 (art 3), the Court does not regard it as established that judicial corporal punishment is not considered degrading by those members of the Manx population who favour its retention: it might well be that one of the reasons why they view the penalty as an effective deterrent is precisely the element of degradation which it involves. As regards their belief that judicial corporal punishment deters criminals, it must be pointed out that a punishment does not lose its degrading character just because it is believed to be, or actually is, an effective deterrent or aid to crime control. Above all, as the Court must emphasise, it is never permissible to have recourse to punishments which are contrary to Article 3 (art 3), whatever their deterrent effect may be. The Court must also recall that the Convention is a living instrument which … must be interpreted in the light of present-day conditions. In the case now before it the Court cannot but be

[61] Fiona de Londras and Kanstantsin Dzehtsiarou, 'Grand Chamber of the European Court of Human Rights, A, B and C v Ireland' (2013) 62 *International and Comparative Law Quarterly* 250. See also Fiona de Londras, 'When the European Court of Human Rights Decides Not to Decide: The Cautionary Tale of *A, B & C v Ireland* and Referendum-Emergent Constitutional Provisions' in Panos Kapotas and Vassilis Tzevelekos (eds), *Building Consensus on European Consensus: Judicial Interpretation of Human Rights in Europe and Beyond* (Cambridge University Press, 2019).

[62] *Tyrer v the United Kingdom* [1978] ECHR 2.

[63] ibid, para 31.

> influenced by the developments and commonly accepted standards in the penal policy of the member States of the Council of Europe in this field.[64]

The approach in *Tyrer* is much more in line with how the Court has tended to respond to arguments that 'internal consensus' might justify a position that seems contrary to the Convention. This is not to say that internal consensus is totally irrelevant. It may well be that where the Court is asked to apply evolutive interpretation, the internal consensus might be one factor in considering whether the moment for possible evolution is ripe.

Expert Consensus

Finally, another rarely used type of consensus is expert consensus. The Court typically uses this type of consensus when it has to assess scientific developments in Europe and worldwide. For instance, in *L and V v Austria*, the applicants challenged Article 209 of the Austrian Criminal Code, which provided for a higher minimum age for consensual homosexual intercourse than for heterosexual intercourse.[65] The Court affirmed the decision in *Sutherland v the United Kingdom*,[66] which referred to 'recent research according to which sexual orientation is usually established before puberty in both boys and girls and to the fact that the majority of Member States of the Council of Europe have recognised equal ages of consent'. It explicitly stated that it was 'opportune to reconsider its earlier case-law in the light of these modern developments'.[67] Although expert consensus can support the Court's decision to resort to evolutive interpretation, it is unlikely that it will be the only, or even the most conclusive, argument used by the Court; rather, expert consensus seems mostly to be used to provide broader context for the Court's decision.

DEBATE 3

IS EVOLUTION NECESSARILY PROGRESSIVE?

We often think about evolution as a linear process that improves human-rights standards and never allows for regression in rights protection: in other words, as a progressive technique. However, this is not necessarily the case. In fact, evolution can indeed be regressive, either because the Court has experienced serious backlash in respect of an attempted progressive evolution, or because there is a trend towards regression in a certain area that the Court is not willing

[64] ibid.

[65] *L and V v Austria* [2003] ECHR 20.

[66] *Sutherland v the United Kingdom* App no 25186/94 (European Commission of Human Rights, 1 July 1997).

[67] *L and V v Austria* (n 65), para 47.

to try to halt. Prisoner voting neatly illustrates the first of these, whilst the Court's case law on Islamic dress illustrates the latter.

In *Hirst v the United Kingdom (No 2)*,[68] the Court ruled that the UK's blanket ban on prisoner voting violated the Convention, but it did not clearly outline what *would* be compatible with the Convention. It appeared clear that the Convention did not require *all* prisoners to be allowed to vote, but there is a considerable space between a blanket ban and blanket permission. The Court addressed this in the next case it decided about prisoners' right to vote: *Frodl v Austria*.[69] In this case it held that disenfranchisement of a prisoner would be Convention-compatible only if it had been decided by a judge in the individual case. This was, clearly, a burdensome standard, requiring the question of disenfranchisement to be individually considered for every prisoner. As we have already discussed in chapter 2, the Court's early approach to prisoner voting resulted in significant backlash, not least from the UK. It was in this context that the Court appeared to evolve its position *regressively* in *Scoppola v Italy (No 3)*.[70] In Italy, those who are in prison for less than three years can vote: this is clearly not a blanket ban, but it is also not the individual determination seemingly required by *Frodl*. In this case, the Court decided that it had gone too far in *Frodl* and found the Italian system compatible with the Convention. In doing so, it stated that its reasoning in *Frodl*

> takes a broad view of the principles set out in Hirst, which the Grand Chamber does not fully share. The Grand Chamber points out that the Hirst judgment makes no explicit mention of the intervention of a judge among the essential criteria for determining the proportionality of a disenfranchisement measure. The relevant criteria relate solely to whether the measure is applicable generally, automatically and indiscriminately within the meaning indicated by the Court. While the intervention of a judge is in principle likely to guarantee the proportionality of restrictions on prisoners' voting rights, such restrictions will not necessarily be automatic, general and indiscriminate simply because they were not ordered by a judge. Indeed, the circumstances in which the right to vote is forfeited may be detailed in the law, making its application conditional on such factors as the nature or the gravity of the offence committed.[71]

In other words, the Grand Chamber in *Scoppola (No 3)* ruled that the Chamber in *Frodl* erred in its reading of what *Hirst (No 2)* required. This illustrates the Court's evolution of its own jurisprudence to seemingly reduce the level of rights protection.

The Court's jurisprudence on religious dress (and particularly Islamic dress) demonstrates the second form of regression through evolution. Article 9 of the Convention protects the right to freedom of religious belief, including the

[68] *Hirst v the United Kingdom (No 2)* [2005] ECHR 681.
[69] *Frodl v Austria* [2010] ECHR 508.
[70] *Scoppola v Italy (No 3)* [2012] ECHR 868.
[71] ibid, para 99.

right 'to manifest … religion or belief'. In the ECHR (as in other international human rights systems) there is a distinction between the right to *have* a religion or belief (which is unlimited) and the right to *manifest* that religion or belief (which can be limited, under Article 9(2), by 'such limitations as are prescribed by law and are necessary in a democratic society in the interests of public safety, for the protection of public order, health or morals, or for the protection of the rights and freedoms of others'). On the face of it, manifesting religious belief through one's dress seems relatively uncontroversial: it is difficult to see how wearing a kippah, crucifix or niqab might endanger public safety, public order or the rights and freedoms of others, so that one might reasonably expect that to have a right to freedom of conscience or belief includes having a right to dress in a manner that one considers to be compliant with one's religious belief. However, it now appears increasingly clear that this is not the case under the ECHR, especially if you happen to be a Muslim woman who wishes to be covered in public.

In *Leyla Şahin v Turkey*[72] and the previously discussed case of *SAS v France*,[73] the Court upheld prohibitions on the wearing of hijab in public universities (in Turkey) and face coverings in public (in France), finding them to be permissible limitations on the right to freedom of religion. As already discussed, in *SAS v France* this was the case seemingly in contrast with the apparent European consensus, whilst in *Leyla Şahin* the decision was related to Turkey's secular constitutional identity. In *Leyla Şahin*, European consensus was also a point of disagreement between the majority of the Court and the dissenting judges. The Court claimed that there was no consensus in Europe in respect of wearing headscarves in educational establishments. However, if the enquiry were limited to religious dress in universities only (excluding schools, nurseries, etc) then there were only three states in which such a prohibition existed.[74] In the same time period, the mandatory display of the crucifix in Italian schools was said not to violate Article 9 because, the Grand Chamber found, the crucifix was not necessarily a religious symbol.[75] These decisions illustrate that as the Convention develops, or evolves, it does not necessarily do so in a progressive way; rather, it may happen in a way that fundamentally undermines the capacities of people – especially women – to fully exercise their citizenship, broadly construed, by expressing (sometimes complex) personal identities and engaging in the public square.

Cases about Islamic dress are not *solely* about whether a state can tell a woman what she may wear; they are also about the overall potential costs in rights terms of prohibiting a woman from wearing clothing that she considers to be required by her religious beliefs. Where a woman is told, for example, that she may not cover her face in public, but considers herself bound to do

---

[72] *Leyla Şahin v Turkey* App no 44774/98 (ECtHR, 10 November 2005).

[73] *SAS v France* (n 40).

[74] Turkey, Azerbaijan and Albania. See *Leyla Şahin v Turkey* (n 72), para 116.

[75] *Lautsi and Others v Italy* [2011] ECHR 2412.

so by how she interprets her religious belief, she must make a stark choice: to break the law, to act in conflict with her conscience and religious belief, or to shirk the public square and all of the richness of life – and exercise of rights such as association and expression – that comes with it. Thus, cases of this kind have implications that are unquestionably regressive in both doctrinal and 'real' terms, with disproportionate impacts on people who are already often marginalised, in this case Muslim women who wish to dress in a manner that they consider consistent with their religious beliefs.

The discussion about the possibility of regress is not only a question of fact but also a normative question about whether the Court should be open to restricting rights in certain circumstances. Both of these questions are the subject of considerable debate.

As we pointed out above, in *Scoppola (No 3)*, the ECtHR clearly stated that it was overruling its previous decision and establishing a new standard. Often, the Court just subtly reconfigures the standard: it restricts it without saying that it is doing so. In its more recent decision in *Lacatus v Switzerland*,[76] the ECtHR ruled that prohibitions on begging violate the protection of respect for private life under Article 8. Although the conceptualisation of begging as a matter of private life may be open to question, this judgment clearly represents a development of the existing understanding of private life in the case law. Nevertheless, the Court did not make clear what kind of regulation of begging might be compatible with the Convention. In the recent admissibility decision in *Dian v Denmark*,[77] the Court clarified the scope of the right established in *Lacatus*, finding that a regulatory regime that was highly restrictive but that was not an 'absolute' ban was Convention-compatible. Although one might read *Dian* as the Court finessing its developing approach from *Lacatus*, some considered *Dian* a regressive ruling in which the Court 'distort[ed] its own words'.[78] The Court did not explicitly state that *Lacatus* was being overruled; rather, it sought to distinguish *Lacatus* and *Dian* in its decision.

To suggest that the Court can never change a standard once it has been established would impose an unduly rigid restriction on the Court, fetter its discretion and be in tension with the evolutive approach per se, as well as with the ongoing process of considering 'feedback' from stakeholders in the refinement and interpretation of Convention law.[79] The key question here is how much the Court might regressively evolve Convention standards and whether

---

[76] *Lacatus v Switzerland* [2021] ECHR 37.

[77] *Dian v Denmark* App no 44002/22 (ECtHR, 21 May 2024).

[78] Sarah Ganty, 'Sliding Fast Down the Slippery Slope of Criminalization of Poverty in Strugurel Ion Dian Against Denmark (*Strasbourg Observer*, 29 October 2024) at https://strasbourgobservers.com/2024/10/29/sliding-fast-down-the-slippery-slope-of-criminalization-of-poverty-in-strugurel-ion-dian-against-denmark/.

[79] For the Court's engagement with feedback, see Kanstantsin Dzehtsiarou, 'Keep Me in the Loop: Feedback Exchange between the European Court of Human Rights and States' (2023) 22(3) *The Law & Practice of International Courts and Tribunals* 591.

there are any limits to doing so. On this, the views of Judge Serghides, dissenting in *Dian*, are worth considering:

> The doctrine that the Convention is a living instrument to be adapted to present-day conditions cannot be employed in such a manner as to negate a fundamental right ... This doctrine is an aspect or a capacity of the principle of effectiveness and can in no way be used such as to render the right in question neither practical nor effective, or even to abrogate it on the pretext of other considerations.[80]

CONCLUSION

In this chapter, we discussed the need for evolutive interpretation. Although when deploying evolutive interpretation the ECtHR is open to the criticism of judicial activism, the alternative to evolution is that the ECHR will not be able to respond to contemporary developments, thus risking ineffectiveness and related illegitimacy. In order to counter claims of illegitimate activism, the Court adopts techniques such as European consensus to assess whether evolution on any particular issue or at a particular point of time might be apposite. The consensus argument is not homogeneous and the Court uses different evidence to justify the existence of consensus, including comparative legal analysis of the laws and practice of the Contracting Parties, international treaties, expert opinions and popular opinions. Finally, evolution is not necessarily progressive; there are incidents of evolution in fact acting regressively and narrowing the scope of protection allowed by the ECHR.

FURTHER READING

Kanstantsin Dzehtsiarou, *European Consensus and the Legitimacy of the European Court of Human Rights* (Cambridge University Press, 2015), chapters 2 and 3.

Sandra Fredman, 'Living Trees or Deadwood: The Interpretive Challenge of the European Convention on Human Rights' in NW Barber, Richard Ekins and Paul Yowell (eds), *Lord Sumption and the Limits of the Law* (Hart Publishing, 2016) 45.

George Letsas, *A Theory of Interpretation of the European Convention on Human Rights* (Oxford University Press, 2007), chapter 3.

Alastair Mowbray, 'An Examination of the European Court of Human Rights' Approach to Overruling its Previous Case Law' (2009) 9(2) *Human Rights Law Review* 179.

[80] *Mortier v Belgium* [2022] ECHR 764.

5

Accounting for Difference: Proportionality and the Margin of Appreciation

The European Convention on Human Rights (ECHR or the Convention) purports to emanate from and to reflect the common heritages and values of European states (chapter 1). However, the 46 member states of the Council of Europe all have their own distinct histories, constitutional and legal traditions, and contemporary challenges. As a result, there are differences between them as to how they respond to and manage contentious issues, and the same issue may give rise a range of responses across the Contracting Parties. The question for the European Court of Human Rights (ECtHR or the Court) is, inevitably, how to account for difference; to acknowledge that in some cases there might be multiple *legally acceptable* approaches to managing a human rights conundrum, and that an approach may be rights-compliant even if it is not considered to be uniquely appropriate or optimal. This chapter focuses on techniques the Court has developed to attend to difference: the margin of appreciation; proportionality; and process-based review.

The margin of appreciation might be broadly understood as the discretion that states retain to determine their own legal and policy approaches to questions even where those approaches have implications as to rights. It is the 'space for manoeuvre' that the Court is willing to afford the Contracting Parties in fulfilling their obligations under the Convention.[1] The margin of appreciation is closely linked to the test of proportionality. This is essentially a 'test' or a 'principle' that requires that, when acting in a manner that interferes with rights, the state must (i) have a legitimate objective in mind, (ii) be acting in a manner that is related to this objective, (iii) interfere no more than is necessary to achieve that objective, and (iv) strike a reasonable balance between the need to achieve the objective and the interference with rights. The Court will apply this test with varying degrees of strictness depending on the

[1] Howard Yourow, *The Margin of Appreciation Doctrine in the Dynamics of European Human Rights Jurisprudence* (Kluwer Law, 1995) 13; Steven Greer, *The Margin of Appreciation: Interpretation and Discretion under the European Convention on Human Rights* (Council of Europe, 2000) 5.

circumstances: for example, interference with political speech will be subjected to a heightened standard of scrutiny compared to interference with commercial speech.[2] Even where the Court has acknowledged that a state has a margin of appreciation in respect of the particular issue under consideration, it will usually deploy the proportionality test to assess whether the action complained of remains within, or exceeds, that margin of appreciation. Thus, the margin of appreciation impacts on the strictness of scrutiny under the proportionality principle.

The margin of appreciation and proportionality are among the most contested of the Court's methods of interpretation.[3] This is partly because they may lead to different answers to similar questions asked in different contexts, and thus appear to endanger consistency in approach and rights protection across the Contracting Parties. Furthermore, ascertaining (dis)proportionality and identifying the margin of appreciation are not exact sciences. Ultimately, a proportionality analysis seeks to determine whether an appropriate 'balance' has been struck between competing interests. This is not something that is amenable to scientific determination. It is, rather, a matter of *judgement*, in the fullest sense of the word. The resulting lack of precision is one of the primary concerns that might be expressed in relation to proportionality, but it is also one the structure of the test itself attempts to address. The proportionality analysis does not ask whether the optimal or perfect balance has been struck, only whether a *proportionate* balance has been found. Thus, through this analysis the Court is trying to account for difference (of context, experience, expertise, etc) but to do so in a transparent manner, so that at the very least the weighting given to the various factors (eg, the alleged legitimate objective being pursued) is made clear.

This is not to say, however, that the Court will always be able to determine the question of balance; sometimes it will recognise that a topic is of such sensitivity, subject to such profound disagreement and of such centrality to 'national' or 'constitutional' identity that the state ought to be allowed a wide margin of appreciation in relation to it. Once the state stays within that margin of appreciation, its actions will pass muster under the Convention. This is certainly considered important by the Contracting Parties, which seem to want to nudge the Court towards displaying ever more deference towards the decisions of the national authorities. This is reflected in the symbolically important

---

[2] Compare, for example, *Bowman v the United Kingdom*, 19 February 1998, Reports of Judgments and Decisions 1998-I and *Colman v the United Kingdom*, 28 June 1993, Series A no 258-D.

[3] Just to mention a few examples: Yutaka Arai-Takahashi, *The Margin of Appreciation Doctrine and the Principle of Proportionality in the Jurisprudence of the ECHR* (Intersentia, 2002); Eyal Benvenisti, 'Margin of Appreciation, Consensus, and Universal Standards' (1999) 31 *Journal of International Law and Politics* 843; Jan Kratochvil, 'The Inflation of the Margin of Appreciation by the European Court of Human Rights' (2011) 29(3) *Netherlands Quarterly of Human Rights* 324.

decision to mention subsidiarity and the margin of appreciation in the Preamble, which was amended by Protocol 15 that came into force in August 2021.

The margin of appreciation is not limited to the qualified rights in Articles 8–11 of the Convention, which are naturally fit for proportionality analysis. Rather, it can also exercise an independent function within the Convention jurisprudence. Let us take Article 3, the right to be free from torture, inhuman and degrading treatment or punishment, as an example. This is an absolute right that contains at least three levels of protection: first, the state's negative obligation to refrain from torture, inhuman or degrading treatment or punishment; second, its positive substantive obligation to protect people from ill-treatment from other individuals; and, third, its positive procedural obligation to investigate situations of torture, inhuman or degrading treatment or punishment. There is no margin of appreciation as regards to the negative obligation, but the Court has suggested that states do have some margin of appreciation when it comes to the positive obligations of the second and third type.[4]

In this chapter we will first consider whether the proportionality test is needed and desirable in ECtHR adjudication, or whether it is an 'assault on human rights'.[5] The margin of appreciation is no less controversial than the test of proportionality: commentators writing on it can be divided into those who think that there is no place for any margin of appreciation in human rights adjudication,[6] and those who argue that this is an appropriate concept that might be spread even beyond the ECtHR.[7] Debate 2 therefore will shed some light on the reasons behind these conflicting views. One of the key reasons for criticism of the margin of appreciation is that its scope is difficult to define as its boundaries are set on a case-by-case basis. Debate 3 addresses these concerns.

Debate 1

Do We Need a Proportionality Analysis for Rights Adjudication?

Assessing whether a particular law, policy or state action is a proportionate interference with rights involves a number of stages of analysis, and a violation of the Convention can be established at any one of these stages. We will first consider proportionality in relation to negative obligations, namely

[4] See, for example, *Vinter and Others v the United Kingdom* [2013] ECHR 645, para 120.

[5] Stavros Tsakyrakis, 'Proportionality: An Assault on Human Rights?' (2009) 7(3) *International Journal of Constitutional Law* 468.

[6] Examples are multiple, including Benvenisti (n 3); George Letsas, *A Theory of Interpretation of the European Convention on Human Rights* (Oxford University Press, 2009).

[7] See Yuval Shany, 'Toward a General Margin of Appreciation Doctrine in International Law?' (2005) 16(5) *European Journal of International Law* 907; see also Janneke Gerards, 'Pluralism, Deference and the Margin of Appreciation Doctrine' (2011) 17 *European Law Journal* 80; Dominic McGoldrick, 'A Defence of the Margin of Appreciation and an Argument for its Application by the Human Rights Committee' (2016) 65 *International and Comparative Law Quarterly* 21.

whether the state's interference was proportionate to the aim pursued. We will then briefly cover the test of proportionality in relation to positive obligations. Usually, we think about the stages of proportionality as being broken down into questions considered by the Court in turn. The questions are:

1. Was there an interference with an ECHR right?
2. Was the interference legal?
3. Did the interference pursue a legitimate aim?
4. Is the interference necessary in a democratic society?
5. Did the authorities balance the relevant public and private interests properly when they considered the interference?

The Court does not always address each of these steps expressly when considering a claim of disproportionate interference with rights (because, for example, the interference is apparent and not disputed, or the legitimacy of the aim pursued is accepted by all parties), but when analysing the facts of a particular case, these questions provide a useful framework for assessing proportionality.

Was There an Interference with an ECHR Right?

In this 'preliminary' stage of proportionality the Court assesses whether any Convention right is engaged by the impugned action. If not, the Court can either find no violation or declare an application inadmissible. In practice, it is unusual for the parties to dispute whether there was an interference. Commonly, the respondent state accepts the claim of interference but argues that it was justified (ie proportionate). This is not to say that this preliminary question is never disputed, but such disputes are rare.[8]

Was the Interference Legal?

Once an interference has been established, the Court considers legality by asking whether such interference was 'in accordance with the law' (Article 8(2)) or 'prescribed by law' (Article 9(2), Article 10(2), Article 11(2)). At this stage, the Court assesses only whether the respondent state complied with its national law; a lack of legal basis in domestic law will lead to a finding that the Convention has been violated. In *Giacomelli v Italy*, for example, the Court found a violation because the authorities continued to operate a hazardous waste plant although they were obliged to close it under the national law.[9] If there is no legal basis for the action, the test of legality fails and a violation is established; unlawful action cannot be proportionate. Conversely, if the interference

[8] For an example of the claim of interference being (unsuccessfully) disputed by the respondent state, see *S and Marper v the United Kingdom* [2008] ECHR 1581.

[9] *Giacomelli v Italy* [2006] ECHR 916.

is legal under national law, the Court moves to the next stage of the test of proportionality.

Did the Interference Pursue a Legitimate Aim?

Interferences with Convention rights that are in accordance with the national law are then considered from the perspective of the aim that they pursue. At this stage the respondent state identifies the objective that was being pursued by the impugned action. If no legitimate aim is identified, the Court will find a violation of the Convention. The legitimate aims are usually listed in the qualifying clauses of the relevant right in the Convention, for example Article 8(2), Article 9(2), Article 10(2) and Article 11(2). By means of example, Article 9(2) provides (emphasis added):

> 2. Freedom to manifest one's religion or beliefs shall be subject only to such limitations as are prescribed by law and are necessary in a democratic society *in the interests of public safety, for the protection of public order, health or morals, or for the protection of the rights and freedoms of others.*

The ECtHR applies a light touch approach to governments' claims that they pursued a legitimate aim. A violation will be established at this stage only where no such aim is identified, or where the interference cannot be even remotely linked to any of the legitimate aims. This is rare, although not unheard of. For example, in *Catan and Others v the Republic of Moldova and Russia*,[10] the applicants lived in a territory of the self-proclaimed Republic of Transnistria, which is *de jure* a part of Moldova. The authorities of Transnistria decided to close some schools in its territory in which instruction was in Romanian, the official language of Moldova. The Court held that these schools were closed as part of 'entrenching the separatist ideology' of Transnistria and not in pursuit of a legitimate aim. As a result, the Convention had been violated. Conversely, if a legitimate aim can be identified (even presumptively), the Court moves on to the next stage of the proportionality analysis.

Is the Interference Necessary in a Democratic Society?

Articles 8–11 of the ECHR provide that every interference with the rights enshrined in these Articles should be 'necessary in a democratic society'. In considering necessity, the Court assesses whether there is a 'reasonable relationship of proportionality between the means employed and the aim sought to be realised',[11] and whether there were less intrusive ways of achieving the same result. For instance, in the case of *Alekseyev v Russia*, the Court held that the authorities had resorted to measures that were not necessary in a democratic

[10] *Catan and Others v the Republic of Moldova and Russia* [2012] ECHR 1827.
[11] *Lithgow and Others v the United Kingdom* [1986] ECHR 8, para. 120.

society when they banned a Pride march.[12] Here, the Government argued that this parade would provoke counter-demonstrations and cause public disorder. The Court noted that 'the authorities could have made arrangements to ensure that both events [pro-LGBTQAI+ and anti-LGBTQAI+] proceeded peacefully and lawfully, allowing both sides to achieve the goal of expressing their views without clashing with each other'.[13] Doing that did not necessitate banning the Pride parade, which ban was therefore not necessary in a democratic society. This stage of analysis does not concern itself with whether the option taken is fair, or whether the interference is disproportionate to the public interest to be achieved; rather, it is limited to questions of necessity, sometimes implicating the effectiveness of the approach taken.[14] If the Court establishes that the measure is not necessary in a democratic society, it finds a violation; otherwise, it moves to the next stage of the proportionality test.

Did National Authorities Properly Balance the Relevant Public and Private Interests?

This is the *stricto sensu* 'balancing' stage of proportionality analysis. Somewhat controversially,[15] it is not uncommon for the ECtHR to merge the necessity and balancing stages, considering them both as part of its analysis of whether the measures taken were 'necessary in a democratic society'.[16] The key difference is that during the balancing stage the Court is not asking whether the interference was necessary or effective, but rather whether it fairly weighed the competing interests one against the other and reached a balanced conclusion. This complex analysis is not amenable to a scientifically 'correct' answer: rights are often in contest with one another, and finding the right 'balance' between them is always challenging.[17]

Von Hannover v Germany illustrates this well.[18] In this case, the Court considered whether the applicant's right to respect for private life was breached. The applicant, a member of royal family of Monaco, was photographed without her consent, and these photographs were published in a German tabloid. The German courts favoured freedom of expression in this case and did not interfere, finding that whilst there was an infringement of her privacy, this was proportionate to the public interest in her life as a public figure. In contrast, the ECtHR found that there was a violation of Article 8 because the publication of these photographs disproportionately interfered with the applicant's right to a

[12] *Alekseyev v Russia* App nos 4916/07, 25924/08 and 14599/09 (ECtHR, 21 October 2010).
[13] ibid, para 75.
[14] Janneke Gerards, 'How to Improve the Necessity Test of the European Court of Human Rights' (2013) 11(2) *International Journal of Constitutional Law* 466, 471.
[15] ibid, 472–73.
[16] See, for example, *SAS v France* [2014] ECHR 695.
[17] Indeed, sometimes they might be said to 'clash'; see Stijn Smet and Eva Brems (eds), *When Human Rights Clash at the European Court of Human Rights – Conflict or Harmony?* (Oxford University Press, 2017).
[18] *Von Hannover v Germany* [2004] ECHR 294.

private life.[19] In this case, both courts – the domestic court and the European court – considered the same interests but arrived at a different conclusion as to the proportionate balance between them.

Proportionality and Positive Obligations

The proportionality analysis in cases of positive obligations is quite distinct from the one in relation to negative obligations, due to the difference in the nature and diverse requirements of such obligations. Of course, in cases of positive obligations, instead of identifying the interference, the first step would be to establish the obligation of the state to act. Often this depends on whether the significant risk to human rights is known or ought to be known to the state. If the answer to this question is affirmative, the severity and the nature of the risk will have to be dealt with by proportionate actions of the state. For instance, in *Kurt v Austria*, the Court stated:

> [For finding a violation] it is sufficient for an applicant to show that the authorities did not do all that could be reasonably expected of them to avoid a real and immediate risk to life of which they had or ought to have had knowledge. This is a question which can only be answered in the light of all the circumstances of any particular case.[20]

The Court usually establishes a list of obligations with which the state must comply in a particular area, and then considers whether the state indeed fulfilled these obligations. In a sense this is a form of reverse test of 'necessary in democratic society'. Instead of justifying the interference, the state authorities would have to justify why they failed to comply with a particular framework requiring them to act. However, in the case of positive obligations this test is more complex. As Stoyanova has argued:

> [T]he normative starting point is that States have to choose the least restrictive measures when they take actions to limit rights [(negative obligation)]. In this way, their choice of measures is more circumscribed. In contrast, the Court has never formulated a test to the effect that States have to undertake the most protective measures to ensure the rights [(positive obligation)].[21]

In determining the proportionality of positive actions, the ECtHR not only considers what was done but also examines how it was done. In *EG v Moldova*, the Court stated that:

> States have a positive obligation inherent in Articles 3 and 8 of the Convention to enact criminal laws that effectively punish rape, and to apply them in

[19] ibid, paras 78–75.

[20] *Kurt v Austria* App no 62903/15 (ECtHR, 15 June 2021), para 160.

[21] Vladislava Stoyanova, *Positive Obligations under the European Convention on Human Rights* (Oxford University Press, 2023) 14.

> practice through effective investigation and prosecution. That positive obligation further requires the criminalisation and effective prosecution of all non-consensual sexual acts. Implicit in this context is a requirement to act with reasonable promptness and expedition. A prompt response on the part of the authorities is essential to maintaining public confidence in their adherence to the rule of law and preventing any appearance of collusion in or tolerance of unlawful acts.[22]

To sum up, the Court's proportionality test in relation to positive obligations is less structured and one-dimensional due to the very multilayered nature of positive obligations. It still can be said that some form of test of proportionality is applicable to positive obligations of states under the Convention.

Criticisms of Proportionality

Critics of proportionality mount three major arguments: utility; impact on human rights; and interference with substantive decision-making at the national level.

The utility criticism claims that proportionality is not a means of reasoning that helps to resolve cases effectively; rather, it conceals discretionary, *ad hoc* reasoning. This relates to the fact that the structure of the proportionality analysis suggests a kind of precision in respect of identifying or measuring proportionality, when in truth only some elements of the test can be objectively verified (eg, necessity or legality) and the rest of the analysis is a structured, but subjective, assessment. As Fontanelli argues, proportionality 'is a myth in which the form draws its nourishment from an impoverished meaning'.[23] Thus, the heart of this criticism is that the ECtHR represents this as an objective test and does not acknowledge that no precise scale for measuring incompatible interests can be identified. The criticism is not, then, that the assessment of proportionality is subjective per se; indeed, it is inevitably so. It is, rather, that the Court denies this subjectivity when it pursues the appearance of objectivity through a proportionality test. The subjectivity of proportionality analysis is perhaps most clear in the assignment by the Court of varying weights to different interests in any particular scenario. The Chamber judgment in *Osmanoğlu and Kocabaş v Switzerland* is an apposite illustration.[24]

The applicants in this case were Turkish immigrants in Switzerland who wanted their daughters to be exempted from mixed-sex swimming lessons. Their request was refused, which they claimed violated their rights under Article 9. They understood their Muslim faith as requiring a certain approach

---

[22] *EG v the Republic of Moldova* App no 37882/13 (ECtHR, 13 April 2021), paras 39–40.

[23] Filippo Fontanelli, 'The Mythology of Proportionality in Judgments of the Court of Justice of the European Union on Internet and Fundamental Rights' (2016) 36(3) *Oxford Journal of Legal Studies* 630, 632.

[24] *Osmanoğlu and Kocabaş v Switzerland* App no 29086/12 (ECtHR, 10 January 2017).

to raising children, which included not allowing their daughters to undertake swimming lessons together with boys. Switzerland argued that this was not compatible with the Swiss way of life, and that the interference with Article 9 was proportionate in pursuit of public order and morality. To determine the case, the Court ended up comparing the state's interest in integrating immigrants into their society against the applicants' religious beliefs. In this case, the Court considered the state interest to be a legitimate one, the action to be necessary and the interference thus to be a proportionate interference with rights. In other words, the Court prioritised integration over religious belief. One can imagine, however, that the Court might come to precisely the opposite conclusion: it is not clear why the Court here prioritises the integration rationale over religious belief. Either outcome is possible, and the inability to predict which will be arrived at in a particular case makes the result of a complaint difficult to foresee. A lack of foreseeability calls into question the effectiveness of the Convention in ensuring practical protection of rights, including at the stage of making the kinds of policy that mandate mixed-sex swimming lessons, regardless of the likely objections of people who follow a more conservative approach to religious beliefs, and for whom this would likely cause real difficulties, such as Orthodox Jews or devout Muslims. A similar observation could be made about cases in which the Court compares interests such as the right not to be indoctrinated against the need to maintain cultural traditions,[25] or when the right to acquire information clashes with personal privacy.[26] The criticism of proportionality here is not, then, that it arrives at the 'wrong' outcome – one might argue that balancing such interests is so difficult that a range of possible outcomes might be defended – but rather that its pretension to objectivity and exactitude elides the reality of subjective reasoning in any given case.

The second criticism – that of the impact of proportionality on the value of human rights – is somewhat more philosophical. Some commentators argue that proportionality reduces the value of human rights to the level of comparing various interests.[27] In fact, they say, human rights should be more than just personal interests that can be equal or even sometimes subordinate to communal preferences, and that the outcome of a case should follow from moral assessment of the situation involving human rights.[28] Tsakyrakis argues that

> [t]he adoption of a balancing test, according to the principle of proportionality, risks neglecting the complexity of moral evaluation and, especially, the complexity of rights. More specifically, it tends to overlook, or at least not appreciate adequately, the fact that our moral universe includes ideas not amenable to

[25] *Lautsi and Others v Ital* [2011] ECHR 2412.

[26] See *Von Hannover v Germany (No 2)* [2012] ECHR 228.

[27] See, for example, Letsas, 'Rescuing Proportionality' in Cruft, Liao and Renzo (eds), *Philosophical Foundations of Human Rights* (Oxford University Press, 2015).

[28] Ronald Dworkin, *Taking Rights Seriously* (Harvard University Press, 1977) xi.

> quantification, with the result that these ideas are not given due consideration in our reasoning.[29]

This criticism is not accepted by all commentators. Moral reasoning as suggested by Tsakyrakis might lead to even more subjective, speculative and unpredictable results. People disagree about human rights and there is no universally acceptable morality. Therefore, sometimes moral reasoning presents itself in a form of the imposing of the personal biases of the judges sitting in the case. Such an approach undermines the legitimacy of human rights adjudication. The uncertainty and unpredictability of the results and seemingly ad hoc nature of the reasoning in this case will not even be furnished by a structure that proportionality provides.[30]

The final criticism of proportionality is that it involves the Court in a substantive review of decisions taken at the national level. By means of illustration, in the case of *Konstantin Markin v Russia*,[31] the Court considered whether the Russian law prohibiting male military personnel from taking paternity leave was compatible with the Convention. The Court had to balance the state's reasons for prohibiting paternity leave (which related to 'national traditions', military discipline and national security) against considerations of gender equality. The Russian Constitutional Court had already had a chance to balance the same considerations and decided against allowing male military servicemen to have access to parental leave; it considered that the state had struck a permissible balance.[32] The ECtHR, however, forcefully disagreed, holding:

> [T]he core argument of the Constitutional Court in support of the limitation of the rights of servicemen was that military service imposed specific demands in so far as it required uninterrupted performance of duties by them and that, consequently, the taking of parental leave by servicemen on a large scale would have a negative effect on the fighting power and operational effectiveness of the armed forces. The Court finds that argument unconvincing. It notes the lack of concrete evidence to substantiate the alleged damage to national security. There is no indication that any expert study or statistical research was made to assess the number of servicemen who would be in a position to take three years' parental leave at any given time and would be willing to do so. There is accordingly no evidentiary basis for the assertion that the number of servicemen simultaneously taking parental leave would be so significant as to undermine the fighting capacity of the army. It follows that the Constitutional Court based its decision on a pure assumption, without attempting to probe its validity by checking it against statistical data or by weighing the conflicting interests of maintaining the operational effectiveness of the army, on the one hand, and of protecting servicemen

---

[29] Tsakyrakis (n 5) 475.

[30] For more see Kanstantsin Dzehtsiarou, *European Consensus and the Legitimacy of the European Court of Human Rights* (Cambridge University Press, 2015) 116–119.

[31] *Konstantin Markin v Russia* [2012] ECHR 514.

[32] ibid, see the summary in para 34.

> against discrimination in the sphere of family life and promoting the best interests of their children, on the other.[33]

Contrary to the decision of the Russian Constitutional Court, the ECtHR decided that there was a violation of Article 8. For some, such an outcome raises serious questions about whether the ECtHR is adhering to its subsidiary character. In response, one might argue that the ECtHR can only identify violations of the Convention; it does not have any power to invalidate domestic laws, and thus exercises an especially 'weak' form of judicial review that makes substantive review relatively unproblematic. However, that argument ignores the fact that the Court's decision is binding on the respondent state under Article 46(1) (which we consider further in chapter 8), even if the state considers that the ECtHR has got the question of balance 'wrong' or the issue is one on which reasonable people might reasonably disagree so that a 'right answer' might not easily be discernible. Even if the ECtHR's review is 'weak', then, it is still legally binding, a situation that one might argue is particularly troublesome where the test being applied to assess whether there was a violation is an imprecise one, as proportionality is. Perhaps partly in response to these concerns, the Court has increasingly embraced procedural reasoning and analysis in recent years, seeming to 'avoid' substantive adjudication in cases where the relevant domestic authorities have given due consideration to rights concerns and arrived at a view on proportionality of a measure taking that into account. We have discussed this turn to 'process-based review' in chapter 1, but for now it is sufficient to remind ourselves that the turn to proceduralism speaks to concerns about subsidiarity that are implicated in debates on whether proportionality reasoning is desirable in the ECHR system.

Justifications of Proportionality

Given the seemingly compelling arguments against the Court's use of a proportionality analysis, one might wonder why it perseveres with it. The truth is that proportionality analysis is a commonly deployed approach to the difficult question of 'balancing' competing rights and interests in tribunals all over the world.[34] This is not because any system considers that it is perfect or

[33] *Konstantin Markin v Russia* App no 30078/06 (ECtHR, 7 October 2010), para 57.

[34] For a comparative overview, see Benedikt Pirker, *Proportionality Analysis and Models of Judicial Review* (Europa Law Publishing, 2013); and Alec Stone Sweet and Jud Mathews, 'Proportionality Balancing and Global Constitutionalism' (2008) 47 *Columbia Journal of Transnational Law* 73. Some key judgments on proportionality include the following from the European Court of Justice: *Internationale Handelsgesellschaft mbH v Einfuhr- und Vorratsstelle für Getreide und Futtermittel*, [1970] ECR 1125, 1136; UK: *R (Daly) v Secretary of State for the Home Department* [2001] UKHL 26; Germany: the German Constitutional Court began using this principle almost from the very beginning, see BVerfGE 3, 383 at 399 (1954); it is used in Israel: HCJ 2056/04 *Beit Sourik Village Council v The Government of Israel* PD 24 [2004]; and in Canada: *R v Oakes* [1986] 1 SCR 103.

is unaware of the criticisms already outlined, but rather because it is a workable approach that has resonance across different systems of political, legal and judicial decision-making.

First, the structured nature of the proportionality analysis creates an analytical framework for the delicate assessments that competing interests and rights necessitate, which in turn facilitates *some* transparency. Even if the reader might not be convinced of why the Court came to a certain conclusion on the question of balancing, the structure of the analysis at least outlines how it purports to have come to that decision. If the balancing analysis as outlined is inadequate, this is quickly apparent from the text of the judgment, and can form the basis of concerted scholarly engagement with the reasoning and future attempts to convince the Court to revisit its position. Thus, proportionality analysis supports a culture of justification within human rights adjudication:[35] the respondent state must justify its interference and seek to establish its lawfulness by reference to the analytical framework of the proportionality test, and the Court must clearly assess the strength of those arguments using the same framework.

Second, although the outcome of a proportionality analysis is sometimes unpredictable, the highly structured nature of the assessment does bring an element of foreseeability to how the analysis will proceed and to the arguments that a state will need to make to ground a claim of proportionality. This is significant not only in cases before the Court but also potentially in the policy-making process, where the likely assessment of a contentious law in the ECtHR (or a domestic court mirroring the Strasbourg framework of analysis) will require legality, legitimacy, necessity, etc to be established. Thus, the structure of the proportionality analysis in the ECtHR jurisprudence may structure the policy-making process, potentially reducing the likelihood of introduction of a disproportionate law or policy in the first place.[36] Proportionality is not only a legal test but also an expectation of rights-compatible law and policy-making, so that it can be expected to 'reach back' to the original decision-making process and inject within it a rights-related conscientiousness that will improve the quality of decision-making.[37] Indeed, this to some extent underpins the Court's commitment to process-based review as a

---

[35] See, eg, Alain Zysset, "A Culture of Justification or a Culture of Presumption? The Turn to Procedural Review and the Normative Function of Proportionality at the European Court of Human Rights' in Stephanie Schiedermair, Alexander Schwarz and Dominik Steiger (eds), *Theory and Practice of the ECHR* (Hart Publishing, 2021).

[36] In both Ireland and the UK, for example, 'organs of the state' (Ireland) and 'public authorities' (UK) are required to undertake their work in accordance with the ECHR, and can thus be expected to consider proportionality when making policies and proposing laws that have Convention implications. See Human Rights Act 1998, s 6 (in the UK) and European Convention on Human Rights Act 2003, s 3 (in Ireland).

[37] This is not unique to proportionality in the ECHR. See, eg, Fiona de Londras and Jasmin Tregidga, 'Rights, proportionality, and process in EU counterterrorism lawmaking' (2021) 19(2) *International Journal of Constitutional Law* 665.

mode of accommodating difference, recognising that if a domestic system has considered rights effectively in its decision-making process, there should be strong reasons indeed to consider the outcome disproportionate on the basis of balancing.

Third, proportionality is well established as an approach in domestic and international human rights law, as well as in international law more broadly. Indeed, some have gone so far as to describe it as a global constitutional principle.[38] The judges and lawyers of the Court, the lawyers before it, and the lawyers and policy makers at domestic level are now generally familiar with proportionality as a method of reasoning: not only was the principle developed in Strasbourg after the example of, especially, the German Constitutional Court, but so too has its development in the ECtHR influenced the use of proportionality analysis in other Contracting Parties' domestic law. Very simply put, proportionality is now a familiar and, in some jurisdictions, fundamental approach to reasoning about rights that it would be difficult, if not impossible, to abandon.

Indeed, for all its difficulties as outlined above, proportionality has much to commend it as an approach to undertaking judicial review of the Convention compatibility of state action whilst maintaining respect for the principle of subsidiarity. It leaves ample space for subsidiarity and deference through the mode of margin of appreciation: where the issue in question is one in relation to which states enjoy a broad margin of appreciation, the Court will establish a lower threshold of proportionality; whereas where there is a narrower margin of appreciation, the analysis will be stricter. Proportionality thus allows the Court to attempt to walk the very delicate line between supervising the Convention and not trespassing too far on the sovereignty of states.

Debate 2

Should National Authorities Have a Margin of Appreciation in Respect of Human Rights Protection?

The margin of appreciation is a judicial innovation within Convention jurisprudence. Indeed, it was not until Protocol 15 that it was introduced into the Convention text. That Protocol inserted new preambular language acknowledging 'that the High Contracting Parties, in accordance with the principle of subsidiarity, have the primary responsibility to secure the rights and freedoms defined in this Convention and the Protocols thereto, and that ***in doing so they enjoy a margin of appreciation***, subject to the supervisory jurisdiction of the European Court of Human Rights established by this Convention' (emphasis added).

[38] Anne Peters, 'Proportionality as a Global Constitutional Principle' in Anthony F Lang and Antje Wiener (eds), ***Handbook on Global Constitutionalism*** (Edward Elgar, 2023).

Despite its inclusion, now, in the Preamble, there is no single, clear definition of the margin of appreciation. For O'Donnell, the 'margin of appreciation refers to the latitude allowed to the member states in their observance of the Convention',[39] while Yourow defines it 'as the freedom to act; manoeuvring, breathing or elbow room; or the latitude of deference or error which the Strasbourg organs will allow national [authorities ... before it is prepared to declare ... a violation of one of the Convention's substantive guarantees'.[40] The margin of appreciation is, then, a kind of 'discretionary space' for the Contracting Parties: the space for manoeuvre that a state has in assessing whether an interference with a Convention right constitutes a violation of that right or not. This captures what Letsas calls the substantive meaning of the margin of appreciation,[41] which goes to whether the state rightly interfered with personal rights to protect collective goals such as public order or public health or morals. Letsas argues that the margin of appreciation also has a structural dimension, meaning a mode of reasoning by which the ECtHR defers to national authorities' judgement as to Convention compliance to at least some extent.[42]

It is evident that the Court sees the margin of appreciation as having this structural function, having often pointed to it when noting that in principle, national authorities are better placed than the Court to assess the situation and make relevant decisions.[43] Why? First, there is the 'democratic legitimacy' argument, that is, that it is the national authorities, rather than the ECtHR, that have democratic legitimacy to deal with complex human rights issues. Of course, this rests heavily on the assumption that all member states to the Council of Europe are well-functioning democracies, which is certainly not always the case. However, even if this were a sustainable assumption, one might note that a democratic mandate is not the only source of legitimacy that an institution can rely upon in making decisions as to rights.[44] Indeed, it might even be argued that rights are such that perhaps they ought not to be determined solely by majoritarian structures such as parliaments, and that instead process, participation and outcome might all be important sources of legitimacy, as discussed in chapter 1. Thus, whilst the argument of democratic legitimacy provides some grounding for the margin of appreciation, it does not, alone, offer a complete justification.

The second argument for a margin of appreciation is that national authorities have more expertise in solving difficult human rights questions as they arise

[39] Thomas O'Donnell, 'The Margin of Appreciation Doctrine: Standards in the Jurisprudence of the European Court of Human Rights' (1982) 4 *Human Rights Quarterly* 474, 475.

[40] Yourow (n 1) 13.

[41] George Letsas, 'Two Concepts of the Margin of Appreciation' (2006) 26 *Oxford Journal of Legal Studies* 705, 711.

[42] ibid, 720–24.

[43] Gerards (n 7) 104; see also Onder Bakircioglu, 'The Application of the Margin of Appreciation Doctrine in Freedom of Expression and Public Morality Cases' (2007) 8 *German Law Journal* 711, 717.

[44] See, for example, Annabelle Lever, 'Is Judicial Review Undemocratic?' [2007] *Public Law* 280.

at the national level, because they are better exposed to the national dynamics, debates and contexts that influence the 'real world' impact of political and legal decisions in sensitive right areas. The Court itself has tended to endorse this approach, holding that '[b]ecause of their direct knowledge of their society and its needs, the national authorities are in principle better placed than the international judge to appreciate what is "in the public interest"'.[45] To some extent this mirrors arguments about deference to executive and legislative bodies that are familiar to identifying the 'limits' of judicial authority in many domestic jurisdictions. However, just as in domestic law, some question the assumption of expertise that underpins this position. Tsarapatsanis, for example, argues that whether the ECtHR is better or worse at deciding complex human rights dilemmas might depend on a myriad of factors, and without extensive empirical research it is difficult to reach any conclusions. Moreover, such conclusions might differ in relation to different rights and different states, and even different institutions within the same state.[46] In other words, familiarity with the domestic context does not necessarily put the national authorities in a better position to determine questions of rights.

In legal scholarship, a plethora of arguments has been advanced both in favour and against deployment of the margin of appreciation by the ECtHR. For Legg, the margin of appreciation is a useful tool that allows the Court to take into account considerations that are contextual and not immediately relevant to the matter at hand, but at the same time worthy of being weighed in the balance.[47] Legg uses the theory of practical reasoning to argue that in arriving at a particular decision, the ECtHR uses both first-order and second-order reasons. First-order reasons are immediately relevant to the case at hand; they relate directly to the questions raised. Second-order reasons are less manifestly relevant but determine the context in which the case is taking place, such as broader societal conditions or political structures. Legg uses an example of a person who 'because of tiredness decided not to assess whether or not to accept an investment proposal, thus losing the opportunity'.[48] In this example, tiredness is the second-order reason, since it is not directly relevant to the matter at issue but can have a substantive effect on the final decision. The first-order reasons would be the interest that would have been earned if the investment went ahead, the risk assessment, the availability of necessary funds and so on. Tiredness here is an exclusionary second-order reason that prevents any considerations of the first-order reasons.[49] Within Legg's argument, second-order reasons can influence the significance (or

[45] *James and Others v the United Kingdom* [1986] ECHR 2, para 46.

[46] Dimitrios Tsarapatsanis, 'The Margin of Appreciation Doctrine: A Low-Level Institutional View' (2015) 35 *Legal Studies* 675.

[47] Andrew Legg, *The Margin of Appreciation in International Human Rights Law* (Oxford University Press, 2012) 58.

[48] ibid, 18.

[49] For more examples, see ibid, 18–23.

weight) attached to first-order reasons: 'The [Court] considers the first-order reasons, and applies second-order reasons to them. The second-order reasons may cancel out, strengthen or reduce the ordinary weighting of first-order reasons'.[50] Adopting this approach, the margin of appreciation simply allows for decisions as to weighting to be made: where there is a broad margin of appreciation, the first-order reasons for finding violation should be particularly weighty; where there is a narrow or no margin of appreciation, much less convincing first-order reasons can justify a violation of the Convention.

Whilst Legg's argument is attractive in explaining *how* the margin of appreciation can assist in structuring the Court's reasoning, it does not fully address the major criticism that is levied against it: that its impact is such as to leave some people without relief before the Court simply because the rights, topic or context are such that the Court prefers to avoid making a decision as to rights. Macdonald opines that the Court uses the margin of appreciation when it does not want to provide reasons for its decision not to interfere.[51] Benvenisti argues that the margin of appreciation is a dangerous doctrine that undermines the universality of human rights because it introduces varying standards of human-rights protection.[52] The criticism is not limited to scholarly reflection on the margin of appreciation. Judge De Meyer, for example, has famously argued that

> [t]he empty phrases concerning the State's margin of appreciation – repeated in the Court's judgments for too long already – are unnecessary circumlocutions, serving only to indicate abstrusely that the States may do anything the Court does not consider incompatible with human rights. Such terminology, as wrong in principle as it is pointless in practice, should be abandoned without delay.[53]

In spite of all of these criticisms, the margin of appreciation is now clearly established as a core part of Convention jurisprudence, embedded in the preambular text of the Convention, reflected in states' ways of reasoning about the Convention and expectations of the Court, and a useful mode of enacting subsidiarity. If – as we shall see in chapter 8 – settling the division of labour for Convention compliance between states and the Council of Europe is an ongoing and vital piece of rights-related work, the margin of appreciation allows the Court to maintain effective implementation of the ECHR by not doing too much too soon, and thus avoids undermining trust and co-working between the national and European institutions.

Consequently, whether one considers the margin of appreciation to be justifiable is, in essence, connected to how one conceives of the role of the Court.

---

[50] ibid, 195.

[51] Ronald Macdonald, 'The Margin of Appreciation' in R Macdonald et al (eds), *The European System for the Protection of Human Rights* (Martinus Nijhoff, 1993) 85.

[52] Benvenisti (n 3).

[53] *Z v Finland* [1997] ECHR 10, dissenting opinion of Judge De Meyer.

If it is to grant individual justice in all cases that come before it, there seems to be limited justification for the margin of appreciation. However, if the Court's role is more broadly to 'assum[e] a central coordinating role in implementing the ECHR, by closely cooperating with national institutional agents, which comprise legislatures, courts and administrative agencies',[54] the margin may seem a sensible, if not essential, principle for the Court to have developed and to continue to apply.

Debate 3

What are the Boundaries of the Margin of Appreciation?

Even those who agree that the margin of appreciation is conceptually appropriate often criticise how it is applied in practice. Lord Lester famously called it 'slippery and elusive as an eel'.[55] Yourow points out that 'the contours of margin analysis are too vague, that the substantive content of the doctrine is too elusive and that it can be invoked to reach both pro-rights and pro-state holdings without the benefit of developing substantive doctrinal consistency'.[56] Gerards opines that 'the court frequently just mentions the margin of appreciation test and some factors determining its width, without explaining what the precise scope of the margin in the concrete case should be'.[57] In other words: what are the boundaries of a state's margin of appreciation and how are they decided?

The Nature of the Implicated Right

The first stage in deciding how wide the margin of appreciation should be in any case is to determine the quality of the implicated right as it relates to the margin. In this respect, it might be suggested that the rights enshrined in the Convention can be divided into four groups.

First, the Court has never used the margin of appreciation in relation to negative obligations under absolute rights. Having said that, some relativity that is often reflected in the Court's references to the margin of appreciation can even be found in relation to the most absolute of all rights: the prohibition of torture, inhuman and degrading treatment and punishment under Article 3,[58] for example, when determining whether the treatment complained of has reached the minimal level of severity to engage Article 3.

---

[54] Tsarapatsanis (n 46) 684.

[55] Anthony Lester, 'Universality Versus Subsidiarity: A Reply' (1998) *European Human Rights Law Review* 73, 75–76.

[56] Yourow (n 1) 152.

[57] Gerards (n 7) 106.

[58] In order to be prohibited by Article 3, certain treatment should reach a minimal level of severity. Compare the Chamber and Grand Chamber of the ECtHR in *Janowiec and Others v Russia* to see that judges disagree about what this level of severity actually means: *Janowiec and Others v*

The second group is positive obligations under any right of the Convention and its Protocols, in relation to which states do enjoy a margin of appreciation. This is true even in relation to the positive obligations that arise under Article 3: states can decide how to fulfil their obligation to protect people from torture, for example, with the Court's intervening only if the actions are manifestly deficient. The case of *MC v Bulgaria* illustrates this well. The applicant was an underage victim of an alleged rape, which was not prosecuted by the Bulgarian authorities because the victim did not physically resist. It was alleged that this violated the positive obligation to protect people from torture, inhuman and degrading treatment or punishment. Although the Court held that actions of state authorities were so inadequate that they fell outside of Bulgaria's margin of appreciation, it stated that 'in respect of the means to ensure adequate protection against rape, States undoubtedly enjoy a wide margin of appreciation. In particular, perceptions of a cultural nature, local circumstances and traditional approaches are to be taken into account.'[59]

The third group is the qualified rights, in relation to which states enjoy a margin of appreciation. Shany identified three ways in which the Court applied the margin of appreciation to qualified rights: in the application of law to facts; in norm-balancing in law application; and in norm-balancing in law interpretation.[60] The margin of appreciation in the application of law to facts is evident in the so-called immigration cases under Article 8. According to the well-established case law, an immigrant cannot be expelled if his family life will be disproportionately impacted as a result. In these circumstances, the states are given wide margin of appreciation in assessing whether the applicant has indeed established any family life in the host country, that is as to the determination of facts and the subsequent application of law thereto.[61] The margin of appreciation in norm-balancing in law application can be illustrated by reference to the accommodation of religious beliefs under Article 9. For instance, in *Lautsi and Others v Italy*,[62] the Court decided that the Italian authorities could restrict the right of the applicant not to be exposed to religious symbols due to the breadth of the margin of appreciation the authorities enjoyed in accommodation of Article 9. Here, then, the authorities had a wide margin of appreciation in their application of the law (requiring the display of the crucifix in school) to the facts (of a non-Christian pupil's exposure to that crucifix). The margin of appreciation in norm-balancing in law interpretation

Russia App nos 55508/07 and 29520/09 (ECtHR, 16 April 2012) and *Janowiec and Others v Russia* [2013] ECHR 1003.

[59] *MC v Bulgaria* App no 39272/98 (ECtHR, 4 December 2003), para 154. See also *Cannavacciuolo And Others v Italy* [2025] ECHR 29; *MSD v Romania* App no 28935/21 (ECtHR, 3 December 2024).

[60] Yuval Shany, 'All Roads Lead to Strasbourg?: Application of the Margin of Appreciation Doctrine by the European Court of Human Rights and the UN Human Rights Committee' (2018) 9(2) *Journal of International Dispute Settlement* 180.

[61] David Harris et al, *Harris, O'Boyle and Warbrick Law of the European Convention on Human Rights* (3rd edn, Oxford University Press, 2014) 577.

[62] *Lautsi and Others v Italy* (n 25).

arises where the state is determining the scope of a right. This is a particularly challenging aspect of the margin of appreciation, creating problematic differences in standards that in turn might undermine the universality of the human rights standards. The ongoing litigation on whether there is a right for same-sex couples to access marriage under Article 12 illustrates this well. In *Oliari and Others v Italy*, the Court appeared to suggest that the Contracting Parties have a margin of appreciation in deciding whether to implement any legislative reforms as to recognition of homosexual relations, although here the Constitutional Court of Italy called for relationship recognition, which was not provided, thus causing a violation.[63]

A similar outcome was reached in *A, B and C v Ireland*, where the Court held that the extent to which abortion should be legally available was within the margin of appreciation of the states but that where the law did provide for access, this must be facilitated and cannot be illusory.[64] The application of the margin of appreciation in terms of norm-balancing in interpretation readily illustrates how it can help the Court to negotiate the narrow space between a rock and a hard place. Marriage equality, abortion, and the right to choose the time and nature of one's dying are situations in which there are longstanding and unresolved tensions in ethics, politics and international law. It is clear that should the Court require Hungary, for example, to legalise same-sex marriage, or Malta to make access to abortion available without restriction, this would cause an enormous outbreak of criticism, and the judgments would likely not be executed. The key question, then, is whether the Court should be principled and ignore the reality of this likely reaction, or whether it should accommodate the differences in national context and tolerate varying levels of protection across the Continent. Seeing those national contexts as second-order reasons, in Legg's argument, leads one certainly to favour the latter, although that unquestionably causes those likely to be least able to leverage national politics in their favour, in homophobic, misogynistic and socially repressive domestic political environments, to wonder whether and how the ECtHR can truly be said to be a 'beacon of light' from their perspective.

The fourth group of rights comprises the so-called super-qualified rights in relation to which an even broader margin of appreciation is provided. Unlike qualified rights, legal provisions enshrining rights in this category do not list legitimate aims for which they can be restricted; rather, they can be limited in pursuit of any aim, provided that they do not cut into the core of the right. Because these rights are 'so' qualified, the states enjoy a remarkably broad margin of appreciation here. Perhaps the best example is the right to free elections under Article 3 of Protocol 1. This provides:

> The High Contracting Parties undertake to hold free elections at reasonable intervals by secret ballot, under conditions which will ensure the free expression of the opinion of the people in the choice of the legislature.

[63] *Oliari and Others v Italy* [2015] ECHR 716.

[64] *A, B and C v Ireland* [2010] ECHR 2032.

The broad margin of appreciation enjoyed by states in organising their electoral systems under Article 3 of Protocol 1 is well illustrated by *Yumak and Sadak v Turkey*. At the time, Turkish law set a particularly high 10 per cent nationwide threshold for a party to enter parliament. The effect of this was that regional parties, which would practically never reach the threshold, could not enter the national parliament, and any seats they had won would be transferred to the bigger nationwide parties. Although the Court accepted that such a high threshold for entering the national parliament was unusual when compared to the other member states, it did not find a violation, precisely on the basis of the wide margin of appreciation afforded to the respondent states.[65]

Beyond the Nature of the Implicated Right

Although the nature of the right is an important consideration in the Court's assessment of the scope of the margin of appreciation, it is not enough to determine its scope in each case. The Court listed the factors that determine the margin of appreciation in *S and Marper v the United Kingdom*. These include (i) the nature of the Convention right, (ii) the importance of the right for the individual, (iii) the nature and the object of the interference, and (iv) European consensus.[66] It seems that first three criteria are vaguely formulated and cannot determine the scope of the margin with much clarity,[67] and although (as discussed in chapter 4) European consensus reasoning does not always introduce rigour and predictability, it can be used to help determine the first three factors. For example, in *Dickson v the United Kingdom*, the Court pointed out that

> [w]here … there is no consensus within the Member States of the Council of Europe, either as to the relative importance of the interest at stake or as to how best to protect it, the margin will be wider. This is particularly so where the case raises complex issues and choices of social strategy: the authorities' direct knowledge of their society and its needs means that they are in principle better placed than the international judge to appreciate what is in the public interest.[68]

The Decision-Making Process at the National Level

Factors like the democratic legitimacy of the legal provision in question or a higher level of expertise of national decision-makers can also feature in determination of the scope of margin of appreciation. As discussed in chapter 1, in recent years, the Court has become particularly attentive to this through the spreading of the use of what is known as 'process-based review'. If

---

[65] *Yumak and Sadak v Turkey* [2008] ECHR 1887.
[66] *S and Marper v United Kingdom* (n 8).
[67] Gerards (n 7) 106.
[68] *Dickson v the United Kingdom* [2007] ECHR 1050, para 78.

Convention principles have been adequately taken into account in domestic decision-making processes, it is generally considered that the ECHR is effectively embedded and was given appropriate weight, so that the Court in Strasbourg will afford significant deference to the domestic authorities' views on Convention compatibility. In other words, the decision as to whether there has been a substantive violation of Convention rights will be informed – sometimes to a considerable degree – by whether the Convention played a part in domestic decision-making processes.

The Court has long been attentive to the quality of parliamentary decision-making processes as a basis upon which the margin of appreciation might be broadened or narrowed. For example, in *Odièvre v France*, the Court stated that broad margin of appreciation should be given to the national parliament, which had to strike a balance between the interest of a child to know her parents and that of her mother to remain unknown.[69]

Perhaps one of the most well-known examples of the Court's deference to proper parliamentary decision-making is the case of *Animal Defenders International v the United Kingdom*.[70] This case revolved around whether the ban on paid political advertisement is compatible with the Convention. Previously, the ECtHR found a similar ban in Switzerland[71] in violation of the Convention, but it decided differently in *Animal Defenders*. The Court relied on the quality of parliamentary debates in reaching such a decision:

> The prohibition was ... the culmination of an exceptional examination by parliamentary bodies of the cultural, political and legal aspects of the prohibition as part of the broader regulatory system governing broadcasted public interest expression in the United Kingdom and all bodies found the prohibition to have been a necessary interference with Article 10 rights. It was this particular competence of Parliament and the extensive pre-legislative consultation on the Convention compatibility of the prohibition which explained the degree of deference shown by the domestic courts to Parliament's decision to adopt the prohibition. The proportionality of the prohibition was, nonetheless, debated in some detail before the High Court and the House of Lords. Both courts analysed the relevant Convention case-law and principles, addressed the relevance of the above-cited VgT judgment and carefully applied that jurisprudence to the prohibition. Each judge at both levels endorsed the objective of the prohibition as well as the rationale of the legislative choices which defined its particular scope and each concluded that it was a necessary and proportionate interference with the applicant's rights under Article 10 of the Convention. The Court, for its part, attaches considerable weight to these exacting and pertinent reviews, by both parliamentary and judicial bodies, of the complex regulatory regime

[69] *Odièvre v France* App no 42326/98, (ECtHR, 13 February 2003), para 45. See also *Evans v the United Kingdom* [2007] ECHR 264, para 86; *Murphy v Ireland* [2003] ECHR 352, para 73; *Dudgeon v the United Kingdom* [1981] ECHR 5, para 59.

[70] *Animal Defenders International v the United Kingdom* [2013] ECHR 362.

[71] *VgT Verein gegen Tierfabriken v Switzerland* [2001] ECHR 412.

> governing political broadcasting in the United Kingdom and to their view that the general measure was necessary to prevent the distortion of crucial public interest debates and, thereby, the undermining of the democratic process.[72]

While there is a very clear, subsidiarity-based logic to the turn to 'process-based review', questions about its desirability and, indeed, the robustness of the Court's approach undoubtedly remain, especially given the evidence of democratic back-sliding in some Contracting Parties in recent years. As long ago as *United Communist Party of Turkey v Turkey*,[73] the Court remarked that 'the Convention was designed to maintain and promote the ideals and values of a democratic society … The only type of necessity capable of justifying an interference … is therefore one which may claim to spring from a "democratic society"'. A real question thus arises as to whether the state of democracy in a respondent state ought to influence how much deference to afford the state's assertion that the interference complained of is compatible with the Convention. However, the Court is susceptible to failing to recognise or take steps to arrest democratic backsliding that merit airing here.

The Court is inevitably conscious of the precarity of its position vis-à-vis member states, and treads a fine line between individual justice and system legitimacy. There is a risk that where especially vocal or critical states engage in activity suggesting democratic decay, the Court is less willing to step in or recognise its implications for democracy and the rule of law. Some states that are considered 'historically' rule-of-law-respecting arguably receive too great a benefit of the doubt through the application of process-based review, *even if* their posture towards human rights and towards international supervision has shifted significantly and in ways that indicate significant democratic decay, at the very least. There have in the past been indications that the robustness of process-based review might vary across countries. This is not a new concern, although it is one that is gaining significant traction, not least because a of a growing anxiety that states that do not consider themselves – and perhaps are not generally regarded as – countries 'in need of' close international supervision,[74] or what we might call 'consolidated democracies', might benefit too greatly from the turn to process, exacerbating what Başak Çalı has called 'variable geometry' in human-rights protection.[75]

---

[72] *Animal Defenders International v the United Kingdom* (n 70), paras 114–116.

[73] *United Communist Party of Turkey v Turkey* [1998] ECHR 1.

[74] Robert Spano has suggested closer supervision may still be required for states 'that do not respect the rule of law … do not ensure the impartiality and independence of their judicial systems, oppress political opponents or mask prejudice and hostilities to-wards vulnerable groups or minorities': Robert Spano, 'The Future of the European Court of Human Rights – Subsidiarity, Process-Based Review and the Rule of Law' (2018) 18 *Human Rights Law Review* 473, 493.

[75] Başak Çalı, 'From Flexible to Variable Standards of Judicial Review: The Responsible Domestic Courts Doctrine at the European Court of Human Rights' in Oddný M Arnardóttir and Antoine Buyse (eds), *Shifting Centres of Gravity in European Human Rights Protection: Rethinking Relations between the ECHR, EU and National Legal Orders* (Routledge, 2016) 144.

Take for example the case of *Hirst v the United Kingdom (No 2)*. Here, the Court decided that total disenfranchisement of prisoners violated the Convention. Although this question had been considered by Westminster in the 1960s, the Court was not satisfied with the level of debate that took place then. It stated:

> [T]here is no evidence that Parliament has ever sought to weigh the competing interests or to assess the proportionality of a blanket ban on the right of a convicted prisoner to vote. It is true that the question was considered by the multi-party Speaker's Conference on Electoral Law in 1968 which unanimously recommended that a convicted prisoner should not be entitled to vote. It is also true that the working party which recommended the amendment to the law to allow unconvicted prisoners to vote recorded that successive governments had taken the view that convicted prisoners had lost the moral authority to vote and did not therefore argue for a change in the legislation. It may be said that, by voting the way they did to exempt unconvicted prisoners from the restriction on voting, Parliament implicitly affirmed the need for continued restrictions on the voting rights of convicted prisoners. Nonetheless, it cannot be said that there was any substantive debate by members of the legislature on the continued justification in light of modern-day penal policy and of current human rights standards for maintaining such a general restriction on the right of prisoners to vote.[76]

In this case, it seems questionable that the Court should limit the scope of the margin of appreciation of Contracting Parties, mainly on the basis of the absence of any recent consideration of the particular issue by the national parliament. Such a requirement seems very crude and formalistic. In 2011, the Westminster Parliament discussed the issue and concluded that prisoners should continue to be disenfranchised, but does the mere discussion of this expand the margin of appreciation and suggest execution of the *Hirst* decision? Surely not. Thus, a parliamentary debate is a necessary but not sufficient precondition for finding the disenfranchisement of prisoners legal under the Convention. Even the concurring Judges Tulkens and Zagrebelsky, who thought that there was no rational basis for blanket disenfranchisement, were critical of the Court's assessment of the nature of the parliamentary debates in the UK.[77] Of course, this is a variation on a more fundamental question for the Court about how far it can go in scrutinising the decisions of democratically legitimate national bodies. We return to this in earnest in chapter 8.

Although 'variable geometry of protection' may seem justifiable, the intuition that states with lower levels of overall protection require more robust supervision is open to multiple criticisms. First, stemming from formal sovereign equality of the parties to international treaties, the Court should not apply different standards to different equal parties. Second, as we highlighted

[76] *Hirst v the United Kingdom (No 2)* [2005] ECHR 681, para 79.

[77] ibid, joint Concurring Opinion of Judges Tulkens and Zagrebelsky.

in chapter 1, 'good processes' can always lead to 'bad results', even in consolidated democracies. When the Convention was drafted, it was assumed that Western European states would rarely be considered to breach it, and that in contrast it would act as a beacon of hope for the repressed East. We know, of course, that this has not been the case. The Court should not function as an adjudicatory body for a handful of Eastern and Southern European states. Although some degree of 'variable geometry' may be understandable, the Court should not assume an overall level of human-rights protection based on democratic maturity when determining the extent of a state's margin of appreciation.

The Complexity of the Issue

It might be argued that the limits of the Court's expertise should affect the scope of the margin of appreciation. According to this argument, the state should have a wider margin of appreciation in relation to complex technical or scientific issues, the full extent of which can be understood only by specially trained professionals. This is quite in line with the idea of deference on the basis of expertise often found in domestic law. Having said that, the Court could still narrow the margin of appreciation in relation to the procedural aspects of making law and policy relating to such complex technical issues. For example, in *Hatton and Others v the United Kingdom*, the matter at issue was whether the decision of the UK authorities to allow night flights at Heathrow airport violated the Article 8 rights of the applicants.[78] The Court accepted that the national authorities had a wide margin of appreciation in deciding on the means of economic development (which was implicated by decisions as to having open runways overnight), but it scrutinised the surrounding processes, such as consultations during the decision-making process, and decided that the authorities did not violate the Convention.

To sum up, although it is possible to identify some factors that determine the scope of the margin of appreciation, such as the nature of the rights, European consensus (which was discussed in chapter 4) and the character of the matter at issue and decision-making process, it seems safe to conclude that the Court often operates in uncertain conditions. In some novel cases, it is almost impossible to predict what margin of appreciation will be afforded to the respondent state.

Conclusion

Proportionality and the margin of appreciation are key techniques of ECHR interpretation and, unsurprisingly, have generated a great amount of commentary. This is so because these techniques can accommodate differences in the

[78] *Hatton and Others v the United Kingdom* [2001] ECHR 565.

application of human rights across contexts, even though in principle human rights are universal and, within the Convention system, would be expected to apply in the same way across the Council of Europe. Even if one agrees that the practice of human-rights adjudication requires some scope for recognising and accommodating difference, the boundaries of that accommodation are contentious. Although both proportionality and the margin of appreciation make a claim to objectively determine those boundaries, balancing is fundamentally subjective and the scope of the margin of appreciation sometimes seems to be determined on an ad hoc basis. The lack of clear and objective criteria to determine the scope of the margin of appreciation and the outcome of a balancing exercise can call into question the foreseeability and effectiveness of the Convention and, thus, its legitimacy.

Further Reading

Yutaka Arai-Takahashi, *The Margin of Appreciation Doctrine and the Principle of Proportionality in the Jurisprudence of the ECHR* (Intersentia, 2002), pt 1.

Başak Çalı, 'From Flexible to Variable Standards of Judicial Review: The Responsible Domestic Courts Doctrine at the European Court of Human Rights' in Oddný M Arnardóttir and Antoine Buyse (eds), *Shifting Centres of Gravity in European Human Rights Protection: Rethinking Relations between the ECHR, EU and National Legal Orders* (Routledge, 2016) 144.

Andrew Legg, *The Margin of Appreciation in International Human Rights Law* (Oxford University Press, 2012), chapters 4–6.

Stavros Tsakyrakis, 'Proportionality: An Assault on Human Rights?' (2009) 7(3) *International Journal of Constitutional Law* 468.

6

The Convention in Times of Insecurity

Insecurity makes it more difficult for people to enjoy and exercise their rights, both because of the realities of living in and with insecurity, and because of the impacts on rights of security measures introduced and pursued by states. In this chapter, we consider debates on the role of the Convention in situations of insecurity, from armed conflict to public health crises and intimate violence.

Armed conflict (or war) is primarily governed by international humanitarian law. The extent to which international human rights law – including the European Convention on Human Rights (ECHR) – continues to operate in situations where these rules are being applied is a matter of some contention, which we consider in Debate 1. Although the Convention mostly applies in times of armed conflict, a difficult question arises when that armed conflict takes place outside of the territory of the Contracting Party. Article 1 provides that the states parties to the Convention will secure the rights therein protected 'to everyone within their jurisdiction'. Thus, the question of whether the Convention has extraterritorial application is a highly controversial one. We address it here as Debate 2.

Armed conflict is not the only situation of insecurity contemplated by the Convention. Article 15 deals with the application of the Convention in situations of 'public emergency' that 'threaten … the life of the nation'. As we shall see in Debate 3, such situations are not limited to violence but might include public-health emergencies, as some claim was the case during the COVID-19 pandemic.[1] In such circumstances, the Convention permits states to derogate from rights 'to the extent strictly required by the exigencies of the situation', but questions inevitably arise over (i) whether that should be the case at all, (ii) when a state should derogate, and (iii) whether the European Court of Human Rights (ECtHR) takes an effective approach to restraining state action under Article 15 or, instead, is deferential to claims of both the existence of an emergency and the appropriateness of the response thereto. We consider these questions in Debate 3.

[1] See generally Alan Greene, *Emergency Powers in a Time of Pandemic* (Bristol University Press, 2020).

Importantly, insecurity is an alarmingly commonplace experience. Domestic violence and similar forms of interpersonal violence are a major human-rights public-health concern in Europe and worldwide, and raise significant questions about states' obligations to protect people from such interpersonal violence. In Debate 4 we focus on domestic violence, to consider the relationship between the Convention and quotidian, interpersonal insecurity.

Debate 1

Does the ECHR Apply in War?

Although armed conflict is primarily governed by international humanitarian law, international human rights law also applies.[2] For many years, this was a settled position of the ECtHR. As we shall see in Debate 2, for the ECHR to be applicable, the Court needs to establish the jurisdiction of a particular state on the territory of the conflict in question. If nobody has such jurisdiction even within usual boarders of the Council of Europe member states, the practical application of ECHR cannot be secured. In *Georgia v Russia (II)*, the Court concluded that, given the situation of intense conflict, no state party had effective control of the area so that neither had jurisdiction during the relevant five-day period of active hostilities:

> In the event of military operations – including, for example, armed attacks, bombing or shelling – carried out during an international armed conflict one cannot generally speak of 'effective control' over an area. The very reality of armed confrontation and fighting between enemy military forces seeking to establish control over an area in a context of chaos means that there is no control over an area.[3]

Georgia v Russia (II) exposed a potential gap in Convention-related accountability, arguably meaning that 'the ECHR [was] not applicable when it [was] sorely needed',[4] although the applicable rules of international humanitarian law of course continued to apply. Apart from the very particular kinds of circumstances at issue in *Georgia v Russia (II)*, however, both human rights law and international humanitarian law apply in armed conflict. The simultaneous application of international humanitarian and international human rights law is doctrinally and practically challenging. Questions arise as to whether – and if

---

[2] See, for example, *Legal Consequences of the Construction of a Wall in the Occupied Palestinian Territory* (Advisory Opinion) 2004, available at www.icj-cij.org/en/case/131, and *Armed Activities on the Territory of Congo (Democratic Republic of Congo v Uganda)* [2005] ICJ Rep 168; Alexander Orakhelashvili, 'The Interaction between Human Rights and Humanitarian Law: Fragmentation, Conflict, Parallelism, or Convergence' (2008) 19 *European Journal of International Law* 161.

[3] *Georgia v Russia (II)* [2021] ECHR 58, para 126.

[4] Kanstantsin Dzehtsiarou, 'Georgia v Russia (II)' (2021) 115(2) *American Journal of International Law* 288.

so when – international human rights law might be superseded by international humanitarian law, or whether – and if so how – the two bodies of law should be read together in a more harmonious manner to apply concurrently throughout an armed conflict.[5] The potential for the two bodies of law to diverge, converge or be read together is well illustrated by the example of the right to be free from arbitrary detention.

Arbitrary detention is prohibited by Article 5 of the ECHR and remains prohibited in war;[6] but in a situation of armed conflict, how we determine whether a detention is arbitrary or not will be defined by the rules of international humanitarian law. This permits the detention of prisoners of war without charge or trial until the cessation of hostilities, which in real terms can mean years of detention. These rules may permit detention in situations, and for durations, that international human rights law would ordinarily consider to be arbitrary.[7] The ECtHR has shown a willingness to reconcile states' obligations under human rights law with their obligations under international humanitarian law and the perceived realities and necessities of armed conflict. In *Jaloud v the Netherlands*, for example, the Court confirmed that it was

> prepared to make reasonable allowances for the relatively difficult conditions under which the Netherlands military and investigators had to work. In particular, it must be recognised that they were engaged in a foreign country which had yet to be rebuilt in the aftermath of hostilities, whose language and culture were alien to them, and whose population … clearly included armed hostile elements.[8]

The implication of this is that although the Convention continues to apply, the Court is willing to allow a broader decision-making margin to the respondent state in situations of armed conflict. That is not without controversy. For some scholars, such as Silvia Borelli, Convention rights should not be 'refracted' through international humanitarian law. She argues:

> [W]here a State has failed to enter a derogation from its relevant ECHR obligations in relation to military action abroad, the Court should adopt a principled stance and assess the legality of its actions on the basis of the Convention alone, without seeking to qualify or interpret the State's obligations by reference to [international humanitarian law] standards.[9]

---

[5] Orakhelashvili (n 2).

[6] See, for example, Rule 99, ICRC Rules of Customary International Humanitarian Law; Article 42, Geneva Convention IV (1949); Rule 147, Geneva Convention IV (1940); Article 7(1)(e) Rome Statute of the International Criminal Court 1998.

[7] On the right to be free from arbitrary deprivation of liberty generally, see, eg, Fiona de Londras, *Detention in the War on Terror: Can Human Rights Fight Back?* (Cambridge University Press, 2011), chapter 2.

[8] *Jaloud v the Netherlands* [2014] ECHR 1292, para 226.

[9] Silvia Borelli, '*Jaloud v Netherlands* and *Hassan v United Kingdom*: Time for a Principled Approach in the Application of the ECHR to Military Action Abroad' (2015) 16 *Questions of International Law* 25, 27.

However, *Hassan v the United Kingdom*[10] suggests that the Court takes a somewhat different approach. Hassan had been arrested (by UK troops), detained (at a US-run facility) and interrogated (by UK intelligence agents) in Iraq. He claimed a violation of Article 5 of the ECHR. Article 5(1) lists a clearly constrained set of circumstances in which detention is permitted; in contrast, international humanitarian law allows detention on much wider bases. The UK argued that as this was an armed conflict, compliance with international humanitarian law ought to be said to mean compliance with Article 5, notwithstanding the fact that this is not a basis for detention under Article 5 and that the UK had not derogated from the application of Article 5 rights. This was based on the argument that international humanitarian law constituted *lex specialis* that 'might operate to modify or even displace'[11] a Convention provision.

Somewhat unexpectedly, the Court largely acceded to the UK's claims. It found that there was a clear state practice not to require derogation from Article 5 in order to allow for detention compliant with international humanitarian law in armed conflict, that it was obliged to understand and apply the Convention in a manner congruent with general public international law (citing the Vienna Convention on the Law of Treaties (VCLT)), and that it was therefore not precluded from taking international humanitarian law into account when interpreting and applying Article 5. The Court claimed that 'even in situations of international armed conflict, the safeguards under the Convention continue to apply, albeit interpreted against the background of the provisions of international humanitarian law', and effectively 'read in' a provision to Article 5(1) allowing detention compliant with international humanitarian law. In so doing, it rejected the UK's argument that *lex specialis* displaced the Convention, although it came to a remarkably similar conclusion to the one sought by the UK through that claim.[12]

Hassan was a radical step by the Court: it seems not only to take account of context and the challenges of armed conflict, but to go further than this and effectively equate legality under international law *per se* with Convention compatibility. Whilst some praised the Court for asserting its jurisdiction to hear the case in the first place,[13] there are powerful criticisms of the decision, not least in the dissenting opinions, which argue that states such as the UK not only failed to derogate from Article 5 and yet tried to rely on a lower legal standard, but also consistently resist the extraterritorial application of the Convention. In other words, the implicit criticism is that in *Hassan* the Court concedes too much to states; that, as Borelli argues, the way to avoid Article 5

---

[10] *Hassan v the United Kingdom* [2014] ECHR 936.

[11] ibid, para 88.

[12] On the importance of rejecting the *lex specialis* claim, see Lawrence Hill-Cawthorne, 'The Grand Chamber Judgment in Hassan v. UK' (*EJIL: Talk!*, 16 September 2014) at www.ejiltalk.org/the-grand-chamber-judgment-in-hassan-v-uk/.

[13] ibid.

obligations here is to derogate,[14] not to attempt to undermine the Convention protection per se through argumentation of this kind. Whilst for some the Court's 'symbiotic' approach in *Hassan*, reading international humanitarian law and international human rights law together, is commendable,[15] for others it is human rights law that loses out here, providing to states a way to release themselves from rights obligations in practice, if not in law, when acting militarily abroad. Moreover, the usually narrow and strict reading of exceptions to the right to liberty under Article 5(1) was undermined, and it was argued that new grounds for detention were considered by national courts.[16] Notwithstanding these concerns, the approach in *Hassan* continues to be endorsed and applied by the Court,[17] and in its recent case law concerning the Russian invasion of Ukraine, the Court has made clear that the 'the factual basis on which [Russia] obtained exterritorial jurisdiction' (namely through military action) meant it was appropriate to consider the rules of international humanitarian law when interpreting and applying the Convention.[18]

Debate 2

Does the ECHR Have Extraterritorial Effect?

A particular challenge of human rights protection arises in respect of extraterritorial military operations, including those undertaken under a mandate from the UN Security Council. This raises an interesting and controversial question about the Convention: does it apply to the state acting overseas? With a massive increase of military conflicts over the last decade or so, this question is crucial for the effectiveness of human-rights protection in Europe.

It is a general principle of treaty interpretation that treaties ***ordinarily*** do not have extraterritorial effect.[19] This is certainly suggested by the text of the Convention, which requires the Contracting Parties to give effect to the rights protected therein 'to everyone within their jurisdiction'.[20] Whilst being within the jurisdiction of the state is not necessarily the same as being within the territorial boundaries of the state, there is usually a connection between the two. Thus, it can be assumed that the wording of Article 1 was intended to limit

---

[14] See Borelli (n 9).

[15] Cedric De Koker, 'Hassan v United Kingdom: The Interaction of Human Rights Law and International Humanitarian Law with Regard to the Deprivation of Liberty in Armed Conflicts' (2015) 31(81) *Utrecht Journal of International and European Law* 90.

[16] Miles Jackson, 'Judicial avoidance at the European Court of Human Rights: Institutional authority, the procedural turn, and docket control' (2022) 20 *International Journal of Constitutional Law* 112, 128.

[17] *Georgia v Russia (II)* (n 3), para 95; *Ukraine v Russia (Re Crimea)* App nos 20958/14 and 38334/18 (ECtHR, 25 June 2024), para 913.

[18] *Ukraine v Russia (Crimea)* (n 17).

[19] Article 29, VCLT.

[20] Article 1, ECHR.

the obligations to the territory of the state in the ordinary course of events.[21] However, the Court's jurisprudence shows that the reach of the Convention is not *necessarily* territorially bounded; instead, it will apply extraterritorially in exceptional circumstances.

What those exceptional circumstances are is not entirely settled. For some time, it had been thought that *Loizidou v Turkey* provided the answer.[22] In 1974, along with hundreds of thousands of other Greek-Cypriots, Titina Loizidou had been displaced from her home in Northern Cyprus. She tried repeatedly to return, but was always prevented from doing so by Turkish authorities guarding the occupied north of the island. She lodged an application against Turkey claiming a violation of Article 1 Protocol 1, which protects the right to property. Turkey claimed that Loizidou had legally lost the right to her property under the Constitution of the Turkish Republic of Northern Cyprus (TRNC). Turkey maintained that the TRNC was a state that was not a Contracting Party to the ECHR and therefore that the Court had no jurisdiction. However, the TRNC was (and remains) a self-declared state recognised only by Turkey and, citing the special nature of the ECHR as a treaty for the protection of rights and a 'constitutional instrument of European Public Order', the Court held that it should take this into account in determining whether Turkey had responsibility for protecting Convention rights in the territory.

Although the Court noted that Article 1 of the Convention meant that it was primarily limited by territory, it held that obligations under the Convention could arise where a state exercised effective control of an area outside of its national territory as a result of military action. This was the case here: not only had the Turkish troops' invasion led to the establishment of the TRNC and the loss of Loizidou's property, but so too had Turkish troops prevented her from returning to her property on numerous occasions. For the Court, the large number of Turkish troops undertaking active duties in Northern Cyprus was such that the state exercised effective overall control and was liable for violations of the Convention that took place there. *Loizidou* thus stood for the proposition that effective control of an area brought Convention obligations with it. Under *Loizidou*, it seemed irrelevant where the territory over which the state had effective control was: it could be within or outside of the Council of Europe. The controversial case of *Banković* initially seemed to settle this.[23]

Banković related to the NATO-led bombing of Belgrade by a number of Contracting Parties during the Yugoslav war. In the course of the air strikes, a television station was targeted and a number of civilians were killed. Among other things, the applicants in this case claimed that the Contracting Parties in question had violated the Convention by failing to plan the operations in a manner that would minimise the risk of civilian casualties, and had failed to

[21] Ed Bates, *The Evolution of the European Convention on Human Rights* (Oxford University Press, 2010) 111.

[22] *Loizidou v Turkey* (merits), 18 December 1996, Reports of Judgments and Decisions 1996-VI.

[23] *Banković and Others v Belgium and Others* [2001] ECHR 890.

comply with the duty to investigate deaths that arises under Article 2. However, what was then Yugoslavia was not a Contracting Party to the Convention, and so the first and most important question was whether or not the Convention could be said to apply at all.

In answering this, the Court held that the Convention was primarily territorially limited and would apply extraterritorially only in exceptional situations. Where the location of the alleged violation was within the territories of any Contracting Party to the Convention, this was said to be within the legal space – or *espace juridique* – of the ECHR, so that the Convention would apply there.[24] This was justified by the fact that the rights enjoyed by persons within the jurisdiction of a Contracting Party should not be reduced to naught because a different Contracting Party – already subject to those rights standards in the ordinary course of events – was operating upon them in that space.[25] The notion of an *espace juridique* was entirely novel, developed by the Court to try to conceptualise ways of ensuring that those who already enjoyed Convention rights would continue to enjoy them, even in the (rare) event of another European state's 'taking over' some form of control there. However, the delimitation of that space also, of course, identified geographical space outside of the *espace juridique*: space in which the Convention did not ordinarily apply, and in relation to which something *extra*ordinary would need to happen to alter that.

What was then Yugoslavia fell into that space outside of the *espace juridique*, and so the Court was required to elucidate the situations in which the Convention might be said to apply there. According to the Court:

> In sum, the case-law of the Court demonstrates that its recognition of the exercise of extra-territorial jurisdiction by a Contracting State is exceptional: it has done so when the respondent State, through the effective control of the relevant territory and its inhabitants abroad as a consequence of military occupation or through the consent, invitation or acquiescence of the Government of that territory, exercises all or some of the public powers normally to be exercised by that Government.[26]

In this case there was no effective control because there had been no 'military occupation' but rather an air strike. This, combined with the fact that there was no danger that a vacuum of Convention-rights protection would arise, meant that the Convention did not apply in this case.

Banković was heavily criticised in the literature[27] as exposing a kind of illogic at the heart of the Convention, namely that a state would not be bound by

---

[24] ibid, para 80.

[25] ibid. In this the Court also drew on its expressed desire to avoid 'a regrettable vacuum in the system of human-rights protection' in *Cyprus v Turkey* App no 25781/94 (12 May 2014), para 78.

[26] *Banković and Others v Belgium and Others* (n 23), para 71.

[27] See, for example, Marko Milanovic, '*Al-Skeini* and *Al-Jedda* in Strasbourg' (2012) 23 *European Journal of International Law* 121; Michael O'Boyle, 'The European Convention on Human Rights and Extraterritorial Jurisdiction: Comment on "Life After Bankovic"' in Alphonsus

international human rights standards in a particular case simply because that state happened to be acting 'abroad'. On the one hand, that proposition seems to undermine the basic tenet that human rights are universal and enjoyed by all on the basis of humanity alone, but on the other hand it arguably refined that general *normative* principle into a workable set of *legal rules* about the applicability of a certain set of human rights standards *and* their enforceability through the ECtHR on a particular territory. The real difficulty, of course, is with the apparent injustice of the outcome of such a position; the apparent lack of accountability for actions that are often heinous, including death and torture; and perhaps the (unpalatable) implication that whilst these violations were lamentable when they happened outside of the European Public Order,[28] these scenarios were not for the ECtHR to remedy.[29] Were this to be the case, it would, perhaps, not be entirely surprising.

We have already noted that the text of the Convention appears to limit its applicability by reference to the concept of 'jurisdiction'. This is a concept that has real content in international law: it is intended, among other things, to clearly delimit where the authority of one legal system and its enforcement mechanisms ends and that of another begins.[30] Taken as a term of general international law, 'jurisdiction' here would mean in many ways just what the Court in *Banković* said it means: that the Convention applies outside the territory of the Contracting Party only where the state in question has either spatial or personal jurisdiction. Spatial jurisdiction would arise where the 'space' in which the actions complained of took place was under the effective control of the Contracting Party. Personal jurisdiction would arise where, at the time of the actions complained of, the victim was under the effective control of the Contracting Party. In *Banković* neither of these was the case: there was only an aerial campaign and the physical space in question was not under the effective control of the respondent states; neither were the victims under their effective control. Thus, the outcome from *Banković* arguably reflects these specific exceptions to the general rule that the Convention would not have extraterritorial effect, even whilst the articulation and application of a concept of *espace juridique* for the Convention might remain problematic but not particularly material to the outcome in the case per se. As a result, and notwithstanding the criticism of the outcome from the case, the approach taken in *Banković* might have suggested that the Court would develop and apply a relatively strict

---

Coomans and Menno Kamminga (eds), *Extraterritorial Application of Human Rights Treaties* (Intersentia, 2004) 125; and Erik Roxstrom, Mark Gibney and Terje Einarsen, 'The NATO Bombing Case (*Bankovic et al v Belgium et al*) and the Limits of Western Human Rights Protection' (2005) 23(55) *Boston University International Law Journal* 55.

[28] See the reference thereto in *Banković and Others v Belgium and Others* (n 23), para 80.

[29] On this see further Marko Milanovic, *Extraterritorial Application of Human Rights Treaties: Law, Principles, and Policy* (Oxford University Press, 2011) 85–86.

[30] For a comprehensive overview, see Cedric Ryngaert, *Jurisdiction in International Law* (Oxford University Press, 2015).

approach to the proposition that the Convention would apply extraterritorially only where either spatial or personal jurisdiction could be established. This is not only for the reasons of jurisprudential consistency but also (i) in deference to the legal systems of states where the actions complained of may have taken place, and the other parts of general international law that would apply in respect of armed conflict there, and (ii) as an expression of self-restraint on the part of the ECtHR by extending its adjudicatory power beyond the Contracting Party *only* where that is clearly consistent with international legal conceptions of jurisdiction.

However, the reality is that the Court has taken what seems to be a much more constitutionalist approach to the question of extraterritoriality than the strict rules of general international law would seem to require. By this we mean that the Court appears to proceed on the implicit basis that *law follows power*, so that the Contracting Party should be *accountable* under the Convention for actions that appear to violate human rights, even where those actions take place abroad and without appearing to pay particular attention to whether the strict rules of personal and spatial jurisdiction are adhered to. Although this approach might be praised for an increased level of protection, at the same time it injects some uncertainty and unpredictability into the law under the Convention. In turn, such a state of affairs gives some ground to the Contracting Parties to the Convention to claim the illegitimacy of the Court's actions in the area of extraterritorial application of the Convention.

This loose approach to territorial jurisdiction is evident in *Al-Skeini and Others v the United Kingdom*,[31] which concerned five Iraqis who had been killed by UK troops in Basra, in northern Iraq, one of whom had died in a UK detention facility. Following *Banković*, the domestic court had held that the UK could not be held accountable under the Human Rights Act 1998 (incorporating the ECHR) in respect of those who died and were not detained at the time by the UK, because Iraq was outside of the *espace juridique* of the Convention and there was neither spatial nor personal jurisdiction in relation to them: in the judgment of Lord Bingham, *Banković* constituted a 'clear – and clearly restrictive – approach to Article 1 jurisdiction' that justified this way of addressing the question in the domestic court.[32]

In Strasbourg, the Court appeared to abandon the concept of *espace juridique*, at least as a 'hard limit' to the application of the Convention outside of the geographical space of the Convention's Contracting Parties. In a judgment that mentioned *espace juridique* only five times, two of which referred to its usage in the domestic Court, the ECtHR held:

> The Convention is a constitutional instrument of European public order … It does not govern the actions of States not Parties to it, nor does it purport to be

[31] *Al-Skeini and Others v the United Kingdom* [2011] ECHR 1093.

[32] *Secretary of State for Defence v Al-Skeini & Others* [2007] UKHL 26 [131].

a means of requiring the Contracting States to impose Convention standards on other States.

The Court has emphasised that, where the territory of one Convention State is occupied by the armed forces of another, the occupying State should in principle be held accountable under the Convention for breaches of human rights within the occupied territory, because to hold otherwise would be to deprive the population of that territory of the rights and freedoms hitherto enjoyed and would result in a 'vacuum' of protection within the 'Convention legal space' … However, the importance of establishing the occupying State's jurisdiction in such cases does not imply, *a contrario*, that jurisdiction under Article 1 of the Convention can never exist outside the territory covered by the Council of Europe Member States.[33]

With these two paragraphs, then, the Court effectively put an end to the *espace juridique* notion from *Banković*. It returned, in effect, to the position that whilst jurisdiction is primarily territorial under Article 1, the Convention will apply outside of the territory of a Contracting Party where it has effective control over a person or effective control over a territory *whether or not* that territory is within the so-called *espace juridique* of the Convention. According to the Court, the UK did have effective control over the relevant area of Iraq at the time that the five persons in question were killed:

[F]ollowing the removal from power of the Ba'ath regime and until the accession of the Interim Government, the United Kingdom (together with the United States) assumed in Iraq the exercise of some of the public powers normally to be exercised by a sovereign government. In particular, the United Kingdom assumed authority and responsibility for the maintenance of security in South East Iraq. In these exceptional circumstances, the Court considers that the United Kingdom, through its soldiers engaged in security operations in Basrah during the period in question, exercised authority and control over individuals killed in the course of such security operations, so as to establish a jurisdictional link between the deceased and the United Kingdom for the purposes of Article 1 of the Convention.[34]

After *Al-Skeini*, a question remained as to how effective control over either a person or an area would be established. How much control was sufficient to meet the apparent threshold requirement of 'effectiveness' for the purpose of applying the Convention, bearing in mind that extraterritorial application of the Convention is *exceptional* and that it remains primarily territorial in its application? This is particularly difficult to assess in situations where someone is not detained by the military forces of the state in question, or where the geographical area in which the alleged violation took place is not under the state's

[33] *Al-Skeini and Others v United Kingdom* (n 31), paras 141–142. See also *Al-Jedda v the United Kingdom* [2011] ECHR 1092.

[34] *Al-Skeini and Others v United Kingdom* (n 31), para 149.

military control but rather where there is what may seem like a more fleeting engagement between the state forces and the victim of the alleged violation. Just such a set of circumstances arose for consideration in the case of *Jaloud v the Netherlands*.

This case concerned a checkpoint in South East Iraq at which Dutch military officers were stationed. A car that had been ordered to stop refused to do so, and a Dutch lieutenant opened fire, leading to the death of the applicant's son. The Dutch Royal Military Constabulary investigated whether any crime had been committed. It collected evidence, interviewed witnesses, and concluded that the use of force had been justified and no prosecution should follow. The applicant in *Jaloud* claimed that the investigation in question was not sufficient to satisfy the positive obligations relative to the right to life under Article 2 ECHR, but first had to establish that the Convention applied to the incident at all.

The Dutch troops in question were serving as part of a multi-national force and, at the time, were under UK command. However, the Court found that this alone was not sufficient to say that the acts in question could not be attributed to the Netherlands:

> The fact of executing a decision or an order given by an authority of a foreign State is not in itself sufficient to relieve a Contracting State of the obligations which it has taken upon itself under the Convention. The respondent party is therefore not divested of its 'jurisdiction', within the meaning of the Article 1 of the Convention, solely by dint of having accepted the operational control of … a United Kingdom officer … Although Netherlands troops were stationed in an area in south-eastern Iraq where SFIR forces were under the command of an officer from the United Kingdom, the Netherlands assumed responsibility for providing security in that area, to the exclusion of other participating States, and retained full command over its contingent there.[35]

In particular, the Court considered that the checkpoint in question was under Dutch control, and found that this was sufficient to establish personal jurisdiction (ie effective control over the person) for the Netherlands over people passing through the checkpoint.

> The Court … notes that Mr Azhar Sabah Jaloud met his death when a vehicle in which he was a passenger was fired upon while passing through a checkpoint manned by personnel under the command and direct supervision of a Netherlands Royal Army officer. The checkpoint had been set up in the execution of SFIR's mission, under United Nations Security Council Resolution 1483 … to restore conditions of stability and security conducive to the creation of an effective administration in the country. The Court is satisfied that the respondent Party exercised its 'jurisdiction' within the limits of its SFIR mission and for the purpose of asserting authority and control over persons passing through the

[35] *Jaloud v the Netherlands* (n 8), para 147.

> checkpoint. That being the case, the Court finds that the death of Mr Azhar Sabah Jaloud occurred within the 'jurisdiction' of the Netherlands.[36]

The Court went on to find that the duty to investigate under Article 2 had not been satisfied and, thus, that there was a violation of the Convention. Regardless of what might be considered to be the justice of the outcome of the case, *Jaloud* does raise a serious question about the rigour with which the Court is applying the concept of jurisdiction here. It is difficult to reconcile command control over a checkpoint with 'effective control' over a person, particularly in the light of a case like *Banković*, where aerial bombardment of Belgrade did not establish personal jurisdiction over the persons then in the city. Whilst there are some important factual distinctions (eg, the Dutch troops at the checkpoint had the power to order people to stop), these distinctions do not appear to be sufficiently material to properly distinguish the two cases from one another for the purposes of establishing jurisdiction. Instead, some are drawn to the conclusion that the Court here was essentially equating attribution with jurisdiction, that is proceeding on the basis that where an action could be attributed to the state, the state should be answerable for it under the Convention.[37]

The Court's more recent case law has not entirely resolved these persistent challenges with developing a clear and consistent jurisprudential position on extraterritoriality. In *Ukraine v Russia (Re Crimea)*,[38] the Court concluded that Russia had 'extraterritorial jurisdiction over Crimea on account of "effective control"'. Meanwhile, *Ukraine and the Netherlands v Russia* related to the shooting down of a civilian airplane in the Donbass region of Eastern Ukraine, which caused the death of 196 Dutch citizens.[39] In that case, Russia was providing significant support to the local administration since, and the Netherlands claimed that by supplying the missile system used in the shooting and failing to investigate the loss of life, Russia had violated the Convention. The Court found that Russia did indeed effectively control the relevant area via its military, economic, logistics and political support of the separatists who claimed to govern it. According to the Court,

> where there is effective control over an area, whether exercised directly by the Contracting State's own armed forces or via the local subordinate administration, there is *ratione loci* jurisdiction (see paragraph 559 above). For Article 1

[36] ibid, para 152.

[37] For an argument to this effect, see Jane Rooney, 'The Relationship between Jurisdiction and Attribution after *Jaloud v Netherlands*' (2015) 62 *Netherlands International Law Review* 407. This is certainly not accepted by all; see, for example, Marko Milanovic, 'Jurisdiction, attribution and responsibility in *Jaloud*' (*EJIL: Talk!*, 11 December 2014) at www.ejiltalk.org/jurisdiction-attribution-and-responsibility-in-jaloud/.

[38] *Ukraine v Russia (Re Crimea)* (n 17).

[39] *Ukraine and the Netherlands v Russia* App nos 8019/16, 43800/14, 28525/20 (ECtHR, 30 November 2022).

> purposes, therefore, the area in question is treated as being indistinguishable from areas within the controlling State's sovereign borders.[40]

As Nuridzhanian has observed, this case suggests that a military attack occurring wholly on a foreign territory controlled by the state and involving use of a surface-to-air missile system supplied but not directly operated by that state falls within that state's spatial jurisdiction, but an artillery attack launched from the state's own territory or territory but causing damage outside of its controlled territory does not unless there is an ill-defined 'element of proximity'.[41]

However, some are highly critical of the Court's approach to extraterritoriality, accusing it of developing its jurisprudence in an idiosyncratic manner characterised as 'judicial imperialism' that undermines Contracting Parties' military operations.[42] This criticism is not exactly consistent with all cases in which extraterritorial jurisdiction is used. From this point of view, the judgment in *Carter v Russia* attracted very little criticism. The case originates from the claim of the relatives of Alexander Litvinenko, who was poisoned by Russian agents in the United Kingdom.[43] Here, the Court found a violation of Article 2, of course without Russian jurisdiction over a particular place in London where the victim was poisoned. Tzevelekos and Berkes argue that

> with *Carter*, a state that directly caused extrajudicial death overseas has been found liable by the human rights Court of Europe in a case where this state essentially did not exercise any manifest effective control over the territory at issue or the direct victim. *Carter* may be nominally maintaining some type of control as a precondition for extraterritorial negative human rights obligations, but it is drastically contributing into turning the *Bankovic* effective control criterion into an empty shell of a legal ghost from the past.[44]

Although this case was directly relevant to the UK, its authorities did not intervene because to do so they would likely have needed to argue in favour of extraterritorial application of the Convention – something the UK has consistently been opposed to.

In recent years, climate-change litigation has raised novel questions of jurisdiction, the Court's handling of which has been met with disappointment by

[40] *Ukraine and the Netherlands v Russia* (n 39), para 561.

[41] Gaiane Nuridzhanian, 'The admissibility decision in Ukraine and the Netherlands v Russia: implications for state's exercise of extraterritorial jurisdiction in time of war' (2024) at https://ssrn.com/abstract=5054110, 13.

[42] Richard Ekins, Jonathan Morgan and Tom Tugendhat, *Clearing the Fog of War: Saving Our Armed Forces from Defeat by Judicial Diktat* (Policy Exchange, 2015) 9.

[43] *Carter v Russia* [2021] ECHR 766.

[44] Vassilis Tzevelekos and Antal Berkes, 'Turning Water into Wine – The Concealed Metamorphosis of the Effective Control Extraterritoriality Criterion in Carter v Russia' (*ECHR Blog*, 9 November 2021) at www.echrblog.com/2021/11/guest-post-turning-water-into-wine.html.

some.[45] This is clear from the reaction to the Court's decision in *Duarte Agostinho and Others v Portugal and 32 others*.[46] This case was brought by six youth activists based in Portugal, who claimed that the respondent states' greenhouse gas emissions could be linked to present and future adverse climate effects in ways that violated their Convention rights. The applicants here invited the Court to develop a novel approach to extraterritoriality, based on the claim that there is a causal relationship between greenhouse gas emissions in a state's territory and adverse effects via climate change that are experienced by people living outside of that territory. The respondent states thus had 'control over the applicants' Convention interests', it was claimed. While the Court acknowledged that '[c]limate change is a global phenomenon, and each State bears its share of responsibility for the global challenges generated by climate change',[47] it refused to 'creat[e] by way of judicial interpretation a novel ground for extraterritorial jurisdiction' or to expand existing grounds[48] to develop a test for jurisdiction based on control over Convention interests. To do so, the Court concluded, would result in 'a critical lack of foreseeability' and open the door to cases from 'anyone adversely affected by climate change wherever in the world he or she might feel its effects'.[49]

Duarte Agostinho suggests that the Court is reluctant to encroach on the territory of general international law by developing an approach to jurisdiction that opens it up to becoming a system of judicially enforceable human rights for the world at large, at least as it relates to climate change. Quite how to reconcile this with the Court's approach to extraterritoriality in cases relating to overseas military action is unclear. In respect of the latter, it is at least arguable that the Court has at times developed its jurisdiction inconsistently with international legal principles of jurisdiction, thus extending itself into areas that are more properly regulated by other parts of international law. Even if one were to say that this can be justified by the fact that those other bodies of public international law may be incapable of holding a state to account for its actions in that other country, and that individuals who have suffered grave violations of their rights might not have any forum or mechanism by which to attempt to make that state legally responsible, it is difficult to see why that is not similarly the case in respect of the real and often devastating impacts of climate change, which are, by their nature, transboundary harms.

---

[45] See, eg, Melanie Murcott, 'What the ECtHR Could Learn from Courts in the Global South' (2022) *Verfassungsblog: On Matters Constitutional Online* at https://verfassungsblog.de/what-the-ecthr-could-learn-from-courts-in-the-global-south/.

[46] *Duarte Agostinho and Others v Portugal and 32 others* App no 39371/20 (ECtHR, 9 April 2024).

[47] ibid, para 19.

[48] ibid, para 195.

[49] ibid, para 206.

DEBATE 3

SHOULD RIGHTS BE SUSPENDED IN TIMES OF EMERGENCY?

Not all situations of violence and insecurity meet the threshold of 'war' or 'armed conflict'. In Article 15, the ECHR contemplates the existence of a state of emergency that would justify the 'relaxation' of human rights standards so that the state may do things in furtherance of 'security' in those situations that we would not ordinarily permit it to do.[50] Article 15 provides:

> 1. In time of war or other public emergency threatening the life of the nation any High Contracting Party may take measures derogating from its obligations under this Convention to the extent strictly required by the exigencies of the situation, provided that such measures are not inconsistent with its other obligations under international law.
> 2. No derogation from Article 2, except in respect of deaths resulting from lawful acts of war, or from Articles 3, 4 (paragraph 1) and 7 shall be made under this provision.
> 3. Any High Contracting Party availing itself of this right of derogation shall keep the Secretary-General of the Council of Europe fully informed of the measures which it has taken and the reasons therefor. It shall also inform the Secretary-General of the Council of Europe when such measures have ceased to operate and the provisions of the Convention are again being fully executed.

Although allowing states to derogate in times of emergency is part of how international human rights law seeks to balance the regulation through rights of previously sovereign matters (namely the relationship between the state and those within its domestic jurisdiction) with often-robust state action to protect sovereignty and/or the population where significant risks are perceived, the idea that security requires or justifies a reduction in rights has long been controversial.[51] There are three primary areas of concern in this relation: whether a reduction in rights results in an enhancement of security; whether security measures introduced disproportionately and discriminatorily impact on some parts of the community more than others; and whether decisions about necessity and appropriateness of rights-restricting security measures should be subject to scrutiny by (national and international) courts.

At the heart of emergency derogation systems is the implicit claim that at least some crises require measures that would ordinarily be deemed unacceptably restrictive of rights in order to restore 'normalcy'. Some put this claim quite bluntly, asserting that there is a hydraulic relationship between security and

[50] Article 4, International Covenant on Civil and Political Rights; Article 27(1), American Convention on Human Rights.

[51] For a useful overview of the broader political philosophical debates, see, for example, Fernando Teson, 'Liberal Security' in Richard Wilson (ed), *Human Rights in the 'War in Terror'* (Cambridge University Press, 2005) 57.

'liberty' (taken to mean rights, here), and even that an optimal point between them can be found, so that there is a clear relationship between the taking of security measures and the enhancement of rights enjoyment.[52] However, there is no evidence of such hydraulicism,[53] and in any case arguments of that kind tend to be short-term in their nature, failing to take proper account of the long-term costs of security measures such as reduced social cohesion and faith in the state, increased alienation and disenfranchisement, and potentially long-term insecurity.[54] Furthermore, and moving to the second concern, even if there were a relationship between security and rights of this kind, the reality is that very often the people whose rights are effectively reduced through such measures are not the people who perceive their security to have been enhanced. Security-enhancing measures are often imposed disproportionately on people from so-called suspect communities:[55] young men of colour in the UK, Muslim women in France, Kurds in Turkey, political opponents in Azerbaijan, etc. The uneven societal impacts of such measures are a matter of real concern, not only because they may result in social disintegration and a sense of alienation from the state, but also because they may reflect discriminatory application of security measures, laws and policies.[56] This may, in turn, become normalised – seen as part of the everyday policing and governing of the state – so that the popular expectations of what the state can or should do are fundamentally adjusted.

If it is not clear that a reduction in rights protection (through derogation) necessarily increases security, and if it is the case that the application of security measures can result in discrimination and may not be effective in terms of security in the longer term, the question of whether derogation should be permitted clearly arises. Very few would argue that no adjustment or derogation should be permitted at all, either because there is a general (although not universal) understanding that security is required for the purposes of being able to exercise rights, so that a short-term reduction in rights enjoyment might be justifiable for the purposes of restoring security and rights normalcy, or because of the pragmatic position that if the law does not allow states to temporarily adjust their human rights obligations they may simply act in the name of 'security' in violation of the law, so that it is better to have a system of effective supervision within which emergency measures can be taken than not to. This proposition was at the heart of the debate between Greene and Dzehtsiarou

---

[52] See, for example, Eric Posner and Adrian Vermeule, *Terror in the Balance: Security, Liberty and the Courts* (Oxford University Press, 2007).

[53] Andrew Ashworth, 'Security, Terrorism and the Value of Human Rights' in Ben Goold and Liora Lazarus (eds), *Security and Human Rights* (Hart Publishing, 2007) 129.

[54] Fiona de Londras, 'Sustainable Security: A Proposal' in Dapo Akande et al (eds), *Human Rights and 21st Century Challenges* (Oxford University Press, 2020) 108.

[55] Paddy Hillyard, *Suspect Community: People's Experience of the Prevention of Terrorism Acts in Britain* (Pluto Press, 1993).

[56] Peter Burgess and Mederic Martins Maze, 'The Social Impact of EU Counterterrorism' in Fiona de Londras and Josephine Doody (eds), *The Impact, Legitimacy and Effectiveness of EU Counter-Terrorism* (Routledge, 2015) 93.

on whether states should enter derogations to underpin public-health measures during the COVID-19 pandemic.[57] Although COVID-19 affected all European states, the response to it varied significantly across the Continent. Only some states derogated from the ECHR; most did not. Dzehtsiarou argued that the latter response was appropriate, as the proportionality test used by the ECtHR could accommodate the measures that were deployed by states given the severity of the public-health crisis. For Greene, the COVID-19 pandemic was a perfect example of a situation where the derogation clause should be used to ensure tight control of the emergency claim and the repressive measures introduced to protect public health.

That debate demonstrates that the extent to which whether there is an emergency requiring derogation is a matter of interpretation, with states coming to different conclusions even in seemingly similar situations. Article 15 of the ECHR, in principle, outlines an approach to secure appropriate and effective supervision of the law relating to derogation by specifying three requirements a state must comply with to derogate lawfully. These are (i) that the procedural requirements in Article 15(3) would be fulfilled, (ii) that there would be a war or public emergency threatening the life of the nation (Article 15(1)), and (iii) that the measures taken would go no further than is strictly required by the exigencies of the situation (Article 15(1)). There are thus procedural, threshold and substantive requirements.

The Procedural Requirement

The procedural requirement is quite straightforward: a Contracting Party that wishes to derogate must notify the Secretary-General of the Council of Europe of the derogation, the measures taken pursuant to it and the reasons for the derogation. In truth, the notifications provided to comply with this procedural regulation tend to be quite cursory, which is perhaps to be expected as the notification requirement is essentially procedural and there is no real scrutiny of the notification of the state of emergency – or of its cessation – on the part of the Secretary-General.

The Threshold Requirement

Article 15 permits derogation only where there is a war or public emergency threatening the life of the nation. Thus, in cases where derogations have been at issue before the Court, the question of whether there is a war or public

[57] Alan Greene, 'Derogating from the European Convention on Human Rights in response to the coronavirus pandemic: if not now, when?' (2020) 3 *European Human Rights Law Review* 262; Kanstantsin Dzehtsiarou, 'Article 15 derogations: are they really necessary during the COVID-19 pandemic?' (2020) 4 *European Human Rights Law Review* 359; Alan Greene, 'On the value of derogations from the European Convention on Human Rights in response to the COVID-19 pandemic: a rejoinder' (2020) 5 *European Human Rights Law Review* 526.

emergency sufficient to permit derogation has arisen. Whilst the Court has laid down a broad definition of these concepts for the purposes of Article 15, it has been criticised for failing to subject states' claims that such a state of affairs exists to sufficiently rigorous examination.[58] Although this is most commonly associated with violence and significant political upheaval (eg, coups), there is nothing in Article 15 that limits emergencies to situations of violence per se. Indeed, the COVID-19 pandemic made clear that a public-health emergency could 'threaten the life of the nation' in a way that required a derogation, although only a handful of Contracting Parties opted to derogate when introducing (often very restrictive) public-health measures at that time.[59]

In *Lawless v Ireland*, the Court held that a public emergency sufficient to allow for derogation under Article 15 was to be understood as 'an exceptional situation of crisis or emergency which affects the whole population and constitutes a threat to the organised life of which the State is composed'.[60] In the *Greek Case*, the Court added the requirement that the crisis or emergency would be 'actual or imminent'.[61] These two important early cases suggested that an emergency should be truly exceptional; that it should be said to exist only where the normal measures allowed under the Convention – including limitations to rights based on public safety and so on – were clearly inadequate.[62] However, in the intervening decades the apparently strict definition of 'emergency' under Article 15 has been substantially watered down, particularly in the important case of *A and Others v the United Kingdom*.[63]

A and Others v the United Kingdom involved a challenge to measures taken by the UK following the attacks on the United States of 11 September 2001. Although those attacks took place in the United States, the UK declared a public emergency and derogated from the Convention. It was the only Council of Europe state to do so, and in *A and Others* it was claimed by the applicants that there was no public emergency threatening the life of the nation under Article 15 because (i) there was no actual or imminent emergency, (ii) the alleged emergency was not temporary, and (iii) the fact no other states in the Council of Europe had derogated from the Convention suggested that there was no public emergency.

The ECtHR disagreed. Holding that '[t]he requirement of imminence cannot be interpreted so narrowly as to require a State to wait for disaster to strike before

[58] Alan Greene, 'Separating Normalcy from Emergency: The Jurisprudence of Article 15 of the European Convention on Human Rights' (2011) 12(10) *German Law Journal* 1764.

[59] See generally *Communauté Genevoise D'action Syndicale (Cgas) v Switzerland* App no 21881/20 (ECtHR, 27 November 2023); *Pešić and Others v Serbia* App nos 48973/20, 54565/20 and 54676/20 (ECtHR, 5 January 2023) (Pending Applications). For commentary, see Audrey Lebret, 'COVID-19 Pandemic and Derogation to Human Rights' (2020) 7(1) *Journal of Law and the Biosciences* 1.

[60] *Lawless v Ireland* [1961] ECHR 2.

[61] *Denmark and Others v Greece ('The Greek Case')* (1970) 12 CD 186, paras 112–113.

[62] ibid, para. 113.

[63] *A and Others v the United Kingdom* [2009] ECHR 301.

taking measures to deal with it',[64] and referring to how the 9/11 attacks had established the 'danger of a terrorist attack', the Court found that the UK was entitled to rely on the intelligence available to it at the time in order to determine that an attack was imminent and, thus, that the imminence requirement was fulfilled. Consequently, the apparent requirement of 'imminence' was approached with such flexibility as to allow any (presumably good-faith) interpretation of intelligence pointing towards a possible attack to fulfil it. In so doing, the Court arguably undermined a limited definition of 'public emergency' in Article 15(1), and thus loosened one of the constraints designed to ensure that derogations could only exceptionally be resorted to by a Contracting Party.

Further loosening was observed when the Court turned to the question of temporariness. Article 15 does not mention that a public emergency threatening the life of the nation must be temporary, but such a requirement is implicit in the (legal) concept of 'emergency', which is designed to allow the state to take measures that would enable it to restore *normalcy*. Thus, 'emergency' is clearly conceived of as a state of affairs that is limited in time. However, the Court noted that its case law had 'never, to date, explicitly incorporated the requirement that the emergency be temporary'.[65]

Thus, whilst the threshold requirement appears, at first glance, to constrain states' ability to declare an emergency and derogate under Article 15, the Court seems to have interpreted the concept of 'public emergency threatening the life of the nation' in such a way that it can be applied to a great number of situations, even ones that are liable to last for a considerable period of time – years, or perhaps decades.

This has been criticised by some as allowing for the concepts of emergency and normalcy to be 'collapsed' in a manner that gives states far too much leeway to derogate and introduce measures that we would not ordinarily consider to be appropriate or rights-compliant.[66] However, it is arguable that there is some logic to the Court's approach. If the purpose of Article 15 is to allow states to counter 'threat[s] to the organised life of which the State is composed', then it must be capable of allowing effective state responses to contemporary threats. In contemporary Europe, one of these is said to be a kind of persistent, disaggregated, transnational terroristic violence that can emerge suddenly, can persist without much centralised organisation, can be sustained with relatively modest resources, and cannot be 'reasoned' with as its apparent endpoint is not a negotiated settlement to a discrete dispute but rather a more substantial politico-social change across the entire continent (and beyond). The fact that this is not temporary, geographically constrained or organised in a manner similar to a conventional army, for example, does not mean that it is not a public emergency that threatens the life of the nation: the alternative

[64] ibid, para 177.
[65] ibid, para 178.
[66] See Greene (n 58).

is to define it as normalcy and to limit the state to measures that are ordinarily permitted under the limitations built into the Convention rights; and, the argument goes, a state should not be precluded from using the derogation if it considers these to be 'plainly inadequate'.

Although the Court has been at pains to make it clear that whether there is a public emergency as understood under Article 15 is properly subject to judicial supervision by the ECtHR, its settled position is that 'it falls to each Contracting State, with its responsibility for "the life of [its] nation", to determine whether that life is threatened by a "public emergency"'.[67] Perhaps unsurprisingly, then, the Court almost never disagrees with the state that there is in fact an emergency. It did so in the *Greek Case* in 1969,[68] and in the more recent case of *Dareskizb Ltd v Armenia*.[69] In that latter case, the Court found that there was insufficient evidence to conclude that opposition protests following the presidential election results could be considered a public emergency 'threatening the life of the nation' within the meaning of Article 15. However, such situations are notable by their rarity, and for some commentators it is not at all clear that the Court subjects this important threshold decision to meaningful scrutiny,[70] so that the 'degree of scrutiny' it applies 'is hardly different from accepting the parties' own view of the situation'.[71]

The Substantive Requirement

Given the difficulties that perhaps understandably arise in respect of determining the threshold question under Article 15, it might reasonably be expected that the Court would apply the substantive requirement under Article 15 with a closer degree of scrutiny, as indeed it does. The substantive requirement laid out in Article 15 has three parts: (i) that there would be no derogation from non-derogable rights listed in Article 15(2); (ii) that any measures taken pursuant to a derogation would be consistent with the state's other obligations under international law (Article 15(1)); and (iii) that such measures would go no further than 'the extent strictly required by the exigencies of the situation'.

The first of these substantive requirements is easily disposed of at this stage: Articles 3, 4(1) and 7 cannot be derogated from. Nor can Article 2, although, as we have already seen, Article 2 is not violated where a death results from 'lawful acts of war'. Any attempt to derogate from these Articles is, simply, a violation of Article 15 and thus impermissible.[72]

---

[67] *Brannigan and McBride v the United Kingdom* [1993] ECHR 21, para 43.

[68] *The Greek Case* (n 61).

[69] *Dareskizb Ltd v Armenia* [2021] ECHR 760.

[70] See, for example, Oren Gross and Fionnuala Ní Aoláin, 'From Discretion to Scrutiny: Revisiting the Margin of Appreciation Doctrine in the Context of Article 15 of the European Convention on Human Rights' (2001) 23(3) *Human Rights Quarterly* 625.

[71] David Harris et al, *Harris, O'Boyle and Warbrick Law of the European Convention on Human Rights* (3rd edn, Oxford University Press, 2014), 835.

[72] See, eg, *Sanchez-Sanchez v the United Kingdom* [2022] ECHR 925.

The second substantive requirement enables the Court to consider whether a measure introduced pursuant to a derogation violates the state's other international obligations. If it does, it also violates the Convention, not least because Article 53 makes it clear that the Convention is intended to coexist with, and not limit, the rights and freedoms that are guaranteed under other international agreements to which the state is a party. Although one can imagine that this substantive requirement would be amenable to judgment by the Court, the reality is that it has rarely, if ever, had an impact in cases on whether there is a violation of Article 15. Instead of interpreting and assessing compliance with a state's other international obligations in Article 15 cases, the Court has tended to shy away from these questions.

However, the Court does take a more robust approach when considering whether measures introduced are limited to those 'strictly required by the exigencies of the situation'. This requirement means that *even where a state has derogated*, it may only introduce measures that are necessary and proportionate to the emergency in question, and that the principle of the rule of law continues to apply during an emergency.[73] Necessity here ('strictly required') is assessed by considering whether the ordinary law is insufficient to address the emergency,[74] giving considerable weight to the view of the Contracting Party as to both the need for extraordinary measures[75] and the feasibility of alternatives.[76]

Importantly, establishing that a measure was limited to that which was 'strictly required by the exigencies of the situation' does not require the state to prove that the approach taken to the derogation was the best, only or most appropriate one that the state could have taken, although the question of whether a less restrictive alternative might have been adopted will be considered.[77] It does not even have to maintain that the measure was effective in addressing the emergency.[78] The Court affords states a significant margin of appreciation in this relation and will not 'substitute its view as to what measures were most appropriate or expedient'[79] at the time of the derogation; it will simply consider whether the measures introduced went no further than was strictly required by the exigencies of the situation. This is, we suggest, reasonable in principle: as a general matter, it is not for courts to decide on what the state *should* do but only what it *may* do. The former is a question of policy and the latter of law, although the two things are not easily separated in real terms.[80]

---

[73] See, eg, *Piskin v Turkey* [2020] ECHR 902.

[74] *Lawless v Ireland* (n 60).

[75] *Ireland v the United Kingdom* [1978] ECHR 1.

[76] *Brannigan and McBride v United Kingdom* (n 67).

[77] *Lawless v Ireland* (n 60).

[78] *Ireland v United Kingdom* (n 75).

[79] *Marshall v United Kingdom* App no 41571/98 (ECtHR, 10 July 2001).

[80] For a range of views on the challenges for courts in adjudicating in times of emergency, see, for example, Fergal Davis and Fiona de Londras (eds), *Critical Debates on Counter-Terrorism Judicial Review* (Cambridge University Press, 2014).

The Court accordingly takes a highly contextualised approach to such analysis, recognising that what is proportionate in one situation may not be proportionate in another. Whether a measure is proportionate in a particular emergency depends on 'the rights affected by the derogation, the circumstances leading to, and the duration of the emergency situation'.[81] The more severe the emergency, the more severe the measures that might be considered to be strictly required to address it.[82] However, we must recall that both the existence and the severity of the emergency are determined by the Court's giving a high degree of deference to the assessment of the respondent state. The question of duration is particularly important; although, as we have already seen, the Court does not insist that an emergency must be 'temporary' *per se*, it does note that where an emergency is of long duration this will impact on the proportionality of the measures under consideration.[83] In other words, the longer the emergency goes on, the more the state is expected to return to something that resembles 'normalcy' in its attempts to address it.

When considering whether a measure was 'strictly required by the exigencies of the situation', the Court will be attentive to whether there were safeguards in place to protect people who might be subjected to the derogating measures. This is particularly important where emergency measures are introduced to allow for protracted detention without trial, or variations to the trial process itself. In relation to the former, the role that safeguards play in the Court's analysis is readily discernible by comparing *Brannigan and McBride v the United Kingdom*[84] with *Aksoy v Turkey*.[85] Both concerned detention powers in situations of terroristic violence, but in *Brannigan and McBride* the Court noted that there was a right to see a solicitor within 48 hours of being detained and that the writ of *habeas corpus* could be used to challenge detention in any given situation. The Court thus concluded that there were sufficient procedural safeguards in place to protect a detainee against arbitrary detention and mistreatment. In *Aksoy*, by contrast, the law allowed for detention of an individual without bringing them before a judge or other officer for up to 30 days; there was no access to lawyers, family or medics; and there was no way to challenge the lawfulness of detention. The detainee was thus liable to abuse and detention incommunicado, and the Court found (for the first time) that the measures introduced pursuant to the derogation went beyond the strict requirements of the situation. Similarly, in more recent cases, *Şahin Alpay v Turkey*[86] and *Mehmet Hasan Altan v Turkey*,[87] the Court held that while a military coup did pose a severe threat to life and the existence of the nation,

[81] *Brannigan and McBride v the United Kingdom* (n 67), para 43.
[82] *Ireland v United Kingdom* (n 75).
[83] See generally *A and Others v United Kingdom* (n 63).
[84] *Brannigan and McBride v the United Kingdom* (n 66).
[85] *Aksoy v Turkey* [1996] ECHR 68.
[86] *Şahin Alpay v Turkey* [2018] ECHR 253.
[87] *Mehmet Hasan Altan v Turkey* [2018] ECHR 251.

pre-trial detention without the need for reasonable suspicion, introduced in the wake of the coup, was not lawful, as not requiring reasonable suspicion could not be said to have been strictly required by the exigencies of the situation.

Although the Court sometimes concludes that a state has gone beyond what Article 15 permits, this is rare. In Article 15 cases, national governments' assessment is given great weight by the Court. Whilst there are good reasons for affording some margin of appreciation to these assessments, there is much to be said for the contention that the Court gives so much weight to these assessments that it does not effectively enforce the substantive requirements of Article 15. If that is the case then rights-bearers' ability to use these substantive requirements to limit state security action – which, as we know, is often extremely repressive and oppressive – is greatly reduced, and a broad question arises about the effectiveness of the Convention in times of emergency. The derogations regime relies, for its efficacy, both on good faith on the part of governments and rigour on the part of the international supervisory bodies, especially if domestic parliaments and courts have found it difficult to resist the temptation to 'rally around the flag' and enforce rights protection in the face of substantial security risks and state-assertions of necessity.

Debate 4

Does the Convention Protect People from 'Everyday Insecurity'?

Thus far, we have concentrated on what we might call exceptional situations of insecurity; however, in reality insecurity is an everyday occurrence. All over Europe, domestic violence, sexual violence, police violence, corporal punishment and other forms of violent insecurity are prevalent. Such insecurity necessarily implicates rights: not only does one struggle fully to enjoy and exercise rights in situations of pervasive insecurity, but exposure to and failure of the state to prevent violence might, itself, constitute a human rights violation under the Convention. Whilst the jurisprudence of the Court ranges across corporal punishment,[88] conditions of detention (beyond directly inflicted violence, per se)[89] and police violence,[90] we focus here on the ECtHR's approach to domestic violence as illustrative of the Convention's ability to protect against everyday insecurity.

---

[88] See, for example, *Tyrer v the United Kingdom*, 25 April 1978, Series A no 26; *A and Others v United Kingdom* (n 63); *Campbell and Cosans v the United Kingdom*, 25 February 1982, Series A no 48; *Costello-Roberts v the United Kingdom*, 25 March 1993, Series A no 247-C.

[89] See, for example, *Kalashnikov v Russia* [2002] ECHR 596; *Dobri v Romania* App no 25153/04 (ECtHR, 14 December 2010); *Modarca v Moldova* [2007] ECHR 390.

[90] See, for example, *Leonidis v Greece* [2009] ECHR 5; *Iribarren Pinillos v Spain* App no 36777/03 (ECtHR, 8 January 2009).

The law has traditionally been slow and ineffective in addressing issues of domestic violence. Traditionally considered to take place in a 'private' domain in which the state ought not to 'interfere',[91] it was not until the UN Convention on the Elimination of all Forms of Discrimination against Women (CEDAW) that international human rights law took a firm doctrinal stand against the maintenance of the so-called 'public–private divide'.[92] The ECHR might itself be read as a text that impliedly reinforces this divide: privacy and family life are protected from undue interference in Article 8; private property (including the home) is protected in Article 1 of Protocol 1; and whilst Articles 2 and 3 protect the rights to life and to be free from torture, inhuman and degrading treatment or punishment, that protection was originally conceived of as being against state, as opposed to 'private', action.[93] However, over recent years the Court's jurisprudence has developed a substantial body of law on the state's obligation to protect people from domestic violence and to undertake effective investigations where a loss of life was not averted, influenced to some extent by the evolution of international law relating to domestic violence.[94]

This is well illustrated by the case of *Bevacqua and S v Bulgaria*.[95] The applicant in this case claimed that she was regularly beaten by her husband and that these beatings continued after she took their son, left her husband and filed for divorce. Before the finalisation of the divorce, a court order of shared custody was given in respect of the child, requiring continued contact between them. She claimed that every time she pressed charges against him, her husband became more violent. Repeated requests for interim measures of protection were not promptly dealt with, and her then-ex-husband continued to assault her even after their divorce was finalised and she had secured custody of their son. At that time her request for a criminal prosecution was rejected, the authorities claiming that it was a 'private matter' between them. The Court held that the state had failed to fulfil its positive obligations under Article 8 (the right to private and family life), with particular attention to the rights of the

---

[91] The public–private dichotomy has long been critiqued in feminist and feminist legal thought. For its classical criticism in international legal thought, see Hilary Charlesworth and Christine Chinkin, *The Boundaries of International Law: A Feminist Analysis* (Manchester University Press, 2000). See also Alice Edwards, *Violence against Women under International Human Rights Law* (Cambridge University Press, 2011).

[92] Article 2, CEDAW.

[93] The ECHR was not unique in this. For a comprehensive overview, see Dorothy Thomas and Michele Beasley, 'Domestic Violence as a Human Rights Issue' (1993) 15 *Human Rights Quarterly* 36.

[94] *Vuckovic v Croatia*, no 15798/20, (ECtHR, 12 December 2023): in the context of domestic violence, the ECtHR 'has often been guided by the relevant international law standards on the matter, and notably the Istanbul Convention' (para 57). See generally Ronagh JA McQuiggs, *Domestic Violence and the European Court of Human Rights* (Routledge, 2025).

[95] *Bevacqua and S v Bulgaria* [2008] ECHR 498.

child, and stressed that considering these allegations of abuse to be a 'private matter' was clearly incompatible with Article 8.

Even though *Bevacqua* resulted in a finding of violation, it did not focus clearly on the rights of the primary victim of the abuse.[96] However, since then the Court's Article 2 jurisprudence on states' obligations to protect life in situations of domestic violence has developed considerably. In *Kontrová v Slovakia*,[97] the Court considered a case in which the applicant had filed a criminal complaint against her husband for beating her. Shortly thereafter, and accompanied by her husband, she attended at the police station where, with the assistance of an officer, she modified her complaint so that it constituted a minor offence in respect of which no further action was required by law. Less than two months later, her husband murdered their son and daughter. The Court held that Slovakia had violated Article 2: the original complaint meant that the police authorities were aware of the violent situation in the home and had domestic legal obligations to act on this, including to launch a criminal investigation. The fact that the applicant had subsequently modified her complaint, accompanied by her husband, did not mean that the state was relieved of its Article 2 obligation to take all reasonable steps to protect life.

This is not an unusual pattern in these cases: the state is aware of the threat that the assailant poses to family members and yet fails to take adequate steps to protect them. In *Branko Tomašic and Others v Croatia*,[98] court-ordered psychiatric treatment was not effectively administered to the assailant, who subsequently murdered his wife and baby on release from prison. In *Civek v Turkey*,[99] the authorities were aware of the serious threat to life and of the deceased's harassment but failed to take reasonable steps to prevent her husband from murdering her. The key point here is not that the Court expects that states would be able to prevent all instances of fatal domestic abuse, but rather that it has made clear that Article 2 includes an obligation to take seriously the information available to state authorities, and to act in order to protect life in situations of domestic and intimate-partner abuse. Importantly, in *A and B v Georgia*,[100] the Court underlined that when the perpetrator of domestic violence is a serving police officer and abused his official status, the state's obligation to investigate and, where appropriate, to punish is more stringent.

A similar approach is now discernible in the Article 3 jurisprudence, in respect of which it has been found that states have a procedural obligation to ensure effective investigation of allegations of abuse with a view to ensuring

[96] Other cases focusing on Article 8 in this respect include *Hajduová v Slovakia* App no 2660/03 (ECtHR, 30 November 2010); *A v Croatia* App no 55164/08 (ECtHR, 14 October 2010); *Kalucza v Hungary* App no 57693/10 (ECtHR, 24 April 2012).

[97] *Kontrová v Slovakia* App no 7510/04 (ECtHR, 31 May 2007).

[98] *Branko Tomašic' and Others v Croatia* App no 46598/06 (ECtHR, 15 January 2009).

[99] *Civek v Turkey* [2016] ECHR 207.

[100] *A and B v Georgia* App no 73975/16 (ECtHR, 10 February 2022), para 48.

protection from such treatment.[101] The important case of *Opuz v Turkey*[102] significantly developed the Court's jurisprudence in this respect.

The applicant and her mother had been subjected to years of violent abuse by the applicant's husband, and had made frequent complaints to the police. With the exception of one, these complaints had all been withdrawn, the women explaining that the husband had harassed them into doing so, including by threatening to kill them. Each time a complaint was withdrawn the police desisted from any investigation, deeming the situation a 'family matter'. The husband subsequently stabbed his wife, the applicant, seven times, following which he was fined. Although both women claimed that their lives were in danger, he was released by police following questioning. When the women tried to move away, he shot his mother-in-law, killing her. He was convicted of murder and sentenced to life imprisonment; however, he was released pending appeal. His wife, the applicant, claimed that he continued to harass her.

As well as finding a violation of Article 2, the ECtHR importantly concluded that Turkey had violated Article 3 through its failure to protect the applicant. The mistreatment in this case reached the minimum level of severity to be considered inhuman and degrading treatment or punishment – the first time the Court had reached this conclusion in a domestic-violence case – and the state had obligations to protect the applicant from such abuse. Rather than fulfil that obligation, the authorities had not even used the measures available to them (limited as they were) to protect her, and on the whole Turkey did not have an effective legal framework allowing for criminal proceedings in situations of this kind. Furthermore, and extremely importantly in the context of domestic violence, the Court proceeded to find a violation of Article 14 (the right to non-discrimination) in conjunction with Articles 2 and 3, holding that there was a climate of general passivity about domestic violence among the Turkish judiciary, in spite of the high incidence of such violence in the country, which in fact created an atmosphere conducive to domestic violence. The violence experienced by the applicant and her mother could thus be said to be gender-based discrimination resulting from authorities' failure properly to address domestic violence in the country.

Opuz was a landmark in the Court's treatment of domestic violence, recognising not only that domestic violence could engage Article 3 but also that a state's failure adequately to address domestic violence could constitute discrimination under Article 14. This continued with *Eremia v Moldova*,[103] in which the applicants (a woman and her two daughters) complained of the Moldovan authorities' failure to protect them from abuse from their husband and father, who happened also to be a police officer. The Court found violations of Articles 3 and 8, and, drawing on *Opuz*, also of Article 14 combined

[101] See, eg, *Valiuliene. v Lithuania* [2013] ECHR 240; *EM v Romania* App no 43994/05 (ECtHR, 30 October 2012).

[102] *Opuz v Turkey* [2009] ECHR 870.

[103] *Eremia v the Republic of Moldova* [2013] ECHR 601.

with Article 3. As far as the Court was concerned, the authorities' failure to take action to protect the applicant amounted to repeatedly condoning her husband's treatment of her and reflected a discriminatory attitude to her as a woman. All of this was compounded by their unwillingness to act against a fellow police officer. Similar findings of discrimination in respect of domestic violence have since been made in *MG v Turkey* (Article 3 in conjunction with Article 14)[104] and *Halime Kiliç v Turkey* (Article 2 in conjunction with Article 14).[105]

In March 2017, this pattern was consolidated with the important case of *Talpis v Italy*.[106] In this case, the applicant had been abused by her husband on several occasions, as had her children. The police had been called to the scene on the first occasion (when he beat the applicant and her daughter); and on the second occasion (when he attacked the applicant with a knife and tried to force her to go with him and have sex with his friends) she sought assistance from a police patrol on the street, which fined him for carrying a prohibited weapon and suggested Ms Talpis go home. On that occasion she also engaged with an accident-and-emergency unit in a hospital, and then went to a women's shelter, but after three months there she had to leave as they had insufficient space and resources to support her. For a short while she was homeless but subsequently found a job and rented a flat. Her husband continued to subject her to psychological abuse by telephone during this time. In September 2012, Ms Talpis lodged a formal complaint against her husband and sought urgent protection for herself and her children. It was seven months before the police first questioned her, at which stage she mitigated the allegations; in August 2013 the file was closed. Around three months later, Mr Talpis was found intoxicated on the street after the applicant had called the police concerning an argument with her husband. The police urged him to go home, and upon entering the apartment he attacked Ms Talpis and fatally stabbed his son. He also stabbed Ms Talpis in the chest. Her injuries were not fatal. Mr Talpis was subsequently convicted of murder and attempted murder, and was sentenced to life imprisonment. Ms Talpis claimed that there had been a violation of her rights under Articles 2 and 3 in conjunction with Article 14. The Court found multiple violations in this case.

The Court held the Italian authorities had failed to exercise the requisite diligence to act in a timely and effective manner to protect the right to life of Ms Talpis and her son. This related not only to the failure to act promptly after the applicant's complaint in September of 2012, but also to the police failure to take any action to protect Ms Talpis and her children on the night of the stabbing, in spite of having engaged with her husband on a number of occasions that evening and the fact that the police knew, or should have known, that he

[104] *MG v Turkey* App no 646/10 (ECtHR, 22 March 2016).
[105] *Halime Kılıç v Turkey* App no 63034/11 (ECtHR, 28 June 2016).
[106] *Talpis v Italy* App no 41237/14 (ECtHR, 2 March 2017).

posed a real threat to her. Similarly, the unexplained and unjustifiable delay in acting on Ms Talpis' complaint in 2012 resulted in a violation of Article 3, particularly as she was a vulnerable person subjected to violence of sufficient severity to reach the threshold of ill-treatment under Article 3. Finally, the Court reiterated its position from *Opuz* that a state's failure to protect women against domestic violence violates the right to equal protection of the law. Here, the police failures to act to protect Ms Talpis and proceed with investigations in a timely manner was so serious as to effectively endorse the violence in question, constituting discrimination against her as a woman under Article 14. Interestingly, the Court also referred to reports of the UN Special Rapporteur on Violence against Women, the Committee for the Elimination of Discrimination against Women and data from the National Bureau of Statistics to show that domestic violence is a serious and extensive problem in Italy, grounded in discrimination. The violence inflicted on Ms Talpis was, then, also said to be grounded on sex, and thus to be a form of discrimination violating Article 14 in conjunction with Articles 2 and 3.[107]

In *Kurt v Austria*,[108] the Court further developed its case law on states' duty to take preventive operational measures where someone's life is at risk from domestic violence. It clarified that where an allegation of domestic violence is made, authorities must establish whether there is a real and immediate risk to the life of one or more identified victims of domestic violence by carrying out an autonomous, proactive and comprehensive risk assessment. The reality and immediacy of the risk must be examined, taking due account of the particular context of domestic-violence cases. If the outcome of the risk assessment is that there is a real and immediate risk to life, authorities must take adequate and proportionate preventive operational measures to protect life. In recent cases, the Court has clarified the evidentiary burden in relation to proving discrimination in cases of domestic violence. The ECtHR established that if large-scale structural bias is shown to exist, there is no need to demonstrate that this victim was a victim of prejudice,[109] making litigating these cases more realistic.

This jurisprudence signals an important breakthrough in the Court's approach to domestic violence, recognising clearly the role that legislative, administrative and policing frameworks can play in implicitly condoning domestic violence (and thus implicitly acknowledging domestic violence as an outworking of structural inequality), whilst also identifying them as key elements in any attempt to effectively address domestic violence systemically

[107] However, cf the partly dissenting judgment of Judge Spano in this case, and the criticism thereof in Fleur van Leeuwen, 'The Limits of Human Rights Law: Dissenting Androcentric Voices in Talpis v Italy' (*Strasbourg Observers*, 30 May 2017) at https://strasbourgobservers.com/2017/05/30/the-limits-of-human-rights-law-dissenting-androcentric-voices-in-talpis-v-it.

[108] *Kurt v Austria* App no 62903/15 (ECtHR, 15 June 2021). See also *Y and Others v Bulgaria* App no 9077/18 (ECtHR, 22 March 2022).

[109] See *Volodina v Russia* [2019] ECHR 539, paras 111–114; *AE v Bulgaria* App no 53891/20 (ECtHR, 23 May 2023), paras 148–158.

and in individual cases. The Court's broader concentration on investigation, remedy and taking steps to protect persons from rights violation is consistent with its general approach to states' obligations in respect of everyday violence. The Convention, in short, requires states to recognise private violence as having a public dimension, to have in place appropriate legislative frameworks to address such violence, to take steps to protect people from violence, to investigate situations where violence occurs and to ensure the availability of domestic remedies should it fail in so doing. Whilst none of this alone addresses the pervasive and structural prejudices and inequality of power that underpin so much everyday insecurity and violence, these developments in the Court's jurisprudence clearly identify the state's role in attempting to address and undo them, not merely as a matter of good will but as a matter of international legal obligation.

Conclusion

In situations of insecurity, rights matter. In many cases of systemic insecurity, war and emergency, states have not hesitated to interfere with human rights, ostensibly in the name of restoring normalcy. The law accommodates this, and Article 15 allows for reductions in rights protection in times of emergency; however, in order for that allowance to be exercised only when absolutely necessary, a rigorous assessment of states' claims of insecurity and necessity is needed. We have seen in this chapter that such rigour is not always in evidence, even though it seems required to ensure the effective supervision of human rights compliance in times of emergency. Nevertheless, those extraordinary situations are not the only times when insecurity needs to be addressed. Indeed, interpersonal violence is such a serious and widespread experience that insecurity might well be said to be a quotidian condition. In that context, the question becomes whether the ECHR offers any potential to enhance personal security. As the jurisprudence on domestic and intimate violence shows, the Court is developing an approach that takes such insecurity seriously and places clear expectations on states to prevent and protect from these forms of normalised, but gravely serious, everyday insecurity.

Further Reading

Ronagh JA McQuigg, *Domestic Violence and the European Court of Human Rights* (Routledge, 2025).

Alan Greene, 'Separating Normalcy from Emergency: The Jurisprudence of Article 15 of the European Convention on Human Rights' (2011) 12(10) *German Law Journal* 1764.

Alan Greene, *Emergency Powers in a Time of Pandemic* (Bristol University Press, 2020).

Jane Rooney, 'The Relationship between Jurisdiction and Attribution after *Jaloud v Netherlands*' (2015) 62 *Netherlands International Law Review* 407.

7

Socio-Economic Rights and the European Convention on Human Rights

More than a decade after the European Convention on Human Rights (the ECHR or the Convention) was signed into law, international human rights law developed treaties focusing on both civil and political rights (the International Covenant on Civil and Political Rights) *and* socio-economic rights (the International Covenant on Economic, Social and Cultural Rights). Although there are important differences between these international covenants (extensively canvassed elsewhere[1]), the basic principles of indivisibility and universality (ie that both categories of rights are to be universally enjoyed by all human beings *and* are indivisible) underpin them.[2]

Nevertheless, some continue to question the status of socioeconomic rights. The precise contours of this debate do not need to be revisited here,[3] but the broader questions of the role of rights, of courts and of human rights courts per se are relevant to Debate 1 in this chapter: should the ECHR – a 'civil and political rights document' containing 'classic civil and political rights'[4] – be used to protect socio-economic rights? One's preferred answer to this important question depends to some extent on how far we think courts should 'stretch' classically conceived civil and political rights to address poor socio-economic conditions, as well as concerns that socio-economic matters are complex, polycentric issues with inescapable significant resource implications for states that should be approached with caution – if at all – by courts.

These questions were particularly acute during the Global Financial Crises of the late 2000s and the policies of 'austerity' through which governments

[1] For a comprehensive overview on the differences, and similarities, between the two, see Ruth Gavison, 'On the relationships between civil and political rights, and social and economic rights' in Jean-Marc Coicaud et al (eds), *The Globalization of Human Rights* (United Nations University Press, 2003) 23.

[2] See the Vienna Declaration and Programme of Action (1993).

[3] See, for example, Paul O'Connell, *Vindicating Socio-Economic Rights* (Routledge, 2012), chapter 1.

[4] Ingrid Leijten, *Core Socio-Economic Rights and the European Court of Human Rights* (Cambridge University Press, 2018) 25.

sought to respond. These conditions resulted in intense economic hardship and exacerbated structural socio-economic inequalities, particularly in European states most sharply impacted by austerity and financial crises. The attempt to resist an approach to economic recovery that is centred on austerity and the reduction in welfare provision by the state has resulted in litigation in the ECtHR that we consider in Debate 2: can the ECHR be used to challenge austerity?

This leads us, then, to the third debate in this chapter, focused on Article 14 and the anti-discrimination provision in the Convention. Article 14 is, at first glance, a 'relatively insipid'[5] (or some might say 'parasitic'[6]) right, by which we mean that it does not – on the face of it – create a stand-alone right to be free from discrimination (much less to equality) but rather affirms the right to non-discrimination in the enjoyment of *other* Convention rights. It has long been argued that, thus constructed, Article 14 is inadequate to ground an effective jurisprudence of anti-discrimination under the Convention. However, the jurisprudence of recent years gestures towards a shift away from a strict construction of Article 14 in this limited way and towards something more attuned to the protection of a substantive conception of equality. In addition, Protocol 12 to the Convention has created a freestanding right to non-discrimination, although it is far from being ratified by all the Contracting Parties to the Convention and rarely used by the Court. We thus close the chapter by asking whether the right to non-discrimination in the ECHR can promote socio-economic equality.

Debate 1

Should the ECHR Be Used to Protect Socio-Economic Rights?

The ECHR primarily protects civil and political rights, with the exception of rights to education (Article 2, Protocol 1) and to the protection of property and possessions (Article 1, Protocol 1). However, the Court recognised the relationship between these rights as early as ***Airey v Ireland***,[7] when it found that a failure to make civil legal aid available was a breach of Article 6 due-process rights. According to the Court, the Convention 'is designed to safeguard the individual in a real and practical way as regards those areas with which it deals',[8] and where that requires 'extend[ing] into the sphere of social or economic rights', so be it.[9] Indeed, the Court continues to make findings relevant to

[5] Sandra Fredman, 'Emerging from the Shadows: Substantive Equality and Article 14 of the European Convention on Human Rights' (2016) 16(2) *Human Rights Law Review* 273, 273.

[6] *Whaley v Lord Advocate* [2004] SC 78, para 93.

[7] *Airey v Ireland*, (1979–80) 2 EHRR 305.

[8] ibid, para 26.

[9] ibid.

socio-economic rights in the field of access to justice, finding, for example, that unreasonably high fees can result in people's not being able to bring disputes before courts or tribunals.[10]

This brings us to an important point in the discussion of socio-economic rights under the Convention: that the Court has largely addressed them to the extent that they relate to the 'areas with which [the ECHR] deals' rather than on a stand-alone basis. This is perhaps not surprising. The potential for protecting socio-economic rights when they are clearly linked to the civil and political rights expressly protected within the Convention is substantial. For example, there is 'space' within a right to be free from inhuman and degrading treatment to establish a state's obligation to ensure a meaningful and adequate provision of medical care,[11] which bears close resemblance to the right to an adequate standard of healthcare as protected in socio-economic rights instruments and jurisprudence.[12] However, Article 3 does not require states to provide free medical care to all people in all circumstances. States are expected to ensure adequate level of care in prisons and in other closed institutions, but not to all people at all times. Similarly, the right to respect for private and family life can be developed to recognise an obligation to ensure that people can live in a way that accords with their cultural practices.[13] This too might then bear a resemblance in substantive and practical terms to the right to culturally appropriate housing, protected under socio-economic rights instruments and international jurisprudence.[14] Thus, it is clear that there is space for some socio-economic rights to be protected in a practical sense, particularly in relation to the positive obligations that have been developed in Convention jurisprudence to give full effect to the rights protected therein.[15] However, the question that we consider here is whether such jurisprudential developments *ought to be* undertaken.

Perhaps the first argument against such development is that the text explicitly precludes the protection of such rights, largely on the basis that silence might be considered to indicate exclusion, and thus that protecting them – even in effect if not in form – is an unacceptable extension of the Convention beyond its intended meaning. Indeed, in chapter 4 we saw that just such a criticism is levied by some states against evolutive interpretation of the Convention. In relation to those debates, we noted that such a criticism is sometimes rooted in an overly formalistic conception of 'original consent' as determining the extent of a state's international obligations, and furthermore that techniques of

---

[10] See, for example, *Mehmet and Suna Yigit v Turkey* App no 52658/99 (ECtHR, 17 July 2007); *Kreuz v Poland* App no 28249/95 (ECtHR, 19 June 2001), paras 58–67.

[11] *D v the United Kingdom* [1997] ECHR 25.

[12] Article 25, Universal Declaration of Human Rights; Article 12, International Covenant on Economic, Social and Cultural Rights.

[13] See, for example, *Winterstein and Others v France* [2013] ECHR 98.

[14] Article 11, Universal Declaration of Human Rights.

[15] See Ellie Palmer, *Judicial Review, Socio-Economic Rights and the Human Rights Act* (Hart Publishing, 2007), chapter 1.

interpretation have been developed by the Court to establish the legitimacy of such evolutive interpretation, albeit there may still be cases in which the Court might be said to go 'too far' by reference to the text, purpose and understanding of the Convention.[16] Can such arguments also be made in respect of the development of socio-economic protection within Convention jurisprudence? On the face of it, the answer is yes; after all, if evolution is acceptable in some contexts, why not in others? However, the counter-argument might be that whilst evolution of the Convention *in line with the original overall purpose of the treaty* is legitimate and justifiable, evolution *that extends the scope of the treaty beyond its original purpose* is not. In other words, some limits to evolution must be accepted, and those limits might be found in the purpose of the Treaty, as suggested by Article 31(1) of the Vienna Convention on the Law of Treaties (VCLT):

> A treaty shall be interpreted in good faith in accordance with the ordinary meaning to be given to the terms of the treaty in their context and in the light of its object and purpose.

We already saw in chapter 1 that the Convention's perceived purpose was to enable human flourishing, primarily through protecting democracy, the rule of law and participation in government. In that mindset, rights were mostly negative (protections *from* interference) rather than positive (entitlements *to* state action). Accordingly, provision of material human necessities – food, shelter, medical care, for example – was primarily to be achieved through developing individual economic power and resources by freeing markets *not* through legally enforceable rights. Capital was the route to socio-economic security, not state-protected and legally justiciable human rights. Whilst states might provide a welfare net, that was not because *human rights* demanded it but because the concept of statehood and the social contract did; it was for the domestic government – and usually the Executive – to decide on the exact contours of that provision.

Within this framework, socio-economic rights protection largely fell outside the Convention. In the original proposal for the rights to be protected within the Convention, the only aspect that might be defined as a socio-economic right to be found related to property, and even then the proposed protection was for 'freedom from arbitrary deprivation of property'.[17] Even read in line with the original proposal for 'equality before the law',[18] it is difficult to read this as a proposal aimed at redistribution and tackling systemic inequalities.

[16] See, for example, Leonard Hoffmann, 'The Universality of Human Rights' (2009) 125 *Law Quarterly Review* 416.

[17] European Movement, *European Convention on Human Rights*, ING/5/E/R (1949), proposed Article 1(k), as cited in Ed Bates, *The Evolution of the European Convention on Human Rights* (Oxford University Press, 2010) 56.

[18] European Movement (n 17), proposed Article 1(i).

It is, rather, aimed primarily at ensuring that persons can protect what they already have; the least progressive way of conceptualising a right to property that one might imagine from the perspective of concern, for providing the necessities for humans to survive, not least to thrive.

Importantly, the approaches to both negative and positive rights, and the constitutional cultures of the states parties, are now quite different from what they were in the early 1950s. As we have already seen, the Court has developed positive obligations[19] designed to ensure the protection and enjoyment of rights, and is not merely focused on whether states have unjustifiably interfered with protected rights (ie the negative enquiry).[20] In other words, positive obligations have been developed to ensure the fulfilment of rights, which in turn are now sometimes conceptualised as rights *to* and not merely rights *from*. Importantly, the Court never fully excluded the possibility of the Convention's having implications for socio-economic wellbeing. As it held in *Airey v Ireland*, 'the mere fact that an interpretation of the Convention may extend into the sphere of social and economic rights should not be a decisive factor against such an interpretation', as 'there is no water-tight division separating that sphere from the field covered by the Convention'.[21] Expanding the protection thus available under the Convention to address situations of material need, where the state's failure to provide necessities means that the person cannot enjoy the protected right, might be said to be a relatively modest jurisprudential leap if one accepts the development of positive obligations per se. Having said that, these developments must be strictly connected to the rights enshrined in the Convention and not create whole new obligations.

The argument can be understood to mean that inclusion of limited protection of socio-economic right reflects developments in the Council of Europe member states, as they increasingly protect some kind of economic or socio-economic rights by constitution or legislation, and indeed that this is part of constitutional culture in some post-Soviet states in particular, which became members of the Council of Europe following the fall of the USSR. O'Cinnéide has convincingly shown that social constitutionalism is part of European legal heritage and culture(s).[22] If the Convention truly does reflect a

[19] See Vladislava Stoyanova, *Positive Obligations under the European Convention on Human Rights: Within and Beyond Boundaries* (Oxford University Press, 2023).

[20] Jean Francois Akandji-Kombe, *Positive Obligations under the European Convention on Human Rights: A guide to the implementation of the European Convention on Human Rights* (Council of Europe, 2007); Alastair Mowbray, *The Development of Positive Obligations under the European Convention on Human Rights by the European Court of Human Rights* (Hart Publishing, 2004); Brice Dickson, 'Positive Obligations and the European Court of Human Rights' (2010) 61(3) *Northern Ireland Legal Quarterly* 203; Stoyanova (n 19).

[21] *Airey v Ireland* (n 7), para 26.

[22] Colm O'Cinnéide, 'The Present Limits and Future Potential of European Social Constitutionalism' in Katharine Young (ed), *The Future of Economic and Social Rights* (Cambridge University Press, 2017) 324.

'common heritage of political traditions, ideals, freedom and the rule of law'[23] across the member states of the Council of Europe, and if those can evolve as the membership expands, perhaps one can argue that there is a justification from purpose for limited protection of socio-economic goods under the Convention. There is, in other words, at least an argument that the ***purpose*** of the Convention now may be more than simply to protect against tyranny and oppression, but in fact to support human flourishing through the protection of rights. Were such an argument to be considered compelling, the purpose of the Convention ***now*** might be said to include enabling people to make legal claims for socio-economic goods on the state, where these are needed to give effect to the rights protected within the text of the Convention.

This argument potentially falters given that the broader systems of rights protection of which the Convention is a part – the human rights system of the Council of Europe – has developed a parallel mechanism for the protection of socio-economic rights. In 1961, the European Social Charter was introduced to protect socio-economic rights within the Council of Europe system. A system of government reporting was established:[24] this was to be the main enforcement mechanism and there was no way to bring complaints of a breach of the Charter to the ECtHR (although of course the Court could, and increasingly does, refer to the Charter in its case law, just as it does to other international legal instruments[25]). The two systems – Convention and Charter – are separate, with the Charter's enforcement and implementation overseen primarily by a committee of experts now known as the European Committee on Social Rights. Since 1995, the reporting process has been complemented by a system of collective complaints,[26] seemingly motivated by a desire to include more actors in the process of assessing compliance with the Charter and, thereby, increasing the rigour and effectiveness of the enforcement machinery.[27] Unlike the Court, the Committee applying the Charter has been able to establish and enforce substantive socio-economic rights, such as the right to social assistance

[23] Preamble, ECHR.

[24] Pursuant to Article 21 of the European Social Charter, the Contracting Parties are obliged to send to the Secretary-General of the Council of Europe a report at two-yearly intervals, concerning the application of such provisions of Part II of the Charter as they have accepted.

[25] *Demir and Baykara v Turkey* [2008] ECHR 1345, paras 45, 49, 50; *Konstantin Markin v Russia* [2012] ECHR 514, para 55.

[26] According to Article 1 of the Additional Protocol to the European Social Charter Providing for a System of Collective Complaints, the Contracting Parties recognise the right of the following organisations to submit complaints alleging unsatisfactory application of the Charter: (i) international organisations of employers and trade unions; (ii) other international NGOs that have consultative status with the Council of Europe and have been put on a list established for this purpose by the Governmental Committee; (iii) representative national organisations of employers and trade unions within the jurisdiction of the Contracting Party against which they have lodged a complaint.

[27] See Robin Churchill and Urfan Khaliq, 'Violations of Economic, Social and Cultural Rights: The Current Use and Future Potential of the Collective Complaints Mechanism of the European Social Charter' in Mashood Baderin and Robert McCorquodale (eds), *Economic, Social and Cultural Rights in Action* (Oxford University Press, 2007) 195, 200–01.

(protected by Article 13(1) of the Charter), even in the face of a state's claims that it enjoys a wide margin of appreciation in devising and applying conditions for accessing such assistance.[28] Whilst the existence of the Charter and its associated enforcement mechanisms may not convincingly ground an argument that socio-economic rights are adequately protected by another process and thus do not *need* to be protected through the Convention, it does lend weight to the argument that the Convention neither expressly *nor impliedly* protects those rights, and that extending its scope to offer such protection raises legitimacy-related concerns.

There are further, doctrinal concerns with extending the Convention's protection to socio-economic rights. The first, expressed well by Warbrick some years ago, is that the fact such rights are not protected within the text of the Convention may mean that a 'political right not to have destitution thrust upon one by the state' may become conflated with the legal socio-economic right to social support in a way that would hollow out the usefulness of economic or social rights.[29] This is, in effect, an argument that the socio-economic right suffers by being reshaped into a civil and political right under the Convention; an argument that has doctrinal attraction but which might seem less appealing to practitioners, advocacy groups, individuals and communities interested in finding *practical* ways to enforce their (political and legal) socio-economic claims and rights against the state.

A related doctrinal concern is that by using civil and political rights under the Convention to protect socio-economic rights in practical terms, the civil and political rights may suffer; they might also become 'degraded'. This is a complex claim that, when disaggregated, has many layers to it and certainly can be related to the broader, theoretical claim that is still sometimes made that socio-economic rights are *substantively different* from civil and political rights, are not (or should not be) justiciable, and drag courts into inappropriate areas of activity such as resource allocation and reallocation.[30] We do not need to rehearse these broader arguments here, or indeed the many rebuttals to them, but they do provide an important backdrop, as they reflect an intuition on the part of some that socio-economic rights are *less legally important* than civil and political rights. Moving on from that contextual note, let us examine some of the jurisprudence under Article 3 of the ECHR to explore the concern that socio-economic protection under this provision may be damaging to the norm.

Article 3 provides:

> No one shall be subjected to torture or to inhuman or degrading treatment or punishment.

[28] See, for example, *European Roma Rights Centre v Bulgaria* Complaint No 48/2008 (Decision 31 March 2009) (The Collective Complaints Committee on European Social Charter).

[29] Colin Warbrick, 'Economic and Social Interests and the European Convention on Human Rights' in Baderin and McCorquodale (eds) (n 27) 241.

[30] For a comprehensive account of the arguments on social rights per se, see, eg. Conor Gearty and Virginia Mantouvalou, *Debating Social Rights* (Hart Publishing, 2010).

The core underpinning jurisprudential claims in the Article 3 cases are that the negative right to be free from torture, inhuman and degrading treatment or punishment is absolute, that no proportionality analysis is provided, that there is no defence to claims of interference and that violations of this right to be free form torture in particular carry a special stigma.[31] The Court thus treats these violations as particularly serious, as do the Contracting Parties and applicants to the Court. Partly because of this, the Court will find that the right to torture has been violated only where a minimum level of severity in ill-treatment has been reached, and findings of inhuman or degrading treatment or punishment are made sparingly. However, Article 3 has proved to be fertile ground for the development of socio-economic protection before the Court, albeit only in very severe circumstances.

This is well illustrated by *MSS v Belgium and Greece*.[32] This case concerned the conditions of detention of asylum seekers in Greece – conditions in relation to which the Court had already expressed concern.[33] Belgium had sent the applicant back to Greece on the basis that, as this was the first EU country he entered, this was where his asylum application had to be processed. However, in Greece MSS had been detained in appalling conditions before living on the streets without receiving any social assistance or material support from the state. This was so even though Greek law (transposing the relevant EU law) created a national legal obligation to provide accommodation and decent living conditions to asylum seekers.

Noting that human dignity is a foundation of Convention rights, and refusing to accept that Greece's straitened economic conditions should be taken into account when considering whether the treatment of asylum seekers violated Article 3, the Court held that the lack of food, hygiene, a home and material resources, which resulted in MSS's living in extreme poverty, was a violation of Article 3. As a member of a vulnerable group (asylum seekers), the state's positive obligations to protect people from torture, inhuman and degrading treatment or punishment under Article 3 extended to providing him with a home. Belgium was also said to violate Article 3 by sending MSS to Greece and thus exposing him to these inhumane living conditions. Depending on the circumstances, the Court held, a 'serious deprivation of basic human needs' may result in a breach of Article 3.[34]

These circumstances are important. The Court made it clear that whether Article 3 had been violated was to be determined by reference to a six-part test:

[31] On Article 3, see generally Natasa Mavronicola, *Torture, Inhumanity and Degradation under Article 3 of the ECHR: Absolute Rights and Absolute Wrongs* (Hart Publishing, 2021).

[32] *MSS v Belgium and Greece* App no 30696/09 (ECtHR, 21 January 2011).

[33] See, for example, *SD v Greece* App no 53541/07 (ECtHR, 11 June 2009); *Tabesh v Greece* App no 8256/07 (ECtHR, 26 November 2009); *AA v Greece* App no 12186/08 (ECtHR, 22 July 2010), para 160.

[34] *MSS v Belgium and Greece* (n 32), para 252.

1. Was the person in a condition of particular severity, which meant that they were unable to cater for their most basic needs?[35]
2. Was the person a member of a 'particularly underprivileged and vulnerable population group in need of special protection'?[36]
3. Was the person 'wholly dependent on State support … faced with official indifference in a situation of serious deprivation?'[37]
4. Did the state take action (on its own initiative) to relieve these conditions as appropriate to the state of vulnerability and insecurity of the person?[38]
5. Could the state have 'substantially alleviated his suffering' through prompt action?[39]
6. Did the state 'have due regard to the applicant's vulnerability'?[40]

This is clearly a demanding test. It does not amount to a 'right to a home' in a general sense. Indeed, the Court expressly precluded giving any such meaning to Article 3. Instead, it means that the state's positive obligations to protect against torture, inhuman and degrading treatment or punishment – long established in the case law of the Court – may require the provision of basic material necessities 'where there are direct and verifiable links between the conduct of the state or its agents and the origins or continuation of conduct that has caused intolerable harm'.[41] Furthermore, the Court placed great emphasis on the concept of vulnerability, which it suggests herein relates to one's membership of a group, as opposed to a particular analysis of individual circumstances.[42] Asylum seekers are, prima facie, vulnerable,[43] according to Judge Rozakis, and thus require an advanced level of protection that enables them to claim material provision under Article 3, although there was not unanimity among the judges on that point.[44]

[35] ibid, para 254.

[36] ibid, para 251.

[37] ibid, para 253.

[38] ibid, para 259.

[39] ibid, para 262.

[40] ibid, para 263.

[41] Elizabeth Palmer, 'Protecting Socio-economic Rights through the European Convention on Human Rights: Trends and Developments in the European Court of Human Rights' (2009) 2(4) *Erasmus Law Review* 397, 414.

[42] Although see also *Sufi and Elmi v the United Kingdom* [2011] ECHR 1045, applying the vulnerability test from *MSS v Belgium and Greece* (n 32).

[43] The Court's use of vulnerability has been criticised. Peroni and Timmer note that by focusing mostly on group-based vulnerability, the Court has failed to give proper consideration to individual vulnerability (Lourdes Peroni and Alexandra Timmer, 'Vulnerable Groups: The Promise of an Emerging Concept in European Human Rights Convention Law' (2013) 11(4) *International Journal Constitutional Law* 1056); Corina Heri, *Responsive Human Rights: Vulnerability, Ill-Treatment, and the ECHR* (Hart Publishing, 2021); Katie Morris, 'Vulnerability, Care Ethics and the Protection of Socioeconomic Rights via Article 3 ECHR' (2023) 23 *Human Rights Law Review* 1.

[44] See the Opinion of Judge Sajó on this point. *MSS v Belgium and Greece* (n 32), Partly Concurring and Partly Dissenting Opinion of Judge Sajó.

In extreme cases such as *MSS*, the protection of socio-economic rights does not degrade the protection against torture per se under Article 3. The threshold test applied is clearly a high one;[45] and as Thornton notes, the extent of the lack of social support that seems necessary to trigger an Article 3 obligation is such that *MSS* cannot be said to provide for a right to social protection, or even to indicate especially clearly the usefulness of Article 3 as a vehicle for protection of socio-economic rights.[46] The threshold – namely, one of utter destitution resulting directly from state actions and relating to persons wholly dependent on the state for their subsistence[47] – is so high that most situations of hunger, homelessness and material need simply would not meet it, notwithstanding the degradation often experienced in situations of extreme poverty.

Instead, what *MSS* suggests – and it is not the only case to do so – is that the Convention might be used to require a state not to impose destitution or socio-economic devastation upon someone (including by deporting them to a state where their basic socio-economic needs, such as healthcare needs, would not be met,[48] or by inflicting 'policy-induced suffering'[49]), but not to require the state to materially support persons as a matter of human rights law per se. If that truly is the extent of the protection for socio-economic wellbeing under the Convention, one might argue that it does not require too great a level of anxiety about undue expansionism into the field of socio-economic rights protection by the Court. Indeed, it could be read in contrast as a 'substantively suspect' 'reluctance to "extend" Article 3's positive obligations' reach into the socio-economic sphere'.[50]

Debate 2

Can the ECHR Protect Socio-Economic Wellbeing in a Time of Austerity?

Realistically, many millions of people live in situations of socio-economic need without reaching the threshold of destitution. In Europe, as elsewhere, many people experience structural inequality, related to attributes such as race, ethnicity, gender, disability and sexual orientation that have manifest implications

[45] See also the admissibility decision in *Budina v Russia* [2009] ECHR 1104.

[46] Liam Thornton, 'European Convention on Human Rights: A Socio-Economic Rights Charter?' in Suzanne Egan, Liam Thornton and Judy Walsh (eds), *Ireland and the European Convention on Human Rights: 60 Years and Beyond* (Bloomsbury, 2014) 227.

[47] See Dimitrios Kagiaros, 'Vulnerability as a path to a "social minimum": An analysis of ECtHR jurisprudence' in Toomas Kootkas, Frans Pennings and Ingrid Leijten (eds), *Specifying and Securing a Social Minimum in the Battle Against Poverty* (Hart Publishing, 2019) 245.

[48] See *D v United Kingdom* (n 11); *Sufi and Elmi v United Kingdom* (n 42).

[49] Lutz Oette, 'Austerity and the Limits Of Policy-Induced Suffering: What Role for the Prohibition of Torture and Other Ill-Treatment?'(2015) 15(4) *Human Rights Law Review* 669.

[50] Natasa Mavronicola, *Torture, Inhumanity and Degradation under Article 3 of the ECHR: Absolute Rights and Absolute Wrongs* (Hart Publishing, 2021) 136–38.

for their socio-economic wellbeing. Sometimes, these attributes are intersectional, meaning that the combination of factors makes the person even more vulnerable than any person with only one of such attributes.[51] Law including law of the ECtHR sometimes takes into account only some attributes of vulnerability without looking at them holistically.

Some dimensions of economic inequality with serious implications for the enjoyment of civil and political rights are structural. By this we mean that this economic inequality emerges not 'merely' from the individual circumstances of the person in question, but also from a socio-political inequality of power that marginalises some groups and makes them more likely to experience economic disempowerment compared with other sectors of the population. The causes of such structural inequality are complex and often combine historical marginalisation, extractivism, colonialism and corruption with sexism, racism, disablism, and other prejudices and biases that permeate society, resulting in disadvantage in social matters, lack of access to public services such as education or healthcare, and entrenched inequality in labour markets. Asylum seekers, children, women, older people, ill people, people with disabilities, and ethnic and religious minorities are among those most likely to experience structural inequality, and at the same time are those least able to access political power to address it. For marginalised groups, then, litigation and the law may be useful avenues towards attempting to address material conditions of inequality that undermine them in attempting fully to enjoy and exercise their human rights in the civil and political sphere, even bearing in mind the shortcomings of courts and litigation as a mode of addressing deeply-embedded, structural inequalities.

The Global Financial Crises of the late 2000s ushered in a period of structured and severe 'austerity' across Europe, and particularly in countries (such as Greece, Portugal, Ireland and Spain) that had been 'bailed out' by the International Monetary Fund, the European Central Bank and the European Commission (ie 'the Troika'). These austerity programmes raised severe concerns in respect of socio-economic rights: they brought about serious decreases in welfare payments and social protection, often resulted in the dramatic reduction of available public-health and educational facilities, and had especially serious negative implications for people and groups already economically disadvantaged, primarily because the bail outs were conditional on substantial fiscal cuts that, in the case of Greece for example, were said to have brought about 'a welfare state retrenchment unprecedented in the post-war period'.[52] Austerity has had significant negative impacts on the enjoyment of social and economic rights, not only in countries that were 'bailed out' but also in other

---

[51] See Jens T Theilen, 'Intersectionality's Travels to International Human Rights Law' (2024) 45(2) *Michigan Journal of International Law* 233.

[52] Aristea Koukiadaki and Lefteris Kretsos, 'Opening Pandora's Box: The Sovereign Debt Crisis and Labour Market Regulation in Greece' (2012) 41(3) *Industrial Law Journal* 276, 276–77.

Council of Europe states that have introduced reductions in social protection (or 'welfare') in order to 'balance the books'.[53]

Litigation under the ECHR has successfully been used in the attempt to construct rights-based resistance to austerity. Similarly to the Article 3 cases considered above, however, a particularly high threshold of socio-economic deprivation must be met for the Court to intervene. This is well illustrated by *Nencheva and Others v Bulgaria*.[54]

The applicants' children were profoundly disabled and resided in a state institution. However, austerity measures imposed by the Government following a recession in Bulgaria meant that the institution could not provide sufficient food, lighting, sanitation or medical treatment to these children, who subsequently died. In this case, the municipal authorities and those working within the institution in question had attempted to secure further resources from the central state authorities, but were granted only very limited additional funds. The applicants claimed that the failure properly to resource the institution resulted in a violation of Article 2 in this case, that is the right to life. The Court agreed, but repeatedly noted the exceptional circumstances at play here: the state authorities were aware of the 'real and imminent risk' of death[55] and failed to respond adequately in order to protect the children's right to life. This has clear parallels with cases where the failure to respond to known situations of domestic and intimate violence resulted in the death of children,[56] and is thus a significant acknowledgement that protecting the right to life under Article 2 can require ensuring adequate material resources to prevent death, albeit only in exceptional circumstances. Relevant too is the fact that these children were in the direct care of the state.[57]

Compare this to situations where the state reduces salary or social-security payments, potentially leading to a failure to access food, shelter, electricity, healthcare and so on for the people in receipt thereof. In these cases, much of the case law has focused on Article 1 of Protocol 1: the right to the peaceful enjoyment of possessions. In *Koufaki and Adedy v Greece*,[58] deemed inadmissible in 2013, the Court noted that the reduction by 20 per cent in the remuneration, benefits and pensions of public servants did not mean the applicants were unable to subsist, and thus did not disproportionately interfere with property rights. According to the Court, such a reduction in the remuneration of public servants could be justified in a time of economic hardship.

[53] On the impact of the Global Financial Crises on rights generally, see, for example, Council of Europe, *Safeguarding Human Rights in Times of Economic Crisis* (Council of Europe, 2013).

[54] *Nencheva and Others v Bulgaria* [2013] ECHR 554.

[55] ibid, para 121.

[56] *Opuz v Turkey*, [2009] ECHR 870.

[57] Similar findings have been made in relation to the state's obligation to ensure the provision of food, shelter, sanitation, medical treatment, etc for those in state detention. See, for example, *Ananyev and Others v Russia* [2012] ECHR 21.

[58] *Koufaki and Adedy v Greece* App nos 57665/12 and 57657/12 (ECtHR, 7 May 2013).

In *Žegarac and Others v Serbia*, the Court considered claims of a violation of Article 1 of Protocol 1 regarding the reduction of state pensions between November 2014 and September 2018.[59] Those reductions were part of a wider package of austerity measures, and were repealed once it was considered that wider public debt had been reduced to an appropriate level. Concluding that the relevant complaints were manifestly ill-founded, the Court held the authorities had struck a fair balance between ensuring the financial stability of the pension system (which was in the general interest of the public) and protecting the applicants' property rights to prevent them from bearing an excessive burden. This reflects the Court's general position that the margin of appreciation accorded to states in the area of social rights is relatively wide, as it considers that states are in principle better placed to appreciate what was in the public interest on social or economic grounds than international courts. The Court has thus made clear that it will generally respect a legislature's policy choice in this area, unless that choice was manifestly without reasonable foundation.[60]

This is also well demonstrated by *LF v the United Kingdom*.[61] The applicant in this case was excluded from social housing owned by a charity catering for the Orthodox Jewish Community because she was not a member of that community. The Court held that a policy like this fell within the state's wide margin of appreciation as it did not result in the loss of the applicant's only home (she already had temporary social housing) and the impact of the charity's allocation policy in the social housing market, agreed by the local authorities, had been minor.

This does not mean that austerity measures can never be found to violate Article 1 of Protocol 1. In *NKM v Hungary*, for example, the Court found a violation where the Government introduced a backdated tax of 98 per cent on severance pay for civil servants beyond a certain threshold.[62] Notwithstanding the fact that the Court usually allows a wide margin of appreciation in matters of taxation, the applicant had completed 30 years as a civil servant, was deemed to have 'already earned' her severance pay, and was now being asked to endure what the Court considered to be an excessive burden of addressing Hungary's poor economic situation.[63] Judge Tulkens, writing extrajudicially, argues that this case is particularly significant; for her it indicates that the Court is increasingly realising the interdependence of socio-economic and civil and political rights.[64] However, there are important differences between protecting someone from a negative interference with already-owned property to alleviate economic hardship, and compelling the state to distribute its resources

[59] *Žegarac and Others v Serbia* App no 54805/15 (ECtHR, 17 January 2023).

[60] *Luczak v Poland* App no 77782/01 (ECtHR, 27 November 2007), para 48.

[61] *LF v the United Kingdom* App no 19839/21 (ECtHR, 24 May 2022).

[62] *NKM v Hungary* App no 66529/11 (ECtHR, 14 May 2013).

[63] ibid.

[64] Francoise Tulkens, 'The European Convention on Human Rights and the Economic Crisis: the Issue of Poverty' (EUI AEL; 2013/08; *Distinguished Lectures of the Academy*, 24 June 2013).

in a manner that addresses socio-economic inequality.[65] Thus, *NKM* is a case that illustrates the usefulness, but also the limitations, of 'classical' protections against negative interferences with property for attempting to address the societal impacts of austerity.

Consequently, whilst the Convention is useful in resisting austerity in situations of extreme hardship, it does not seem especially likely that it can or will fundamentally reshape or determine the imposition of austere fiscal and economic measures in times of recession in a rights-compliant manner. Instead, other processes designed specifically to protect socio-economic rights should be relied upon. In the Council of Europe context, of course, this points us towards the European Social Charter. A short detour to the Committee's approach to austerity measures, introduced as part of the negotiated 'bail out' of Greece by the IMF, ECB and European Commission, illustrates the potential for these mechanisms more fully to appreciate and address the socio-economic impact of austerity.[66]

General Federation of Employees of the National Electric Power Corporation (GENOP-DEI) and Confederation of Greek Civil Servants' Trade Unions (ADEDY) v Greece[67] concerned a cut to the minimum wage for workers under the age of 25. The claim was that this cut breached the right to fair remuneration in Article 4(1) of the Charter, which provides:

> With a view to ensuring the effective exercise of the right to a fair remuneration, the Parties undertake:
>
> … to recognise the right of workers to a remuneration such as will give them and their families a decent standard of living …

The Committee found that the acceptability of the reduction in the minimum wage for young people must be assessed by reference to proportionality, with particular attention to whether there was an objective justification and whether the measure was proportionate to achieving that. Here, the extent of the reduction in the minimum wage was disproportionate to the objective (of getting younger people into the labour market at a time of economic crisis) and, regardless of the fact that such a reduction was required by the bail-out conditions, it violated the Charter rights of younger people. Let us imagine the potential outcome if the measure had been challenged before the ECtHR instead: it did not relate to already earned or clearly identifiable finances and so Article 1, Protocol 1 likely would not have been violated,[68] and it did not

---

[65] So too does it differ from requirements to transfer property in times of socio-political transition, as illustrated in, for example, *Jahn and Others v Germany* [2005] ECHR 444.

[66] See also *Federation of Employed Pensioners of Greece (IKA-ETAM) v Greece*, Complaint 76/2011.

[67] *General Federation of Employees of the National Electric Power Corporation (GENOP-DEI) and Confederation of Greek Civil Servants' Trade Unions (ADEDY) v Greece*, Complaint 66/2011.

[68] Although cf the Court's case law on pensions: *Lakićević and Others v Montenegro and Serbia* App nos 27458/06 and 3 others (ECtHR, 13 December 2011); *Gaygusuz v Austria* [1996] ECHR 36; *Wieczorek v Poland* [2009] ECHR 2025.

impose destitution causing death or other severe consequences to younger people so that Articles 2 and 3 would unlikely be considered to have been violated, not least because the Court would have demonstrated deference to the means in which the state party was attempting to address an extremely poor national economic situation. The Charter and the Committee supervising it could thus recognise, address and attempt to remedy the rights-related implications of the imposed measures in a way that the Court applying the Convention likely would have struggled to do.

This raises important questions about the effectiveness of the Convention, which connect inevitably with the matter of 'purpose' already considered in Debate 1 and, indeed, in chapter 1 of this book. Taking human rights in the round, it is unquestionable, as Salomon has put it, that 'the governance of the [global financial] crises in the European Union has led to massive violations of human rights'.[69] Although those rights are primarily socio-economic in nature, their violation of course has implications for civil and political rights: for the ability to support one's children and thus avoid state intervention and keep one's family together (enjoying Article 8 rights), for the ability to access education (enjoying Article 2, Protocol 1 rights), for the ability to access appropriate medical care and thus avoid death (enjoying Article 2 rights), and so on. The divide between civil and political and social and economic rights might be artificial in real terms, but it is nevertheless reflected in international human rights law instruments. Within that framework the ECtHR's mandate is to protect civil and political rights as outlined in the Convention. As a result, socio-economic rights can be protected only when there is a clear connection to the enjoyment of those rights. Thus, whilst the Court and Convention can be used to try to prevent some rights violations flowing from austerity measures, they seem ill-equipped effectively to address austerity and its exacerbation of socio-economic inequality per se.

Debate 3

Can the Right to Non-Discrimination Promote Socio-Economic Equality?

In many ways, the debates that we have outlined already in this chapter point to a broader contestation not only about the Convention, but also about the function of human rights law per se. Human rights law was traditionally considered as a means of limiting state power to protect those within states' jurisdiction from repression, oppression and violation of classical civil liberties. Whilst the broader literature on and international legal instruments of human rights law have moved on from that relatively limited, but nevertheless important,

---

[69] Margot Salomon, 'Of Austerity, Human Rights and International Institutions' (2015) 21(4) *European Law Journal* 521, 522.

conception of the purpose of human rights law, the ECHR remains a classically constructed civil and political rights instrument reflecting this conception of the purposes of human rights law. Bearing that in mind, it is perhaps unsurprising that the original Convention text did not include any right to equality, or even any general, stand-alone right to non-discrimination, but rather merely provided in Article 14 for what McCrudden calls the non-discriminatory 'distribution of the other human rights protected by the ECHR'.[70] Article 14 states:

> The enjoyment of the rights and freedoms set forth in this Convention shall be secured without discrimination on any ground such as sex, race, colour, language, religion, political or other opinion, national or social origin, association with a national minority, property, birth or other status.

Whilst the list of grounds is somewhat outmoded, the Court has stressed that it is not exhaustive ('such as …' and 'other status') but rather is illustrative.[71] The Court has thus used Article 14 to consider discrimination claims in relation to sex,[72] sexual orientation,[73] health,[74] age,[75] 'illegitimacy',[76] disability,[77] language,[78] race and ethnicity,[79] and more.

Article 14 creates a right to non-discrimination in the enjoyment of other Convention rights and *not* a right to non-discrimination as such. Recognising this, Protocol 12 was introduced in 2000. This provides:

> The enjoyment of any right set forth by law shall be secured without discrimination on any ground such as sex, race, colour, language, religion, political or other opinion, national or social origin, association with a national minority, property, birth or other status. No one shall be discriminated against by any public authority.

---

[70] Christopher McCrudden, 'Equality and Non-Discrimination' in David Feldman (ed), *English Public Law* (Oxford University Press, 2004), chapter 11, para 11.86.

[71] *Salgueiro da Silva Mouta v Portugal* [1999] ECHR 176.

[72] *Nurcan Bayraktar v Türkiye*, no 27094/20, (ECtHR, 27 June 2023) on equality in marriage; *Moraru and Marin v Romania* App nos 53282/18 and 31428/20 (ECtHR, 20 December 2022) and *Pająk and Others v Poland* App no 25226/18 (ECtHR, 24 October 2023) on retirement ages; and *Tkhelidze v Georgia* App no 33056/17, (ECtHR, 8 July 2021) and *AE v Bulgaria* App no 53891/20 (ECtHR, 23 May 2023) on domestic violence.

[73] See the cases cited in n 72.

[74] *Kiyutin v Russia* [2011] ECHR 439.

[75] *Schwizgebel v Switzerland* App no 25762/07 (ECtHR, 10 June 2010).

[76] *Inze v Austria*, 28 October 1987, Series A no 126.

[77] ibid, para 80.

[78] *Paun Jovanović v Serbia* App no 41394/15 (ECtHR, 7 February 2023).

[79] *Ádám and Others v Romania* App nos 81114/17, 49716/18, 50913/18, 52370/18, 54444/18, 54475/18 (ECtHR, 13 October 2020); *Basu v Germany* App no 215/19 (ECtHR, 18 October 2022); *Wa Baile v Switzerland* App nos 43868/18 and 25883/21 (ECtHR, 20 February 2024).

Protocol 12 thus introduced a general prohibition on discrimination into the Convention,[80] but as it has been ratified by only about half of the Contracting Parties, it has not yet given rise to a substantial body of case law.[81] The Debate with which we close this chapter, then, is as to whether the right to non-discrimination as protected in the ECHR can promote socio-economic equality.

It is important at the outset to acknowledge the general shortcomings of non-discrimination as a vehicle to achieving equality. It is widely recognised in much of the equality and non-discrimination literature that *a right not to be treated differently* is not the same as *a right to be treated equally*, particularly as non-discrimination requires treating similar cases alike, whereas equality may require more. The analytical structure of discrimination law is itself limiting: there must be a comparator (*treated differently compared to whom?*), and as conventionally understood it 'squeezes' people and their experience into a category that is often simplistic and rarely captures the complexity of lived, intersectional experiences of differential treatment.[82] That is not unique to the ECHR. Non-discrimination as it is currently understood and constructed in law accords far more with what is termed 'formal equality' than it does 'substantive equality'. Formal equality concerns itself with consistency of treatment; as Barnard and Hepple put it, it 'embodies a notion of procedural justice which does not guarantee any particular outcome'.[83] Whilst formal equality might be helpful to ensure that, for example, women and men are paid the same salaries for comparable work, it does nothing to address inequalities of opportunity that may mean that women are far more likely to be in types of lower-paid work than men, or the capacity of 'the market' to pay people for their work at a rate that is too low for one to live on. In other words, formal equality works *within* existing economic, political, legal and social structures, but it cannot address the inequalities that those structures produce, reflect and perpetuate. Substantive equality, on the other hand, recognises and attempts to address these structures and has, Fredman argues, four key aims: redistribution, recognition, participation and transformation.[84] The two, then, are clearly vastly different things.

[80] *Sejdić and Finci v Bosnia and Herzegovina* App nos 27996/06 and 34836/06 (ECtHR, 22 December 2009).

[81] At the time of writing (2025), only 20 (out of 46) member states have ratified Protocol 12: see at www.coe.int/en/web/conventions/full-list?module=signatures-by-treaty&treatynum=177. A significant number of states signed but never ratified this Protocol. Some states, for example, the UK, have neither signed nor ratified the Protocol.

[82] See broadly Shreya Atrey, *Intersectional Discrimination* (Oxford University Press, 2019); Shreya Atrey, 'Structural Racism and Race Discrimination' (2021) 74 *Current Legal Problems* 1.

[83] Catherine Barnard and Bob Hepple, 'Substantive Equality' (2000) 59(3) *Cambridge Law Journal* 562, 563.

[84] Sandra Fredman, 'Substantive Equality Revisited' (2016) 14(3) *International Journal of Constitutional Law* 712; see also Sandra Fredman, 'Providing Equality; Substantive Equality

If the right to non-discrimination within the Convention – either in Article 14 or in the stand-alone Protocol 12 form – reflects this formal conception of equality then it seems unlikely to be able to promote socio-economic equality *even if* the Convention protects socio-economic rights, which, as we have already seen, it might be said to do in a quite limited sense. The earlier jurisprudence on Article 14 certainly suggests its interpretation and application as an instrument of formal equality, resulting in what O'Connell calls the 'failure of the Strasbourg Court to promote a substantive conception of equality which would address questions of systematic disadvantage and oppression'.[85] Indeed, whilst this criticism is directed at the cases in which Article 14 was used by the Court, it is important to note that there were many cases in which Article 14 was pleaded but where the Court made its decision solely on the basis of other Articles,[86] such as *Sander v the United Kingdom*,[87] in which a violation of Article 6 was found in respect of racist comments by jury members but in which Article 14 is hardly discussed at all.[88]

The structure of Article 14 means that any attempt to establish impermissible discrimination must first satisfy the Court that the behaviour complained of falls within the 'ambit' of another Convention right. In many cases, the Court has given scant, if any, attention to the ambit requirement, albeit largely by dealing with the complaint under another Article altogether. For example, in LGBTQAI+ rights cases, the Court has primarily considered the claims under Article 8 alone, and not as discrimination under Article 14 taken in conjunction with Article 8.[89] Johnson argues that finding a violation of the discrimination provisions

> matters because it sends the clear and unequivocal message that a violation of human rights has occurred because of unacceptable prejudice. In contrast, when the Court says it is not necessary to examine a complaint about a difference in treatment based on sexual orientation under [Article 14] it fails to explicitly 'call out' prejudice against gay and lesbian people.[90]

---

and the Positive Duty to Provide Resources' (2005) 21 *South African Journal on Human Rights* 163, 167.

[85] Rory O'Connell, 'Cinderella comes to Ball: Article 14 and the right to non-discrimination in the ECHR' (2009) 29 *Legal Studies* 211, 212.

[86] For analysis, see Colin Harvey and Steven Livingstone, 'Protecting the Marginalised: The role of the ECHR' (2001) 51 *Northern Ireland Legal Quarterly* 445.

[87] *Sander v the United Kingdom* [2000] ECHR 194.

[88] For critique, see Marie-Benedicte Dembour, 'Still Silencing the Racism Suffered by Migrants … The Limits of Current Developments under Article 14 ECHR' (2009) 11 *European Journal of Migration and Law* 221.

[89] See, for example, *Lustig-Prean and Beckett v the United Kingdom* [1999] ECHR 71.

[90] Paul Johnson 'Sexual orientation discrimination and Article 14 of the European Convention on Human Rights: the problematic approach of the European Court of Human Rights' (2023) 6 *European Human Rights Law Review* 548, 563.

Although this might be said to sidestep the prima facie restrictiveness of the ambit requirement, it remains challenging to address socio-economic inequality by using this approach, not least because the Court is largely limited to considering socio-economic matters within the context of expressly protected civil and political rights. However, the Court has shown some creativity in bringing socio-economic matters within the ambit of rights, even finding that welfare payments can fall within the ambit of Article 1 of Protocol 1, notwithstanding its general position that money is not property.[91] It has also been proactive in the context of employment, finding, for example, that an employment ban might have an impact on the right to respect for private life under Article 8 because it removes the capacity to make a living.[92]

Importantly, there is no requirement that the 'primary' right be violated for the Court to find that Article 14 has been violated;[93] in other words, even if the right to property is not violated, it might be discriminatorily applied in a manner that violates Article 14. This principle of autonomy is critical to the non-discrimination case law of the Court,[94] not least because it allows for the Court to bring socio-economic matters within the 'ambit' of a Convention right for the purposes of Article 14, with relatively little attendant risk of allegations of illegitimacy.[95]

Finding that alleged discrimination falls within the ambit of the rights protected by the Convention is only the first step of the test of discriminatory treatment used by the Court. After finding that the treatment complained of falls within the ambit of a Convention right, the Court considers whether there is indeed a difference in treatment, and then whether there is an objective and reasonable justification for such difference. For some time, the Court took a relatively conservative approach to this latter question, focusing largely on whether differences in treatment could be justified through the application of a proportionality test:[96] a classically 'formal' approach to equality. However, in recent years some scholars have discerned important shifts in the Court's approach, even to the extent that, Fredman argues, 'recent jurisprudence … contains many glimmers of substantive equality'.[97] Fredman finds this not only

[91] *Gaygusuz v Austria* (n 68); *Luczak v Poland* [2007] ECHR 986 (but cf *Stec and Others v the United Kingdom* [2006] ECHR 1162.

[92] *Sidabras and Džiautas v Lithuania* App nos 55480/00 and 59330/00 (ECtHR, 27 October 2004).

[93] This was not always the case; earlier case law required a breach of the original right (making an Article 14 analysis somewhat unnecessary); see Fredman (n 5).

[94] *Case 'Relating to Certain Aspects of the Laws on the Use of Languages in Education in Belgium' (merits)*, 23 July 1968, Series A no 6.

[95] On ambit and its connection to autonomy, see Aaron Baker, 'The Enjoyment of Rights and Freedoms: A New Conception of the "Ambit" under Article 14 ECHR' (2006) 69(5) *Modern Law Review* 714.

[96] *Belgian Linguistic Case* (n 94); *Abdulaziz, Cabales and Balkandali v the United Kingdom*, 28 May 1985, Series A no 94.

[97] Fredman (n 5) 274.

in what she called the 'elasticity of grounds' (ie the Court's willingness to recognise non-articulated grounds of discrimination, considered above), but also in the gradual move away from focusing exclusively on a formal assessment of whether treatment was 'equal'. In *Thlimmenos*, the Court found that excluding all those with criminal convictions from admission to the profession of accountant discriminated against those, like the applicants, whose criminal convictions related to conscientious objection (in this case to military service, grounded in religious belief). The Court thus accepted that discrimination could arise where 'States without an objective and reasonable justification fail to treat differently persons whose situations are significantly different'.[98] In *DH v Czech Republic*, the Court then established the important principle that indirect discrimination could violate Article 14, so that 'a difference in treatment may take the form of disproportionately prejudicial effects of a general policy or measure which, though couched in neutral terms, discriminates against a group',[99] even if that was not its intent.[100] Whilst Article 14, then, has its limitations, it clearly has the capacity to be deployed in a manner that tackles some serious socio-economic inequalities *where they relate to the exercise of Convention rights.*

On the face of it Protocol 12's protection against discrimination should offer a greater scope for transformative change. Like Article 14, it lists indicative and non-exhaustive grounds, and it can be deployed in respect of any right 'set forth by law'. Although the case law on Protocol 12 is limited,[101] the Explanatory Report to Protocol 12 suggests that its scope is intended to be rather wide, applying where a person is discriminated against:

(a) In the enjoyment of any right expressly granted under national law;
(b) In the enjoyment of any right that can be inferred from a clear obligation of a public authority under national law;
(c) By a public authority in the exercise of a discretionary power;
(d) By any other act or omission of a public authority.[102]

The first case relating to Protocol 12 was a Grand Chamber judgment in *Sejdic' and Finci v Bosnia and Herzegovina*.[103] Part of this judgment was concerned with the fact that in Bosnia, only people who declared themselves as Bosniacs, Croats and Serbs could run for the presidency: the applicants were none of these. As the right to free elections in Article 3 of Protocol 1 does not cover presidential elections, Article 14 was inapplicable, but Bosnia and Herzegovina had ratified Protocol 12. The Court found a violation of Article 1 of Protocol 12

[98] *Thlimmenos v Greece* [2000] ECHR 162, para 44.
[99] *DH and Others v the Czech Republic* [2007] ECHR 922, para 184.
[100] *Oršuš and Others v Croatia* App no 15766/03 (ECtHR, 16 March 2010), para 150.
[101] The Court's case law database HUDOC shows only 16 Chamber and 2 Grand Chamber judgments that involved considerations of Protocol 12.
[102] Council of Europe, Explanatory Note to Protocol No 12 to the Convention for the Protection of Human Rights and Fundamental Freedoms (2000).
[103] *Sejdić and Finci v Bosnia and Herzegovina* (n 80).

since the applicants, who identified as Roma and Jewish respectively, could not run for these positions. In doing so, the Court held that the meaning of discrimination under Protocol 12 was the same as under Article 14, so that justification for differences in treatment was possible. However, in this case no sufficiently robust justification for the difference in treatment between the applicants existed. Accordingly, the right to non-discrimination had been violated. Similarly, in *Kovačević v Bosnia and Herzegovina*, the Court held that the applicant's inability to vote for the candidate of his choice due to a combination of ethnic and territorial requirements violated Article 1 of Protocol 12.[104]

The fact that Protocol 12 is not considered where an application can be decided under Article 14,[105] combined with the relatively low number of ratifications of Protocol 12, means that the case law is scant. However, in the existing case law there are indications that it is enabling some expansion of the protection against discrimination, largely because it is not limited to discrimination in enjoyment of Convention rights. Thus, the capacity of the Convention to progress socio-economic equality in Europe will depend on the extent to which the germs of substantive equality discernible in more recent jurisprudence are developed in the future.

Conclusion

The traditional division between socio-economic rights and civil and political rights is artificial. The relationships between these bodies of rights are complex but clear, and it is through recognising these relationships that the ECtHR has managed to develop a jurisprudence that is concerned with conditions of material wellbeing. However, the Court is unquestionably limited by the text of the Convention, which is largely concerned with civil and political rights, whilst the Social Charter and its Committee have a clearer focus on socio-economic rights. These limitations have meant that the Court has exercised understandable caution in addressing socio-economic wellbeing, tending, for example, to require extreme deprivation before intervening. Of course, the Court's role in achieving substantial equality is clear; however, what is also clear is that the ECtHR was not created to achieve this objective. This in turn means that certain occupations of limited activity of the Court in this area are clearly misplaced.

Further Reading

Sandra Fredman, 'Emerging from the Shadows: Substantive Equality and Article 14 of the European Convention on Human Rights' (2016) 16(2) *Human Rights Law Review* 273.

[104] *Kovačević v Bosnia and Herzegovina* [2023] ECHR 625.
[105] *Sejdić and Finci v Bosnia and Herzegovina* (n 80), para 51.

Corina Heri, *Responsive Human Rights: Vulnerability, Ill-Treatment, and the ECHR* (Hart Publishing, 2021).

Katie Morris, 'Vulnerability, Care Ethics and the Protection of Socioeconomic Rights via Article 3 ECHR' (2023) 23 *Human Rights Law Review* 1.

Alastair Mowbray, *The Development of Positive Obligations under the European Convention on Human Rights by the European Court of Human Rights* (Hart Publishing, 2004).

Margot Salomon, 'Of Austerity, Human Rights and International Institutions' (2015) 21(4) *European Law Journal* 521.

8

Implementing the Convention: The Execution of Judgments of the Court

Throughout this book we have considered several debates relating to the interpretation and application of the European Convention on Human Rights (the ECHR or the Convention). However, we have largely left unconsidered whether the Convention really 'works' as a framework for the protection of rights; whether it is *effective*. This question is complex. It relates to a whole host of different sub-issues, including the extent to which national parliaments take account of the Convention, whether it is integrated into policy and decision-making processes, and so on. The issue of effectiveness of the Convention is in the heart of the most recent developments within the system. For instance, during the most recent Summit of the heads of states and governments in Reykjavík in 2023, execution of judgments was a prominent discussion point. The final Declaration of the Summit makes a direct reference to execution of judgments: the heads of state reaffirmed 'our unconditional obligation to abide by the final judgments of the European Court of Human Rights in any case to which we are parties'.[1] In this chapter, we look critically at the implementation of the jurisprudence of the European Court of Human Rights (the ECtHR or the Court).

First, we consider the Court's capacity to order remedies in situations where a breach of the Convention is found. To that end, Debate 1 asks what remedies the Court can order. This is more than a simple doctrinal or formal question. As will become clear, over the years the Court has evolved its remedial capacities from merely delivering declaratory judgments and ordering just satisfaction (the payment of monies to successful applicants) to requiring action that might address underlying causes of violations.

This active approach to the development of remedies in the Court goes fundamentally to the question of whether and, if so, how the Court can effectively address rights violations by the Contracting Parties, and indeed how far the Court should go in developing mechanisms to make its own judgments more

[1] Reykjavik Declaration at https://rm.coe.int/4th-summit-of-heads-of-state-and-government-of-the-council-of-europe/1680ab40c1, 4.

effective. There is a clear international *legal* obligation on a respondent state to execute the judgment of the Court and implement the remedies as ordered (Article 46). However, in Debate 2 we go beyond this purely doctrinal legal duty to explore broader and more contentious questions of states' resistance to execution of ECtHR judgments. What arguments do states make when they are not inclined to abide by the legal obligation in Article 46, and how might these arguments be addressed?

Moving beyond the strictly doctrinal question of whether states are legally obliged to execute the judgments of the Court is important for two reasons. The first, which we consider in Debate 2, is that it is increasingly clear that the 'mere' fact of legal obligation is not sufficient to compel some states to remedial action. Instead, at least some Contracting Parties to the Convention resist execution based on resource constraints, alleged incompatibility with domestic law, or arguments of the democratic illegitimacy of the ECtHR when considered alongside domestic political and legal institutions. Developing convincing arguments in response to such recalcitrance is clearly fundamental to the future effectiveness of the Convention.

The second reason why it is important to develop arguments in favour of the implementation of the Court's judgments that go beyond bald statements of legal obligation is reflected in Debate 3. In this debate, we consider whether non-respondent states should give effect to ECtHR judgments. Although non-respondent states are not legally 'bound' by the ECtHR's judgments, the effective implementation of the Convention is best achieved through the Contracting Parties' taking steps to ensure compliance with the Convention before the point is reached where litigation in Strasbourg is required. It is thus important to consider whether and, if so, why states *ought to* give effect to these judgments, even if they are not strictly obliged to do so.

Finally, in Debate 4 we reflect on whether the new advisory opinions by the ECtHR can enhance Convention's domestic embeddedness. If advisory opinions prove to be effective, the principles articulated therein can be implemented in the practice of national courts even before the legally binding judgment is delivered by the ECtHR. The current and potential future utility of advisory opinions is discussed here.

Debate 1

What Remedies Can the Court Order?

At the start of its operation, the ECtHR issued only declaratory judgments, meaning that if the Court had found a violation of the Convention, it would not prescribe the exact measures that the Contracting Parties should undertake to ensure compliance with the Convention. Although the judgments of the Court are binding on respondent Contracting Parties under Article 46, this approach meant that the Court would avoid interfering with (or being accused of interfering with) the sovereignty of the Contracting Parties by dictating the mode of execution of a particular judgment. The Committee of Ministers would then decide whether the measures adopted by the respondent state were sufficient to implement the judgment. In recent years, the Court has become more prescriptive about the measures a respondent state needs to undertake to comply with the Convention. Before we consider the evolution of the Court's attitude to remedies, we first examine what remedies are available to the Court.

These remedies are known as individual and general measures, and it is assumed that the states will react to an adverse judgment by instigating such measures to address the violation that has been identified. Still, in most cases, the Court does not specify these measures beyond financial remedy (ie just satisfaction) but leaves it to the states and the Committee of Ministers to work out the means of execution. In *Marckx v Belgium*, for example, the Court stated that 'the Court's judgment is essentially declaratory and leaves to the State the choice of the means to be utilised in its domestic legal system for performance of its obligation'.[2] Over recent years, however, the Court has begun to be more specific relating to what respondent states must do to execute a judgment.

Individual measures normally include just satisfaction that must be paid to the applicant to cover their pecuniary and/or non-pecuniary damages. Just satisfaction is governed by Article 41 of the Convention, which states that if the Court finds that there has been a violation of the ECHR, and if the internal law of the Contracting Party concerned allows only partial reparation to be made, the Court shall, if necessary, afford just satisfaction to the injured party. On the face of it, Article 41 seems to require that the national law of the Contracting Party would not be sufficient to provide for compensation, and that national compensation is allocated before just satisfaction from the ECtHR could be awarded. While the Court originally stuck firmly to the principle that both requirements would have to be fulfilled, and would sometimes deliver a separate judgment on the matter, it now tends to analyse just satisfaction in the final paragraphs of the operative part of almost every judgment.[3] Indeed, the award of just satisfaction has become more or less standard, with very little attention given to the apparent requirements of Article 41.[4]

This raises a question of whether it is appropriate for the Court to award such compensation almost automatically and without carefully considering the constraints enshrined in Article 41. This debate is of importance beyond the seemingly simple question of adherence to Article 41: the ECtHR was not created to replace national mechanisms for compensation but to be subsidiary to them, so that its function should be about articulating and applying the Convention standards, rather than awarding monetary compensation per se. This is not least because the Convention will be most effective if an adverse finding in Strasbourg results in a change to state practice, and not merely the

[2] *Marckx v Belgium*, [1979] ECHR 2, para 58.

[3] See, as one example of many, *Ananyev v Russia* [2009] ECHR 1241, para. 64.

[4] Compare, for example, the Court's handling of just satisfaction in *De Wilde, Ooms and Versyp v Belgium (Article 50)* [1972] ECHR 1 and *Manerov v Russia* [2016] ECHR 19.

payment of monetary compensation, as states have sometimes argued is the extent of their remedial obligation.[5]

This is not to suggest that the payment of monetary compensation is unimportant; for many, access to the ECtHR may be their last chance of recognition of rights violation and the payment of appropriate compensation following a lack of success in the domestic legal system. Moreover, since the Court has relatively few tools of implementation in its arsenal, just satisfaction in the form of monetary compensation may, in some cases, act as a sufficient incentive for implementation of the judgment and better compliance with the Convention. To some extent, this is likely to depend on the context in which the state is engaging with the Court: should the state not be minded, or able, to pay compensation or to engage constructively with the Convention system, 'simple' monetary awards against it are unlikely to nudge it towards rights adherence. Instead, the state may simply refuse to pay, and thus not to execute the judgment. Indeed, this is what Russia did in the case of *OAO Neftyanaya Kompaniya Yukos v Russia*[6] and what Turkey (as it then was) did in the case of *Cyprus v Turkey*,[7] both highly sensitive decisions in their domestic political contexts. However, in most cases, the Contracting Parties pay just satisfaction within three months of the judgment's becoming final. It is another aspect of individual measures – namely the precise actions that are required from the state in a particular case – that is the subject of more contestation.

Although the Court still delivers declaratory judgments in most cases, there are some instances in which it articulates the measures it expects the respondent state to take in order effectively to execute its judgments.[8] One of the first judgments in which the Court took this approach was *Assanidze v Georgia*.[9] In

[5] See Kanstantsin Dzehtsiarou and Alan Greene, 'Legitimacy and the Future of the European Court of Human Rights: Critical Perspectives from Academia and Practitioners' (2011) 12 *German Law Journal* 1707, 1709.

[6] *OAO Neftyanaya Kompaniya Yukos v Russia* [2011] ECHR 1342. The Constitutional Court of Russia declared this case unexecutable. See Judgment of 19 January 2017 No 1-П/2017 in the case concerning the resolution of the question of the possibility to execute in accordance with the Constitution of the Russian Federation the Judgment of the European Court of Human Rights of 31 July 2014 in the case of OAO Neftyanaya Kompaniya Yukos v Russia in connection with the request of the Ministry of Justice of the Russian Federation. A courtesy translation is available on the website of the Russian Constitutional Court, at www.ksrf.ru/en/Decision/Judgments/Documents/2017__January_19_1-P.pdf. On 16 March 2022, Russia was expelled from the Council of Europe. Just satisfaction in this judgment has not been paid and there is little prospect that it will be in future.

[7] *Cyprus v Turkey (just satisfaction)* App no 25781/94 (12 May 2014). The response of Turkey: 'Turkey won't pay Cyprus despite decision in Strasbourg' (*Deutsche Welle*, 13 May 2014) at www.dw.com/en/turkey-wont-pay-cyprus-despite-decision-in-strasbourg/a-17631966.

[8] On the prevalence and effect of specifying such measures see Alastair Mowbray, 'An Examination of the European Court of Human Rights' Indication of Remedial Measures' (2017) 17(3) *Human Rights Law Review* 451.

[9] *Assanidze v Georgia* [2004] ECHR 140.

this case, Georgian authorities had illegally detained the applicant in violation of Article 5 of the Convention, in respect of which the Court held:

> As regards the measures which the Georgian State must take, subject to supervision by the Committee of Ministers, in order to put an end to the violation that has been found, the Court reiterates that its judgments are essentially declaratory in nature and that, in general, it is primarily for the State concerned to choose the means to be used in its domestic legal order in order to discharge its legal obligation under Article 46 of the Convention, provided that such means are compatible with the conclusions set out in the Court's judgment. This discretion as to the manner of execution of a judgment reflects the freedom of choice attached to the primary obligation of the Contracting States under the Convention to secure the rights and freedoms guaranteed. However, by its very nature, the violation found in the instant case does not leave any real choice as to the measures required to remedy it.[10]

The case of *Oleksandr Volkov v Ukraine* is an example of an even more directive approach to individual measures by the Court.[11] The case concerned the irregular dismissal of a member of the Supreme Court of Ukraine, in respect of whom the Court held that it

> cannot accept that the applicant should be left in a state of uncertainty as regards the way in which his rights should be restored. The Court considers that by its very nature the situation found to exist in the instant case does not leave any real choice as to the individual measures required to remedy the violations of the applicant's Convention rights. Having regard to the very exceptional circumstances of the case and the urgent need to put an end to the violations of Articles 6 and 8 of the Convention, the Court holds that the respondent State shall secure the applicant's reinstatement to the post of judge of the Supreme Court at the earliest possible date.[12]

Both cases illustrate the Court's development – on its own initiative – of a far more assertive role in, and more directed approach to, remedies for violation of the Convention. Whilst this might be attributed to a concern with the number of clear violations coming before the Court, and unenthusiastic or incomplete execution of judgments, questions about the legitimacy and potential impacts of the Court's having developed individual measures of this kind do arise. One might question the Court's authority in this relation: there is no clear textual mandate within the Convention for instructing states to take such measures and, as a subsidiary international court, it might be considered that its role is to identify violations and then leave it to domestic authorities to determine *how* (although not *whether*) to address them through execution of the ECtHR's

[10] ibid, para 202.
[11] *Oleksandr Volkov v Ukraine* [2013] ECHR 32.
[12] ibid, para 208.

judgment. This in effect creates a feedback loop between the Strasbourg system of human rights protection and domestic authorities, through which the optimal standard can be developed.[13] On the other hand, one might argue that remedial innovation of this kind is a logical development of the Court's jurisdiction over individual complaints, which was originally optional but has now developed into a cornerstone of the Convention system automatically applicable to all state parties. Without the potential to direct individual measures to remedy the identified rights violations in a particular case, one might question the usefulness of the Court per se. Furthermore, the Court had earlier been criticised for its lack of willingness to identify specific remedies, which some considered to be an impediment to the effective execution of its judgments.[14] The Court thus began to develop its more specific remedial approach, moving away (in large part) from providing primarily declaratory relief.[15]

General measures 'adopted ... [to] prevent ... new violations similar to that or those found or [to] put ... an end to continuing violations'[16] require substantial and sometimes systemic change in domestic law, and are, perhaps unsurprisingly, thus sometimes met with considerable controversy. In some cases, the Court *only* required general measures for execution of the judgment. For instance, in the case of *Hirst (No 2)* the Court found that the blanket disenfranchisement of prisoners in the UK violated the Convention[17] and that a change of law on prisoner disenfranchisement (a general measure) was required for UK law to comply with the Convention.

For some, the development and deployment of explicit references to general measures in the Court's judgments in recent years illustrates its increasing willingness to be 'active' (or some might say 'activist') in response to structural problems in human rights protection in a particular country. Indeed, the development of pilot judgments also suggests that the Court is trying to find ways to address systemic human rights challenges in the Contracting Parties.

Rule 61 of the Rules of Court provides that the Court may initiate a pilot-judgment procedure, and adopt a pilot judgment where the facts of an application reveal the existence of a structural or systemic problem or other

---

[13] For an in-depth discussion of feedback loops, see Kanstantsin Dzehtsiarou, 'Keep Me in the Loop: Feedback Exchange between the European Court of Human Rights and States' (2023) 22(3) *The Law & Practice of International Courts and Tribunals* 591.

[14] European Commission for Democracy Through Law (Venice Commission), *Opinion on the Implementation of the Judgments of the European Court of Human Rights*, Opinion no 209/2002 (December 2002); Philip Leach, 'No longer offering fine mantras to a parched child? The European Court's developing approach to remedies' in Andreas Føllesdal, Birgit Peters and Geir Ulfstein (eds), *Constituting Europe: The European Court of Human Rights in a National, European and Global Context* (Cambridge University Press, 2013) 142.

[15] See the analysis of this in Laurence Helfer, 'Redesigning the European Court of Human Rights: Embeddedness as a Deep Structural Principle of the European Human Rights Regime' (2008) 19 *European Journal of International Law* 125.

[16] Appendix 4 (Item 4.4), Rules of the Committee of Ministers for the Supervision of the Execution of Judgments and of the Terms of Friendly Settlements, Rule 6, Section 2.

[17] *Hirst v the United Kingdom (No 2)* [2005] ECHR 681.

similar dysfunction in the Contracting Party that has given rise, or may give rise, to similar applications. Rule 61 also establishes that the Court should, in its pilot judgment, identify both the nature of the structural or systemic problem or other dysfunction as established, and the type of remedial measures the Contracting Party concerned is required to take at the domestic level to address it. The Court can also set a deadline for the implementation or, in some cases only, initiation of its proposed reforms. The Court identified the rationale behind the pilot judgments as follows:

> [T]he pilot-judgment procedure was conceived as a response to the growth in the Court's caseload, caused by a series of cases deriving from the same structural or systemic dysfunction, and to ensure the long-term effectiveness of the Convention machinery. [The Court] reiterates that the dual purpose of the pilot-judgment procedure is on the one hand, to reduce the threat to the effective functioning of the Convention system and, on the other, to facilitate the speediest and most effective resolution of a dysfunction affecting the protection of the Convention rights in question in the national legal order.[18]

The pilot-judgment procedure is important but does not completely strip the Contracting Parties of the power to frame their internal policies. In pilot judgments, the Court does not specify in a detailed way the shape that the proposed reform should take, and the respondent state retains considerable discretion. Moreover, the ECtHR does not really develop its case law in pilot judgments but usually re-emphasises the well-established standard that the respondent state fails to implement. Pilot judgments usually follow a number of similar cases. The majority of recent pilot judgments deal with conditions of detention and relatively straightforward violations of the right to a fair trial (Article 6). Moreover, none of the pilot judgments in the years 2014–24 were delivered by the Grand Chamber of the Court – the formation that is usually entrusted with case-law development.

The addition of pilot judgments to the ECtHR's toolkit was a significant step towards the Court's attempt to ensure 'embeddedness' of the Convention in domestic systems,[19] but it is not without its risks. An obvious danger of the pilot-judgment procedure is that the Contracting Parties might not be willing actively to engage with it; that the Court would outline a clear remedy but find its judgment unexecuted, potentially calling its authority and effectiveness into question. In truth, the pilot-judgment procedure has been something of a mixed bag in terms of success.

In *Burdov v Russia (No 2)*, the Court considered an issue of non-execution of the enforceable judgments of national courts.[20] Such non-execution violates Article 6 of the Convention: the right to fair trial. The Court found that

---

[18] *Cannavacciuolo and Others v Italy* [2025] ECHR 29, para 489. A similar statement can be found in *Wałęsa v Poland* [2023] ECHR 9344, para 316.

[19] See further Helfer (n 13).

[20] *Burdov v Russia (No 2)* [2009] ECHR 86.

this was a widespread problem, not limited to the case before it, and indicated general measures that Russia should take to address it. In particular, the Court held that

> the respondent State must introduce a remedy which secures genuinely effective redress for the violations of the Convention on account of the State authorities' prolonged failure to comply with judicial decisions delivered against the State or its entities. Such a remedy must conform to the Convention principles as laid down notably in the present judgment and be available within six months from the date on which the present judgment becomes final.[21]

Russia requested the extension of the six-month term for execution, and after about 12 months introduced a new law that provided a domestic remedy for failure to execute the final judgments of domestic courts.[22] While the ECtHR initially indicated that the remedy was prima facie effective and thus required applicants to exhaust it before applying to Strasbourg,[23] it has since become clear that the Russian legislation introduced following *Burdov (No 2)* was not effective in resolving the identified issue. Thus in *Ilyushkin v Russia* and *Kalinkin v Russia*, the Court held there was still no effective domestic remedy by which to complain of delays in executing domestic judgments.[24] While in this case the remedy was established, and this allowed for resolution of the problem, albeit partially, there are examples in which the ECtHR had effectively to admit defeat. In the pilot judgment dealing with similar issue as in *Burdov (No 2)* but in Urkaine – *Ivanov v Ukraine* – the Court stated that

> the respondent State must grant adequate and sufficient redress, within one year from the date on which the present judgment becomes final … In the Court's view, such redress may be achieved through implementation proprio motu by the authorities of an effective domestic remedy in those cases … If, however, the respondent State fails to adopt such measures following a pilot judgment and continues to violate the Convention, the Court will have no choice but to resume the examination of all similar applications pending before it and to take them to judgment so as to ensure effective observance of the Convention.[25]

The Court could not fulfil its promise, however, and did not ensure that the standard set in *Ivanov* could be effectuated at the national level. In 2017, the Court pronounced a judgment in *Burmych and others v Ukraine*, in which it stated that

---

[21] ibid, para 141.

[22] Federal Act 68-Ø from 30 April 2010, 'On compensation for a violation of the right of trial in reasonable time or right for a judicial act to be executed in reasonable time'.

[23] *Nagovitsyn and Nalgiyev v Russia* [2010] ECHR 1331.

[24] *Ilyushkin and others v Russia* App nos 5734/08 et seq (ECtHR, 17 April 2012); *Kalinkin and others v Russia* App no 34006/02 (ECtHR, 14 September 2006).

[25] *Yuriy Nikolayevich Ivanov v Ukraine* [2009] ECHR 1570, para 99.

> despite the significant lapse of time since the delivery of the Ivanov pilot judgment on 15 October 2009, the Ukrainian Government have so far failed to implement the requisite general measures capable of addressing the root causes of the systemic problem identified by the Court and to provide an effective remedy securing redress to all victims at national level.[26]

To the significant dissatisfaction of some judges, who even called it a 'denial of the right to individual application',[27] the ECtHR decided to transfer a high number of similar applications to the Committee of Ministers without a judgment.

In other cases, pilot procedures have helped to nudge change, even in highly contentious areas. *Greens and MT v the United Kingdom*[28] followed *Hirst (No 2)* and persistent structural problem of a blanket ban on voting for convicted persons held in detention. At the time of the decision, the UK Government had not yet executed *Hirst (No 2)* and the Court had received a further 2,500 applications relating to the ban on prisoner voting. In *Greens*, the Court adjourned examination of all pending applications on the matter and prescribed general measures to the UK in the following terms:

> [T]he respondent State must introduce legislative proposals … within six months of the date on which the present judgment becomes final, with a view to the enactment of an electoral law to achieve compliance with the Court's judgment in *Hirst* according to any time-scale determined by the Committee of Ministers.[29]

Although the Government did introduce legislative proposals that would allow some prisoners to vote, these proposals were originally rejected by an overwhelming majority of Parliament.[30] Meanwhile, numerous 'clone' cases against the UK progressed, all resulting in findings of Convention violations.[31] However, in late 2017 the UK Government proposed an approach to prisoner voting that was confirmed as sufficient by the Council of Europe, and which resulted in administrative changes enabling offenders released on licence to vote. Finally, in September 2018, the Committee of Ministers confirmed that it considered *Hirst (No 2)* to have been executed.[32] Whether this outcome can be attributed to intervention via a pilot judgment per se is unclear, and the minimally compliant nature of the change eventually introduced has certainly

---

[26] *Burmych and Others v Ukraine (striking out)* [2017] ECHR 894, para 146.

[27] ibid, Joint Dissenting Opinion of Judges Yudkivska, Sajó, Bianku, Karakaş, De Gaetano, Laffranque and Motoc, para 9.

[28] *Greens and MT v the United Kingdom* [2010] ECHR 1826.

[29] ibid, para 115.

[30] The Backbench Parliamentary Debates, 'Prisoners' Right to Vote' at www.publications.parliament.uk/pa/cm201011/cmhansrd/cm110210/debtext/110210-0002.htm.

[31] *Firth and others v United Kingdom* [2014] EHRR 874; *McHugh and others v United Kingdom* App no 51987/08 (ECtHR, 10 February 2015).

[32] Council of Europe, Committee of Ministers 1324th meeting, 7 September 2018.

attracted critical comment, not least because it did not result in any legislative change.

It is thus reasonable to ask whether the pilot judgment truly made any significant difference to rights-related remedy in any of these cases, or indeed whether it is effective in remedying structural or systemic rights violations per se (as opposed to effective in managing the Court's workload). The truth is that most of the Court's judgments are routinely executed: in general terms, only those judgments that are politically sensitive or require major resource (re)allocation to ensure their execution become problematic. The protracted tension between the Court and the UK on the question of prisoner voting exemplifies this, as does the arguably unsatisfactory way in which it was resolved, without legislative change and with a material change to voting rights for only a very small number of prisoners.

This reflects the concern that execution of pilot judgments (or indeed any judgments of the Court) may have as much to do with domestic political conditions as with the form of the judgment and the measures directed within it.[33] A judgment of the ECtHR might be particularly politically sensitive if the domestic parliament can block execution (for example by voting against legislative change required for execution), if it concerns unpopular minorities without the political power to exert sufficient pressure on the institutions of the state to create significant political costs for non-execution, or if the government operates in an environment in which the ECtHR is perceived to be actively and illegitimately interfering with the sovereignty of the respondent state.

Pilot judgments represent a relatively recent strategy on the part of the Court to be more prescriptive about general measures. That is not to say that declaratory findings of human rights violation are not useful: a merely declaratory finding should be sufficient to prompt political and legal reform to address the underpinning issue from which the rights violation might be said to flow. Combined with just satisfaction (where awarded), it can fulfil the two classical functions of remedy in public law, to 'redress the wrong done to the plaintiff … [while] … ensuring that future public action complies with the requirements of the law'.[34] However, the transformative potential of declarations of violation is very much dependent on its reception within the politico-legal context to which it is directed. Given the very wide range of domestic legal and political systems to which the ECtHR speaks, it is perhaps not surprising that it has supplemented declaratory relief and its ability to order just satisfaction with other approaches, including pilot judgments.

---

[33] Although specifying general measures in the operative part of the judgment does seem to enhance execution, the sample numbers are relatively small compared to the general number of cases before the Court. See further Mowbray (n 8).

[34] Aruna Sathanapally, *Beyond Disagreement: Open Remedies in Human Rights Adjudication* (Oxford University Press, 2012) 11.

DEBATE 2

MUST RESPONDENT STATES EXECUTE JUDGMENTS OF THE COURT?

Article 46 of the ECHR is very clear: the judgments of the Court are binding on the respondent states. As a result, there is an international legal obligation to execute them. We have already seen, in Debate 1, that the Court can order a range of remedies, some of which may be less challenging for a state to execute than others. However, notwithstanding the fact that execution may involve different challenges and different techniques depending on the form of remedy that is ordered, the Article 46 obligation to execute continues to apply. It does not discriminate between the different remedial forms.

Thus, the simple question of whether a respondent state *must* execute the judgments of the Court is amenable to a straightforward answer as a matter of international law: 'Yes'. Without equivocation, then, we can and should say that execution of ECtHR judgments is very simply a requirement of the rule of law: adherence to an existing legal obligation.[35] However, one might imagine a number of arguments against suggesting that respondent states must *always* execute the judgments against them that are handed down by the Court. We can divide these into arguments of principle, arguments of the constitution and arguments of practicality. We first outline some of the contours of each of these arguments, before suggesting an argument for execution despite them.

Arguments of Principle

Many of the member states of the Council of Europe are healthy democracies where laws are made by an elected parliament, whose role it is to reflect the will of the electorate in compliance with domestic and international legal obligations. Indeed, this is one of the bases upon which the turn to process-based review, which we considered in chapter 1, is predicated. It is inevitable that there will sometimes be situations in which being required to change the law following a decision of a 'foreign' court may cause tensions, notwithstanding the fact that doing so is a requirement of the rule of law.[36] If we leave to one side, for a moment, the *legal* argument of obligation, we can ask whether the proposition that a domestic parliament might resist execution and, through doing so, enter into a kind of feedback exchange with Strasbourg may not be not entirely outrageous in principle, particularly if the individual remedies (if any) that are ordered by the Court are given effect to but the general measures (such as legal change) are not. After all, if the implementation of the Convention is a matter for all the institutions of the state and not *only* the courts (as it is), then why is it that the courts may enter into a dialogue of contestation (as

[35] See, for example, Alice Donald, 'Tackling Non-Implementation in the Strasbourg System: The Art of the Possible?' (*EJIL: Talk*, 24 February 2018) at www.ejiltalk.org/author/adonald/.

[36] See also Article 27, VCLT.

considered in chapter 2 and further in Debate 3 below) but the other institutions of the state may not?

One answer to this provocative question may be that parliamentarians are likely to be swayed by popular opinion and a need to satisfy electoral wiles in a way that independent courts are not, and – if rights are about human dignity and not about bestowing upon people privileges that 'the majority' decides they should have – mere politics ought not to have the same dialogical status as courts. This argument might have an instinctive attraction in most European states, but it is a little more difficult to sustain within the constitutional tradition of the UK where, indeed, the constitution – including constitutional rights – *is* political and where Parliament is recognised as having a role (if not the ultimate role) in determining its content.[37] The argument may also be somewhat more difficult to sustain in states where the judiciary is compromised, either by a lack of judicial independence or by the design of judicial institutions in a way that privileges the views, policies and politics of the ruling party.[38] In recent years, there have been attempts to reshape the constitutional courts in Hungary and Poland, for example, to ensure that the government's desired outcome is likely to be shared by the majority of judges (even to the extent that the ECtHR has concluded that a Polish court was not 'a body compatible with the rule of law requirements' of the Convention[39]); and the courts of Türkiye were purged of approximately 4,000 so-called 'traitors' following the coup against President Erdoğan in 2016.

It is thus by no means clear that either the parliaments or the courts of the member states of the Council of Europe uniformly have the accountability, independence and respect for the rule of law on which such an argument is predicated. However, where the institutions in question *do* have those characteristics (at least to the extent possible in any polity), there are likely to be questions on which reasonable people might reasonably disagree,[40] and in relation to these the simple argument of legal obligation under Article 46 may not be sufficient to satisfy the dissenter who considers the decision of the domestic institutions to have a greater claim to authority, given its roots in a democratic, deliberative and reflective exercise, than that of the ECtHR.

One possible solution to this challenge would be the development of different standards for different member states, depending on how democratic they

[37] For the classical argument, see John Griffith, 'The Political Constitution' (1979) 42 *Modern Law Review* 1.

[38] For a recent analysis of judicial independence across Europe, see Consultative Council of European Judges, *Challenges for Judicial Independence and Impartiality in the Member States of the Council of Europe* SG/Inf(2015)3rev.

[39] *ML v Poland* App no 40119/21 (ECtHR, 14 December 2024), para 174. See also *Baka v Hungary* App no 20261/12 (ECtHR, 23 June 2016).

[40] Jeremy Waldron, 'The Core of the Case Against Judicial Review' (2006) 115 *Yale Law Journal* 1346.

are and how independent their judiciary is. One could argue that this approach has already been subtly adopted by the ECtHR, as some states are treated with more deference than others. However, this approach is deeply problematic – not only because the Court could be accused of applying double standards, but also because assessing the level of democracy and judicial independence is an increasingly complex task. These factors are not binary – they evolve over time, and explicitly taking them into account could lead to legal uncertainty and unpredictability in the Court's case law. This is precisely what the Court seeks to prevent within national legal systems and must be careful to avoid in its own practice.

Arguments of the Constitution

Situations where domestic constitutional law and international law are in conflict are particularly complex, but again domestic law may well have something to say about the relationship. A wide variety of approaches can be identified across Europe.[41]

The first is one that recognises the effective primacy of the international legal norm over the domestic constitutional norm. In such situations, a finding of incompatibility between the domestic constitutional provision and the international obligation will lead to a change in the domestic constitution, which will be given effect by the appropriate mechanism according to domestic law. For example, Article 11 of the Slovak Constitution provides that international treaties on human rights and basic liberties that were ratified by the Slovak Republic and promulgated in a manner determined by law take precedence over its own laws, provided they secure a greater extent of constitutional rights and liberties than domestic law does.[42]

The second approach is to recognise the domestic constitution as a 'block' on internationalism, so that the authority of an international provision is recognised as 'trumping' domestic law *inasmuch as it does not conflict with the Constitution*. Usually, this principle is developed and applied by the domestic courts themselves. In Italy, the ECHR is placed between the Constitution and the national statutes: below the former but above the latter.[43] Attaching a super-legislative status to the ECHR means that the Constitutional Court needs at least to consider the case law of the ECtHR. Yet the Italian Constitutional Court has limited the impact of the Strasbourg case law by suggesting that

[41] For a useful, although incomplete account, see Helen Keller and Alec Stone-Sweet (eds), *A Europe of Rights: The Impact of the ECHR on National Legal Systems* (Oxford University Press, 2008). See also Giuseppe Martinico and Oreste Pollicino (eds), *The Interaction between Europe's Legal Systems* (Edward Elgar, 2012); Iulia Motoc and Ineta Ziemele (eds), *The Impact of the ECHR on Democratic Change in Central and Eastern Europe Judicial Perspectives* (Cambridge University Press, 2016).

[42] See also Article 10 of the Constitution of the Czech Republic.

[43] Judgments Nos 348 and 349 (24 October 2007) (It).

Italian judges should give effect to 'consolidated law' or 'pilot judgments'.[44] In Germany, the Constitution has primacy over the ECHR.[45]

The third approach is to provide that a domestic court may specifically deem the decision of an international court to be incapable of execution because it conflicts with the domestic constitution. While it was a member of the Council of Europe, the Russian Federation was the only state in the Council of Europe in which such an approach was taken explicitly.

The fourth approach is expressly to incorporate the international standard at a sub-constitutional level, so that incompatibility with the Convention can result in, for example, a domestic court's 'interpreting up' a statute, but does not disturb the constitutional standard in question. This is the approach taken in Ireland, for example, under the ECHR Act 2003. In such a system, the incompatibility between the Convention and the Constitution may lead to constitutional change *where politics determines that it should*, but domestic law does not require such a change to be introduced.

The fifth approach is to give the ECHR – or the domestic statute implementing it – a constitutional status, so that it can only be changed in accordance with the requirements for amending constitutional statutes in the domestic legal system. This is what happened in Austria, where the ECHR has constitutional status and conflicts between the Convention and the *Bundes-Verfassungsgesetz* (which is the primary constitutional text) are satisfied by application of *lex posteriori derogat legi priori* principle (ie that a later law repeals an earlier law).[46] In the UK, the Human Rights Act 1998 has the status of a constitutional statute, so that the doctrine of implied repeal does not apply to it as it does to most statutes in the UK.[47] Whilst this does not give the ECHR the status of domestic constitutional law, it brings it obliquely into the constitutional realm through the obligation of the courts to account for ECtHR jurisprudence (under section 2), the power to interpret domestic statutes as far as possible in line with the Convention (under section 3) and the inclusion of much of the Convention text as a schedule to the Act.

All of these approaches reflect the complexity of the relationship between a domestic constitutional provision and the Convention. Whilst a domestic statute is an expression of democratic will refracted through parliamentary processes, a Constitution is something more: it is a mechanism for restraining political and democratic will, a superior law usually entrenched in some

[44] Judgment No 49 (26 March 2015) (It).

[45] This is laid down in *Görgülü* 2 BvR 1481/04 (14 October 2004) BVerfGE 111, 307 (Ger); see further Kanstantsin Dzehtsiarou and Natasa Mavronicola, 'Relation of Constitutional Courts/Supreme Courts to the ECtHR' in *Max Planck Encyclopaedia of Comparative Constitutional Law* (Oxford University Press, 2017).

[46] On the ECHR in Austria, see Daniela Thurnherr, 'The Reception Process in Austria and Switzerland' in Helen Keller and Alec Stone-Sweet (eds), *A Europe of Rights: The Impact of the ECHR on National Legal Systems* (Oxford University Press, 2008).

[47] *Thoburn v Sunderland CC* [2002] 4 All ER 156; *R (HS2 Action Alliance Ltd) v Secretary of State for Transport* [2014] UKSC 3.

way, often an expression of domestic values and not uncommonly a key mechanism in the creation of domestic constitutional culture. It is thus difficult when that domestic constitutional culture is at odds with a transnational legal order of which the state is a part (through membership) but which may not always accord with what governments sometimes describe as 'national values'. These contentious questions are often, but not always, associated with issues relating to societal norms, such as the definition of marriage. However, where a domestic constitution is understood as according the right to marry to opposite-sex couples only, for example, or as precluding the legalisation of abortion, one might argue that incompatibility with an international standard ought not be sufficient to force a change in that constitutional order, but that such change should emerge from domestic, organic processes of constitutional evolution.

Whilst that argument has a certain intellectual attraction to it, in practice international litigation is often a key lever for domestic activists and advocates who wish to bring about a shift in national constitutional provisions and constitutional cultures and values. Processes of constitutional change are not always accessible to marginalised groups and individuals, and sometimes an international 'nudge' is required to force an issue onto the agenda, or indeed to 'compel' the constitutional change itself. If this is acceptable in the case of ordinary legislation, one might argue that the acceptability of the same principle in relation to the Constitution ought to be conceded, and that it is only an unjustified veneration of the constitutional text as communicating some sense of common identity and values from which these marginalised individuals are often excluded that holds one back from taking such a position.

Arguments of Practicality

In some cases, non-execution is justified by the Contracting Parties because of practicality. This argument, once more, holds no truck from a strictly doctrinal perspective. It is nevertheless interesting, sometimes made by states, and thus worth considering. It can emerge in several ways.

First, and perhaps most obviously, where the ECtHR requires general measures, it simply may not be possible to undertake the legal change that this entails. If it requires fresh legislation, a parliamentary majority might not be secured. Where the legal change is constitutional, this may be even more complex. Although constitutional change is brought about by legislation in many states (such as Bulgaria (for most constitutional provisions)), it is common for legislation changing the constitution to require a 'super majority', as is the case in Czechia. Even a government with a simple majority may not be able to secure a super majority, and the upper house in bicameral systems may not be controlled by the federal government. It may operate without a whip,[48] have

[48] For example, there is no formal 'whip' in the UK's House of Lords.

unelected and non-party affiliation structures,[49] or represent states/cantons/länder and not be susceptible to control by the national governing parties, for example.[50] Some states even require an election to amend the Constitution. In Belgium, the law proposing constitutional change must be published, following which there is a general election; only after that can the proposed amendments to the Constitution be introduced (with a two-thirds majority in both Houses of Parliament), with the election as a *quasi*-referendum on the proposed change. In Denmark, a proposed change must be approved by parliament, following which a general election must be held. The new parliament elected in that general election must then approve the proposed amendment again, and there must then be a referendum of the people. Where constitutional change requires a referendum (as it also does in Ireland and Switzerland, for example), the referendum, even if put to the people, simply may not pass. It may well be the case that the people determine that *regardless of what the ECtHR says*, they want to maintain a constitutional position that is at odds with the Convention. If the ultimate decision-maker on constitutional change is the electorate, the most a government can realistically do by means of execution is to make a proposal and argue for its adoption: it cannot guarantee the required legal change. Thus, the very nature of bringing about constitutional change may be a real practical barrier to execution.

Even if complex legal change is not required, resource constraints may make execution of an ECtHR judgment difficult to achieve. In some cases, the general measures to be implemented – for example, to greatly accelerate criminal justice processes in order to tackle undue delay resulting in Article 6 violations – might often be achieved at an enormous cost, and there is an argument that allocating budget and prioritising between different areas of required investment is a matter that is best decided upon by governments themselves. This is, one might argue, particularly the case in situations of extremely limited resources, austerity, mass unemployment and high levels of poverty (including among children); conditions that prevail today in some European states. It is sometimes supposed that only socio-economic rights are costly to implement, but some civil and political rights are also resource-intensive: consider the price, for example, of improving the physical infrastructure of state's prisons, of establishing voting processes in extremely remote locations, or of providing free legal aid to all indigent criminal defendants. States' resources are not boundless, and their distribution always requires policy decisions by political institutions. In other words, prioritisation always operates when decisions about expenditure are being made, so one might argue that it is no effective defence to say 'we could not afford to execute the judgment', or 'we preferred to invest our resources elsewhere'. Indeed, the Court has made it clear

[49] For example, the Irish Senate is almost all unelected and is not organised in party-political terms.

[50] For example, in Germany.

that financial constraints cannot justify a failure to protect Convention rights.[51] That argument, which at first seems one of simple practicality, relates as closely to concepts of sovereignty as do arguments of principle and the constitution. At their heart, they are all arguments that come from a basic claim: *the ECtHR should not be able to tell us what to do.*

The Argument for Execution

Despite these arguments against execution, states have an obligation to execute judgments against them under Article 46. Indeed, there is also a broader international law obligation to do so: Article 26 of the Vienna Convention on the Law of Treaties (VCLT) requires states to respect the international treaties they have ratified, and Article 27 provides that provisions of domestic law cannot be relied upon to justify a failure to perform a treaty. The argument for executing judgments under Article 46(1), then, is one of legal obligation. That legal obligation relates to the broader project of creating an international rule of law: of recognising international legal obligations as legally binding (thus endorsing international law's status *qua* law) and of recognising the decisions of international courts as binding in the same way as those of domestic courts (thus recognising an international rule of law that cannot be subverted by simple will).

Of course, this is not to say that the decisions of international courts are in all senses *the same* as the decisions of domestic courts. In many significant ways they are different, and indeed domestic legal systems often have in-built mechanisms to reject the decisions of courts, not as to the outcome in a particular case but as to the broader legal framework. Thus, for example, if the Irish Supreme Court finds that a provision of the Constitution has a meaning that the Government does not consider workable or favourable, the Government can propose a change to the Constitution to the people and thus attempt to change the baseline legal norm.[52] The electorate, then, has the ultimate say. But in the meantime, the decision of the Supreme Court would be complied with; it is the authoritative legal instrument until a more authoritative one (in this case emanating directly from the people) comes into existence.

In other systems, it is Parliament that would decide on whether to change the Constitution, but the same general point stands: domestic legal systems tend to have processes that allow for ensuring the Court does not have 'the final say', so to speak, on the broader legal standard.[53] There is no consensus about the forms of democratic override in Europe: as we demonstrated, it can

[51] See, for example, *Azinas v Cyprus* App no 56679/00 (ECtHR, 20 June 2002), para 41.

[52] For more, see Fiona de Londras and David Gwynn Morgan, 'Constitutional Amendment in Ireland' in Xenophon Contiades (ed.), *Engineering Constitutional Change: A Comparative Perspective on Europe, Canada and the USA* (Routledge, 2012) 179.

[53] For a broader discussion, see Fiona de Londras, 'In Defence of Judicial Innovation and Constitutional Evolution' in Laura Cahillane, James Gallen and Tom Hickey (eds), *Judges, Politics and the Irish Constitution* (Manchester University Press, 2017) 9.

be done in some states, but the forms of such override are very diverse. At first blush, this is not as clearly present in the ECHR: whilst states can propose and initiate changes to the Convention text that may lead to the amendment of the Convention in due course, this is complex and requires widespread agreement – and ratification – from the other Contracting Parties. However, states *do* have ways to engage with the Court to try to revisit the baseline legal standard: through various feedback loops, through imaginative arguments before the Court, through 'signalling' disagreement with the Court's approach by means of parliamentary debates and so on.[54] The Court has ways of listening: through European consensus, through evolutive interpretation and through the margin of appreciation. Thus, whilst the system is different from that often found in domestic legal systems, this kind of response from states is possible and, sometimes, successful. Thus, the rule of law demands compliance with judgments of the Court in respect of a particular case, but that does not mean the system has no space within it for contestation and refinement of the standards in question per se.

This points to an important distinction in considering the question of non-execution: the distinction between *whether* to execute and *how* to execute. Whilst there is no question *in law* about whether a state must execute, there may be a question *in fact* about how the state has gone about this process of execution. Thus, the discourse that takes place between the Committee of Ministers and the state, and the possibility to seek clarification on what a judgment requires from the Court (under Article 46(3) and potentially Article 46(4)) are important mechanisms for figuring out whether the state's purported actions to execute the judgment suffice, whilst still ensuring that a state – even one that wants to mount a challenge to or is unhappy with the legal interpretation applied by the Court in the case – is positively engaged with the process of execution.

That engagement – that willingness to execute even if the state does not agree with the judgment as an expression of 'diffuse support'[55] for the Court – is of fundamental importance. Not only does it underpin the status of the Convention as law, and the rule of law in Europe, but it also protects the system against contagious non-execution, where states begin to claim not only that they can contest how to execute, but also that they can decline to execute at all. As the former Council of Europe Commissioner for Human Rights, Nils Muižnieks wrote, 'A future where each Council of Europe member state reorganises its internal constitutional hierarchy so that the Convention can be trumped is a danger to the rule of law in that state and in all other states.'[56]

---

[54] See, see Dzehtsiarou (n 13).

[55] See, for example, Yonatan Lupu, 'International Judicial Legitimacy: Lessons from National Courts' (2013) 14 *Theoretical Inquiries in Law* 437.

[56] Nils Muižnieks, 'Non-implementation of the European Court of Human Rights' Judgments: Our Shared Responsibility' (*electronic immigration network blog*, 23 August 2016) at www.ein.org.uk/blog/non-implementation-courts-judgments-our-shared-responsibility.

This reinforces the fact that the Council of Europe is a community of states, and that the Convention and the protection of rights thereunder is a collective enterprise. The action of one state, particularly a 'norm entrepreneur',[57] in undermining the Convention through a refusal to execute has potentially deleterious impacts on the entire system by encouraging or implicitly endorsing a similar approach in others.[58] Thus, there is a moral responsibility on states to engage positively and constructively with execution for the good of the system as a whole, and in order to ensure that the post-war European project(s) continue to be effective in protecting rights and freedoms across the Continent.

We know, however, that this moral and legal duty to execute judgments does not always translate into action, and thus a question as to whether states can be compelled to execute judgments arises. In practice, the Committee of Ministers mostly uses diplomatic pressure on Contracting Parties that have not executed judgments against them; an approach that is sometimes ineffective. The Committee also, however, has the legal power to initiate infringement proceedings under Article 46(4), which provides:

> If the Committee of Ministers considers that a High Contracting Party refuses to abide by a final judgment in a case to which it is a party, it may, after serving formal notice on that Party and by decision adopted by a majority vote of two-thirds of the representatives entitled to sit on the committee, refer to the Court the question whether that Party has failed to fulfil its obligation under [Article 46(1)].

Whether the infringement proceeding under Article 46(4) is useful is the subject of substantial debate. On the one hand, the Parliamentary Assembly of the Council of Europe, human rights activists and some commentators encourage the Committee of Ministers to use infringement proceedings against states on which other forms of pressure have been ineffective.[59] On the other side of this debate are those who think that utilisation of Article 46(4) has limited practical effect on improving the enforcement of the Court's judgments.[60]

Article 46(4) provides that if the Committee of Ministers considers that a Contracting Party refuses to abide by a final judgment in a case to which

---

[57] Norm entrepreneurs can be understood as those 'with the skills and resource to undertake a project or to make things happen' (Annie Herro, 'Norm Entrepreneurs Advocating the Responsibility to Protect, and Peacekeeping Reform Proposals' in David Curran et al (eds), *Perspectives on Peacekeeping an Atrocity Prevention* (Springer, 2015) 41). In this context, they are states with the ability to change the behaviour of others through their leadership, behaviour and representations.

[58] See, for example, Ed Bates, 'The Continued Failure to Implement *Hirst v UK*' (*EJIL: Talk*, 15 December 2015) at www.ejiltalk.org/the-continued-failure-to-implement-hirst-v-uk/.

[59] Karin de Vries, 'Implementation of Judgments of the European Court of Human Rights' (PACE, Report, 9 September 2015, Doc 13864); Donald (n 35).

[60] Fiona de Londras and Kanstantsin Dzehtsiarou, 'Mission Impossible? Addressing Non-Execution through Infringement Proceedings in the European Court of Human Rights' (2017) 66(2) *International and Comparative Law Quarterly* 467.

it is a party, it may, after serving formal notice on that Party and by decision adopted by a majority vote of two-thirds of the representatives entitled to sit on the Committee, refer to the Court the question whether that Party has failed to fulfil its obligation to implement the judgment. If the ECtHR finds that the state has failed to execute the judgment, this constitutes a further violation of the Convention (this time of Article 46(1): the obligation to execute).

The idea behind Article 46(4) was to give the Committee of Ministers an enforcement tool that would be more effective than diplomatic actions such as resolutions and discussions with the state, but less detrimental to the Council of Europe than suspending a state's membership. We have previously raised significant questions about the utility of Article 46(4), arguing that it will be almost impossible for the Committee of Ministers to initiate such proceedings,[61] and indeed between 2010, when Protocol 14 entered into force, and 2025 this procedure was used only twice. The reasons for this minimal deployment of this mechanism include the fact that a significant number of states need to effectively admit that the Committee is unable to execute the judgment; that this might halt the ongoing implementation if any; and finally that it would single out a particular state from the other states that might also have human rights issues. These challenges were overcome in two cases, both of which dealt with political prisoners. Arguably, a third case would have been sent to the Court under Article 46(4) – *Navalnyy v Russia* – if Russia had not been expelled from the Council of Europe.

We have also argued that the effectiveness of this procedure is questionable. We will now consider how useful the Court's two Article 46(4) judgments proved to be. For the first time, the Court delivered Article 46(4) judgment in the case of *Ilgar Mammadov*.[62] In 2014, the Court had found that the arrest and detention of Mammadov, a high-profile political opponent in Azerbaijan, violated Articles 5 and 18 of the Convention, specifically because the actions were politically motivated. The Court did not specify the individual measures to be taken to remedy that violation, but the Committee of Ministers quickly concluded that Mammadov was to be released 'without delay'.[63] Azerbaijan disputed this, and the standoff between them continued for three years, during which time a second case – *Mammadov v Azerbaijan (No 2)*[64] – was concluded in which the Court held that criminal proceedings

---

[61] ibid.

[62] *Proceedings under Article 46(4) in the case of Ilgar Mammadov v Azerbaijan* App no 15172/13 (ECtHR, 29 May 2019). See also 'Committee of Ministers Launches Infringement Proceedings against Azerbaijan', *Council of Europe Newsroom*, 5 December 2017 at www.coe.int/en/web/portal/-/council-of-europe-s-committee-of-ministers-launches-infringement-proceedings-against-azerbaijan.

[63] Resolution DH-DD(2014)1450.

[64] *Mammadov v Azerbaijan (No 2)* App no 919/15 (ECtHR, 5 March 2018).

against Mammadov also violated Article 6 of the Convention. The Committee of Ministers initiated infringement proceedings under Article 46(4) in 2017. In the Article 46(4) proceeding, the ECtHR concluded that Azerbaijan had failed to execute the first judgment.[65] The Court reached this conclusion by considering that the only logical remedy to a violation of Articles 5 and 18, that is a politically motivated arbitrary detention, was the expunging of charges and release of the detained person. Although the case left some things unanswered,[66] it is nevertheless an important indication that the Committee of Minister and the Court are prepared to address non-execution head on. Azerbaijan released Mammadov in August 2018, before the infringement proceedings had been concluded. In 2020, the Supreme Court of Azerbaijan acquitted him and ordered compensation.[67] One might argue that this Article 46(4) judgment was a clear success, effectively 'forcing' Azerbaijan to release Mammadov. However, one might also suggest that this judgment was successful in very specific situation, and this ad hoc success cannot be used to conclude that every Article 46(4) judgment will be effective.

The second Article 46(4) judgment, in *Kavala v Türkiye*, proved that the concerns about the effectiveness of Article 46(4) were not groundless.[68] This case was also about a political leader who was arrested by the authorities, and where the ECtHR found violations of Articles 5 and 18 and ordered the immediate release of the applicant. This was not done, and the Committee of Ministers requested an Article 46(4) judgment. In 2022, in the infringement proceedings, the Court decided that Turkey had not complied with its initial judgment:[69] the conclusion was hardly surprising, and one might argue that it did not require confirmation from 17 Judges of the Grand Chamber. Unlike Mammadov, Kavala has not been released; moreover, in the meantime Turkish courts have sentenced Kavala to life imprisonment. It seems that in this situation, Article 46(4) proved to be much less effective. Moreover, the fact that two judgments of the Court have now been ignored by the authorities in Türkiye arguably undermines the legitimacy and reputation of the whole system. One might wonder whether this failed attempt to put pressure on Türkiye could mean the end of this procedure, or whether the Committee of Ministers will be willing to use it again.

[65] *Proceedings under Article 46(4) in the case of Ilgar Mammadov v Azerbaijan* (n 62).

[66] See, eg, Basak Çalı, 'No Going Nuclear in Strasbourg' (*Verfassgunsblog*, 30 May 2019) at https://verfassungsblog.de/no-going-nuclear-in-strasbourg/; Kanstantsin Dzehtsiarou, 'Mammadov v Azerbaijan (Eur Ct HR)' (2020) 59(1) *International Legal Materials* 35.

[67] Council of Europe, 'Azerbaijan Supreme Court acquits human rights defenders to execute the European Court's judgments', 28 April 2020 at www.coe.int/en/web/execution/-/azerbaijani-supreme-court-acquits-human-rights-defenders-to-execute-the-european-court-s-judgments.

[68] *Kavala v.Turkey* [2019] ECHR 898.

[69] *Kavala v Türkiye (infringement proceedings)* App no 28749/18 (ECtHR, 11 July 2022).

Debate 3

Should Non-Respondent States Give Effect to Judgments of the Court?

Judgments of the ECtHR do not have *erga omnes* effect. In other words, they are legally binding on the respondent states *only*. The Court's judgments commonly include both a determination of the dispute before it *and* often statements on the meaning of the Convention and its provisions. Such statements are, of course, of relevance beyond the particular facts of the case before the Court; while the ECtHR has the role of developing an autonomous and determinative interpretation of the Convention, responsibility for implementation of the Convention is predominantly the responsibility of the Contracting Parties. This reflects the principle of subsidiarity that underpins the Court's jurisdiction.[70] Thus, any expectation that the Convention *as interpreted by the Court* would be applied and implemented at national level is a logical consequence of the functioning of the system. Reflecting this, it is now widely accepted that decisions of the ECtHR enjoy *res interpretata*, that is the principle that judgments of the Court have interpretive authority.[71] This is relevant to all parts of the state: the executive is expected to plan policy by reference to its Convention obligations, the legislature to attempt to legislate only in compliance with the Convention, public authorities to apply and implement the law and bureaucracy of the state consistent with Convention rights, and courts to take account of the Convention and case law of the ECtHR to the extent permissible by domestic law. All must thus be cognisant of how the Court has interpreted the Convention.

It is on domestic courts and their role in implementing the Convention that we concentrate here. Consideration of this requires a preliminary appreciation of the different approaches to the role of international law in domestic legal systems across the Council of Europe. It is sometimes said that the relationship between municipal and international law can be roughly categorised as either monist or dualist, with monist systems treating international law as having domestic effect upon ratification, and dualist systems requiring explicit implementation (usually by legislation) before an international legal instrument can be relied on as binding authority in domestic law. However, as we have already

[70] See Dean Spielmann, 'Judgments of the European Court of Human Rights Effects and Implementation', Keynote Speech at www.echr.coe.int/Documents/Speech_20130920_Spielmann_Gottingen_ENG.pdf, 5; Robert Spano, 'Universality or Diversity of Human Rights?' (2014) 14(3) *Human Rights Law Review* 487.

[71] See, for example, Oddny Arnardottir, '*Res Interpretata, Erga Omnes* Effect and the Role of the Margin of Appreciation in Giving Domestic Effect to the Judgments of the European Court of Human Rights' (2017) 28(3) *European Journal of International Law* 819; Adam Bodnar, '*Res Interpretata*: Legal Effect of the European Court of Human Rights' Judgements for other States Than Those Which Were Party to the Proceedings' in Yves Haeck and Eva Brems (eds), *Human Rights and Civil Liberties in the 21st Century* (Springer, 2013) 223.

seen, across the Council of Europe there is a wide variety of approaches even within these two broad schools.

Even if the Convention has domestic legal effect, however, the domestic impact of judgments from Strasbourg against other Contracting Parties is a matter of some contention, not least because there is no international legal obligation for the national authorities to execute those judgments: such obligation exists only in relation to the respondent state in a particular case. Much depends on judicial approaches towards such judgments. In some states, such as Lithuania and Croatia, these judgments are treated as effectively binding; in others, such as the UK and Ireland, they are explicitly non-binding, although they are to be taken into account when considering Convention-related cases. Where domestic law has made the jurisprudence of the ECtHR binding on its courts then there is little to debate; the principled decision on the role of these judgments has been taken *as a matter of domestic law* and that domestic law is simply applied. However, where domestic law allows for the domestic court to take account of *but not be bound by* these judgments, debates about what this does – and should – mean may ensue. This is the case in the United Kingdom.

Section 2 of the Human Rights Act 1998 requires domestic courts to take account of Strasbourg jurisprudence; almost identical wording is used in the European Convention on Human Rights Act 2003 in Ireland. On the face of it, this means that such decisions ought to be treated just as other persuasive sources are, that is, that parties may rely on them to try to convince the court to take one approach or another to a question, and judges may use them in reaching decisions. In all circumstances, the use of so-called 'foreign law' for the purposes of domestic law interpretation and adjudication is contentious.[72] Caution about reliance on such sources largely emanates from a concern for judicial legitimacy. For some scholars, courts are *always* treading on sensitive ground: they do not have domestic democratic legitimacy that might come from direct election from the people, and they may well make decisions that upend the acts of parliament or the government, the members of which *are* directly elected. This is not the place to engage in this much wider debate about the limits and legitimacy of the judicial role, but it is worth noting at this stage that the debate about the role of ECtHR judgments in domestic law is related to that larger and very longstanding academic and judicial debate about the role of 'foreign' law per se.

It does, however, have a somewhat different character in the context of the interpretation and application of the Convention and, where relevant, its implementing provisions in domestic law. It is beyond dispute that the ECtHR has the ultimate role of interpreting and applying the Convention.[73] As a matter of

[72] On the broader debates on this see, for example, Sandra Fredman, 'Foreign Fads of Fashions? The Role of Comparativism in Human Rights Law' (2015) 64(3) *International and Comparative Law Quarterly* 631.

[73] Pursuant to Article 32, ECHR, the jurisdiction of the Court shall extend to all matters concerning the interpretation and application of the Convention and the Protocols.

international law, the ECHR means what the Court says it means. It is, thus, relatively uncontroversial to suggest that where a domestic court is assessing what the Convention per se might mean, and where there is a judgment on this from Strasbourg, the domestic court might *ordinarily* follow that judgment and then consider its implications for the questions of domestic law that arise.

This is not to suggest that the ECtHR and its domestic counterparts have no necessary or productive relationship in the context of the development and implementation of the Convention; quite to the contrary, in fact. The ECtHR is connected to domestic courts and their work, as considered in chapter 2. What we mean by this is that all these courts have a role in developing and implementing the corpus of European human rights law that forms part of the so-called European Public Order.[74] In respect of the relationship between domestic courts and the ECtHR, this means that there is an important role for (informal) cooperation and collaboration, and indeed at times for contestation and disagreement, on the meaning of the Convention. In order to formalise such informal communications, the Court launched the Superior Court Network. It was created in 2015 with the aim to 'enrich dialogue and the implementation of the Convention'.[75] Now it includes 111 of the highest courts from all 46 Contracting Parties to the Convention.[76] The main rationale for this Network is to share relevant information. The national courts can request information on the European Court's case law or practice, 'where the Jurisconsult's contribution offers added value in relation to external sources'.[77] The ECtHR itself can also request information from the national courts, which it can use in its comparative law reports that are often presented in the judgments and usually form a basis for the Court's conclusion about European consensus.[78] Such discourse and quiet collaboration do not undermine the authority of the European Court: its decision in a particular case remains binding as against the parties, and the respondent state must still execute it. In this way, such *judicial* contestation is distinct from the *political* contestation that underpins much of the non-execution we have considered in Debate 1 of this chapter.

Within a framework of this kind, there must – one might argue – be some space for contestation, so that domestic courts might consider themselves able to express disagreement with the decision of the ECtHR about the meaning of any particular provision. In situations where the judgments were not handed down against the state in question, there is no reason in international law why the domestic courts might decide to treat the cases in question as not being binding upon them.

[74] See further Kanstantsin Dzehtsiarou, *Can the European Court of Human Rights Shape European Public Order?* (Cambridge University Press, 2021).

[75] See at www.echr.coe.int/Pages/home.aspx?p=court/dialoguecourts/network&c=.

[76] See at www.echr.coe.int/Documents/SCN_Members_ENG.pdf.

[77] Operational Rules, para 17.

[78] See, for example, in *Bayatyan v Armenia* [2011] ECHR 1095, paras 46–49.

The collaborative engagement on the meaning of the Convention involves domestic courts and judges with Strasbourg institutions, surfaces some practical or doctrinal complications with the ECtHR's approach that were not otherwise apparent, and seeks to help domestic courts and judiciaries to develop a sense of co-ownership over, and co-authorship of, the Convention and its jurisprudence. After all, only a very small proportion of the cases that concern the Convention ever get to the Court, and fewer still get past the admissibility stage. Most Convention matters are addressed domestically, through legislation, or practice or judicial decisions. The effectiveness of the Convention as part of a system for the protection of human rights calls for engagement between domestic and European judiciaries to better embed the Convention and ensure that its principles and rights are protected, even without the need to take a case to the Court.

The controversy, of course, arises when we distil that general principle (that collaboration between domestic judiciaries and the Court is to be welcomed) into rules of law that might determine how that collaboration would work in practical terms when a case raising a Convention issue comes before the domestic courts. What weight ought the domestic courts to give to the jurisprudence of the ECtHR, which, as we have already noted, is not binding on them as a matter of international law? The simple answer to this question is that it is a matter for domestic law to decide.

In the UK, the early approach under the Human Rights Act 1998 – which was largely similar in Ireland under the 2003 Act – was to treat Strasbourg jurisprudence as if it were *effectively* binding, so that domestic law would be a 'mirror' of Convention law.[79] Over time, this has diminished somewhat, and domestic courts now exhibit a more 'assertive stance',[80] deviating from Strasbourg jurisprudence in a wider set of circumstances, including where the domestic court considers Strasbourg to have been mistaken[81] or that taking a mirroring approach would have negative implications in domestic law.

Despite this, however, it remains politically popular to claim, in the UK context, that the ECtHR is essentially making decisions that properly belong to the domestic courts, and until very recently there were ongoing attempts to change domestic law to make it clearer that domestic courts were permitted to reach outcomes in direct conflict with established Strasbourg jurisprudence.[82] This sense of tension between 'foreign' and domestic courts is not unique to the UK, but it arguably misunderstands the *status quo* by emphasising the 'foreignness' of the ECtHR and de-emphasising the extent to which Strasbourg jurisprudence is a produce of cross-jurisdictional dialogue. Decisions of the ECtHR are subject to (and sometimes emergent from) substantive feedback

[79] *R v Special Adjudicator, ex parte Ullah* [2004] UKHL 26.

[80] Lewis Graham, 'The Modern Mirror Principle' [2021] 3 *Public Law* 523.

[81] Note that this is controversial, including among judges. See, eg, the dissenting judgments in *In the matter of an application by Siobhan McLaughlin for Judicial Review* [2018] UKSC 48.

[82] See Clause 3(3)(b) of the (now abandoned) Bill of Rights Bill 2022.

from domestic courts, and frequently involve the Court in taking domestic law into account to consider, for example, whether there is any European consensus on the legal question before it. Thus, whilst they ultimately emanate from the ECtHR, they are products, often, of the intermingling of the legal traditions across the Continent, which emerges from the make-up of the Court and its Registry, the arguments put to the Court and the practice of undertaking comparative law research in the Court. Second, this argument fundamentally misunderstands Strasbourg decisions as being binding on non-respondent states. Neither the Convention nor the Human Rights Act 1998 *requires* domestic institutions to treat ECtHR decisions as having *erga omnes* effect. Instead, it was UK courts – particularly in the case of *Ullah*[83] – that interpreted a UK Act of Parliament (the Human Rights Act 1998) as effectively requiring these decisions to be treated as *quasi*-binding, albeit subject to some exceptions. Thus, it is open to domestic legal processes to refine this position as, indeed, the courts in the UK have done.[84] When state authorities or politicians persist in presenting the so-called bindingness of Strasbourg jurisprudence as a problem with the Convention per se, then, they are either inadvertently or purposefully passing off what is a *domestic* legal arrangement as the product of a misrepresentation of what *international* legal arrangements require.

Debate 4

Are Advisory Opinions Effective in Embedding the Principles of the Convention Domestically?

Protocol 16, also known as the Protocol of Dialogue, entered into force in August 2018 and introduced new advisory opinions. It allows the highest courts and tribunals of a Contracting Party to request that the ECtHR give advisory opinions on questions of principle relating to the interpretation or application of the rights and freedoms defined in the Convention and relating to cases pending at national level. This is considerably wider than the pre-existing provision for advisory opinions in Article 47 of the Convention.[85] The ECtHR has discretion whether to accept a request or not, but where a request is accepted by a five-judge panel of the Court, a non-binding, reasoned opinion is given by the Grand Chamber. Protocol 16 does not specify the possible ground for refusing requests for advisory opinions, but the Court's *Guidelines* suggest that advisory opinions might be sought where a domestic proceeding raises a novel question of ECHR law, where the facts of the case do

[83] *ex parte Ullah* (n 79).

[84] Graham (n 80).

[85] *Advisory Opinion on Certain Legal Questions Concerning the Lists of Candidates Submitted with a View to the Election of Judges to the European Court of Human Rights (No 1)*, 12 February 2008; *Advisory Opinion on Certain Legal Questions Concerning the Lists of Candidates Submitted with a View to the Election of Judges to the European Court of Human Rights (No 2)*, 22 January 2010.

not lend themselves to straightforward application of the ECHR or where the ECtHR's case law appears inconsistent on a pertinent point.[86] Between 2018 and 2025, the ECtHR delivered seven advisory opinions and rejected four requests.

The advisory opinion mechanism under Protocol 16 was intended to intensify dialogue between the highest national courts and the ECtHR and, thereby, to enable the greater embedding of the ECHR in national law and support the shared responsibility for Convention compliance between national and Council of Europe institutions. This in turn was anticipated to assist with the Court's long-term workload. While that may well be considered generally desirable, concerns had been raised about both the procedural and substantive implications of the new advisory opinion process.[87] The procedural concern related to the questionable utility of advisory opinions in a practical sense, given that seeking an advisory opinion would require domestic proceedings to be adjourned, resulting in delays in domestic courts, as well as adding further cases to the docket for the Grand Chamber. The substantive concern related to what legal effect advisory opinions would have. Although advisory opinions are not legally binding on the national courts that requested them, one might reasonably expect that a national court that requested such an opinion would be unlikely to reject the interpretation therein expressed, but much might depend on how the advisory opinions are written. Moreover, the national court could have a set of expectations about the particular advisory opinion, and if the ECtHR did not fulfil these expectations, the national court might be reluctant to comply.

In practice, the procedural concern has not been borne out. National courts are advised to make a request for an advisory opinion only once all the relevant facts and points of law have become clear,[88] which in turn enables them to make a clear, precise advisory request to the Court, and advisory opinion procedures have tended to progress in a timely manner.

The substantive concern has also been less acute in practice than was anticipated, but certain conditions need to coincide for advisory opinions to be effective. The request by the national court should concern a genuinely novel issue or an issue where an evolutive interpretation of the Convention is possible. Second, the Court's opinion should be precise enough for the national

[86] *Guidelines on the implementation of the advisory-opinion procedure*, adopted by the Plenary Court on 18 September 2017 and updated on 25 September 2023 at www.echr.coe.int/Documents/Guidelines_P16_ENG.pdf, para 5. See also *Advisory Opinion on the Procedural Status and Rights of a Biological Parent in Proceedings for the Adoption of an Adult* [GC], request no P16-2022-001, Supreme Court of Finland, paras 25–26, 13 April 2023.

[87] Kanstantsin Dzehtsiarou and Noreen O'Meara, 'Advisory Jurisdiction and the European Court of Human Rights: A Magic Bullet for Dialogue and Docket-Control?' (2014) 34(3) *Legal Studies* 444.

[88] *Guidelines on the implementation of the advisory-opinion procedure*, adopted by the Plenary Court on 18 September 2017 and updated on 25 September 2023 at https://www.echr.coe.int/Documents/Guidelines_P16_ENG.pdf, para 10.

court to follow its guidance should it choose to do so. Third, the national court should present its interpretation of Convention law to the Court. This last condition is important, as it ensures that the ECtHR is aware of the complexities of the situation and that it is the national court that initiates the feedback loop. If the same case then returns to the ECtHR in the form of a contentious application, the feedback loop will be complete, allowing the Court to agree or disagree with the national court's application of the advisory opinion.

Although advisory opinions are not binding per se, national courts are asked to inform the Court what action they have taken based on the advisory opinion, ensuring a feedback loop between the national and regional court in this respect.[89] However, the principle of *res interpretata* applies; advisory opinions enjoy interpretive authority in the same way as all opinions of the Court. Thus, all Contracting Parties would be expected to take notice of the general principles interpreted and outlined in advisory opinions and to treat them as authoritative interpretations of the Convention. In practice, the Court's opinions are not always very precise, leaving implementing courts with considerable discretion. This means that a national court may attempt to implement an advisory opinion in good faith, only to find itself in a situation where the ECtHR later identifies a violation in a contentious case. One could therefore argue that although advisory opinions have some impact and are taken into account by the requesting courts, it remains unclear whether allocating the Grand Chamber's limited resources to such opinions is truly cost-effective.

Conclusion

The ECHR is a joint and collective enterprise by the Contracting Parties and the bodies of the Council of Europe. Its success relies not only on the approaches and interpretations of the Court, but also on the reception of the Convention in domestic systems, the willingness of states to enforce expectations of compliance with one another, and the extent to which the Convention, as interpreted and applied by the ECtHR, can and does strike a balance between the needs for effective rights protection, predictability and foreseeability of law, feedback loops with national authorities, and evolution to govern novel and complex questions of contemporary governance. At times this has required innovation, either in the interpretation of the Convention or in the (remedial and procedural) tools available to the Court, but that innovation has brought criticism from states and other actors concerned that the Convention is being taken 'too far' by the Court. Resolving those tensions, whilst still protecting individual rights, is the core of the challenge faced by the Convention and, in essence, lies at the heart of almost all of the debates we have considered throughout this book.

[89] ibid, para 33.

Further Reading

Oddny Arnardottir, '*Res Interpretata, Erga Omnes* Effect and the Role of the Margin of Appreciation in Giving Domestic Effect to the Judgments of the European Court of Human Rights' (2017) 28(3) *European Journal of International Law* 819.

Fiona de Londras and Kanstantsin Dzehtsiarou, 'Mission Impossible? Addressing Non-execution through Infringement Proceedings in the European Court of Human Rights' (2014) 66 *International and Comparative Law Quarterly* 467.

Laurence Helfer, 'Redesigning the European Court of Human Rights: Embeddedness as a Deep Structural Principle of the European Human Rights Regime' (2008) 19 *European Journal of International Law* 125.

Alastair Mowbray, 'An Examination of the European Court of Human Rights' Indication of Remedial Measures' (2017) 17(3) *Human Rights Law Review* 451.

Index

abolition of death penalty (Prot. 6, Art. 1), 14
abortion, 6, 10, 97–98, 123, 197
absolute rights, 107, 121
accession to the ECHR:
EU accession to ECHR, 46–49
adjudicatory function of ECtHR, 68–69, 76, 79, 138–39
admissibility criteria, 55–56
admissibility decisions, 26, 55
climate change, 66–68
anonymous applications, 75–76
applicants, 60–61
corporate victims, 65–66
deceased victims, 64–65
potential victims, 61–62
victims of covert activities, 62–64
climate change, 66–68
discretionary decision-making, 70–76
effectiveness, relationship with, 76–79
legitimacy, relationship with, 57–60
manifestly ill-founded, 73–74
Prot. 14, 68
Prot. 15, 68–70
advisory opinions, 184
Art. 47, 17, 208
Prot. 16, 16–18, 208–9
procedural concerns, 209
substantive concerns, 209–10
age:
appointment of judges, 24–25
consensual homosexual intercourse, 99
discrimination claims, 176
minimum wage, 174
retirement of judges, 24–25
Andorra:
abortion, 97
applications to the ECtHR, 60–61
corporate victims, 65–66
deceased victims, 64–65
potential victims, 61–62
victims of covert activities, 62–64
arbitrary detention, 132–33, 152, 203
armed conflicts, 131
derogation in time of emergency (Art. 15)
emergency derogation systems, 145–47
procedural requirements, 147
substantive requirements, 150–53
suspension of rights, 145–53
threshold requirements, 147–50
international humanitarian law, 131–32
UN missions, 50–51
Armenia:
Bayatyan v Armenia, 90–91
Dareskizb Ltd v Armenia, 150
derogation in time of emergency (Art. 15), 150
freedom of thought, conscience and religion (Art. 9), 90–91
asset-freezing:
Al-Dulimi v Switzerland, 51–54
assisted dying, 88
assisted reproductive technologies, 6, 88
attribution, 50, 142
austerity, *see* **deprivation; global financial crises; poverty**
Austria:
consensual homosexual intercourse, 99
Frodl v Austria, 37, 40, 100

in vitro fertilisation, 88
Kurt v Austria, 111, 158
L and V v Austria, 99
lex posteriori derogat legi priori principle, 196
preventive operational measures, 111, 158
prisoner voting, 37, 40, 100
proportionality and positive obligations, 111
SH and Others v Austria, 88
authority and judicial supremacy, 33–41
Azerbaijan:
Ilgar Mammadov v Azerbaijan, 202–3
political opposition, 146, 202–3

B-lawyers, 28
bail-outs, 17–72, 174–75
balancing competing rights and interests, *see* **proportionality**
ban on full-face veils, *see* **religious dress**
begging, 102
Belgium:
ban on full-face veils, 93
conditions of detention of asylum seekers, 168–70
consensus, 94
constitutional amendment, 198
illegitimate children, 85, 94, 185
Marckx v Belgium, 85, 94, 185
MSS v Belgium and Greece, 168–70
bindingness of ECtHR judgments, 14, 33–34, 54, 115, 184, 193, 204–8
interim measures, 95
see also execution of ECtHR judgments
Bosnia and Herzegovina:
Kovačević v Bosnia and Herzegovina, 181
non-discrimination, 180–81
Sejdic' and Finci v Bosnia and Herzegovina, 180–81
***Bosphorus* presumption,** 42–46
Bulgaria:
Bevacqua and S v Bulgaria, 154–55
Capital Bank AD v Bulgaria, 66
constitutional amendments, 197
corporate victims, 66
domestic violence, 154–55
MC v Bulgaria, 122
Nencheva and Others v Bulgaria, 172
positive obligations, 122
socio-economic rights, 172
Bureau of the ECtHR, 19–20, 29
Centre for Legal Recourses (CLR):
applications to the ECtHR, 64–65
Charter of Fundamental Rights of the European Union (CFREU), 45–46, 48–49
Chechnya:
anonymous applications, 75–76
Shamayev and Others v Georgia and Russia, 75–76
children:
approach to raising children, 112–13
austerity, deprivation and economic inequality, 171, 172, 198
best interests, 114–15
discrimination against
Roma children, 10
illegitimate children, 85–86, 92, 94
civil and political rights, 6, 161, 162–63, 167, 171, 173–75, 175–76, 181, 198
climate change litigation, 61, 66–68
extraterritoriality, 143–44
transboundary harms, 143–44
clone cases, 15, 16, 191
colonialism, 3, 171
Committee of Ministers, 14, 191–92
advisory opinions, 17
Al-Dulimi v Switzerland, 53–54
execution of judgments, 200–3
expulsion of Russia, 30–31
judicial appointments, 20–21
prisoner voting cases, 39–40, 191
remedies, 184–85, 187
comparative law, 29
European consensus, 90–93
expert consensus, 99
internal consensus, 96–99
international consensus, 94–96
compensation, 185–86
non-pecuniary damage, 74
Pinto Law, 58–59
compliance, 11, 14, 33–34, 184–92
right to a fair trial, 12–13
EU's presumption of compliance, 44–45, 52
see also execution of judgments
consensual homosexual intercourse, 99
consensus:
European consensus, 90–93
expert consensus, 99
internal consensus, 96–99
international consensus, 94–96

consent:
legitimacy, relationship with, 3–5, 81, 83–85, 163
original consent concept, 3–4, 83–84, 163–64
conscientious objection, 90–91
European consensus as method of interpretation, 91–92
consistency:
legitimacy through consistency, 7–8, 28–29, 87–88, 106, 121, 131, 177
constitutional chrononomy, 82
constitutional law:
ECHR, relationship with, 33, 196–97
Italy, 195–96
Germany, 196
lex posteriori derogat legi priori principle, 196
international law, conflicts with, 195
constitutionalist (meta-function) function of ECtHR, 69–70, 76–77, 79
Convention on the Elimination of all Forms of Discrimination against Women (CEDAW), 154
coronavirus, 131, 147, 148
corporal punishment, 98–99, 153
corporate victims, 65–66
corruption, 171
Council of Europe, 3–4
expulsion, 30–31
Greece, 30
Russia, 30–31
withdrawal, 30
Court of Justice of the European Union (CJEU), 41–43, 44, 46–49, 53
covert activities by states, 62–64
COVID-19, 131, 147, 148
Croatia:
Branko Tomašic and Others v Croatia, 155
court ordered psychiatric treatment, 155
execution of ECtHR judgments, 205
Cyprus:
Avotiņš v Latvia, 44
Bosphorus presumption, 44
compensation, 186
Cyprus v Turkey, 186
extraterritoriality and Cyprus conflict, 136
Loizidou v Turkey, 136
Czechia:
constitutional amendment, 197
death penalty:
abolition/prohibition of death penalty (Prot. 6, Art. 1), 14
deceased victims, 64–65
declaratory judgments, 183, 184–85, 186–87, 192
democracy, 92, 126, 164, 195
democratic back-sliding, 126
democratic override, 199–200
Denmark:
admissibility decisions, 102
constitutional amendment, 198
Dian v Denmark, 102
deprivation:
arbitrary deprivation of property, 164–65
austerity, 168–69, 172, 181
destitution, 167, 170–71, 175–76
inhumane living conditions, 168–69
see also poverty
derogation in time of emergency (Art. 15):
emergency derogation systems, 145–47
suspension of rights
emergency derogation systems, 145–47
procedural requirements, 147
substantive requirements, 150–53
threshold requirements, 147–50
destitution, *see* **deprivation**
detention:
arbitrary detention, 132–33, 152, 203
conditions of detention of asylum seekers, 168–70
dialogue:
dialogue of contestation, 193–94, 206
feedback loops, 34–35
judicial dialogue, 34–35
protocol of dialogue (Prot. 16), 17
vexed dialogue, 40
diffuse support, 2, 200–1
Directorate of Jurisconsult, 21, 28–29, 206
disability and disabled people, 7
non-discrimination, 176
socio-economic wellbeing, 170–71, 172
disadvantage:
non-discrimination, 178
significant disadvantage as a result of a violation
admissibility decisions, 16, 56, 68–70, 71, 72
socio-economic wellbeing, 170–72
discretion:
admissibility criteria, 70–76

discrimination, 10, 114–15
discrimination against women, 154
domestic violence, 132, 153–59
security measures, 146–47
see also non-discrimination
disenfranchisement:
prisoners, *see* prisoners voting rights
domestic law:
ECHR, relationship with, 195–97
democratic illegitimacy of, 184
ECHR's embeddedness, 10–11, 207
tensions between, 34, 108–9, 184, 204–6, 207–8
ECtHR judgments, 13–14, 33, 115, 204–6
deference to national authorities, 11, 106, 117, 124–26, 128, 139
EU law, relationship with, 41
exhaustion of domestic remedies (ECHR Art. 35), 11, 55–56, 57, 58–59, 70, 190
feedback loops, 34–35
margin of appreciation, *see* margin of appreciation
proportionality analysis, *see* proportionality
UN SC resolutions, 51, 53
domestic violence, 132, 153–59
drafting process, 25–26

education:
economic inequality, 171–72
religious dress in educational establishments, 101
right to education, 14, 162, 175
effective control, 132, 135–44
effective remedy, 58–59, 191
effectiveness:
admissibility, relationship with, 76–79
margin of appreciation, relationship with, 129
output legitimacy, relationship with, 9–10
socio-economic rights, 175
embeddedness, 11, 120, 124–25, 184, 189
emergency powers, *see* **derogation in time of emergency**
enforcement of ECtHR judgments, *see* **execution of judgments**
equality:
equality before the law, 164–65
gender equality, 114, 123
socio-economic equality, 162, 177–78
formal equality, 177–78, 179–80
substantive equality, 177–78, 179–80
sovereign equality, 3, 127–28
see also non-discrimination
***erga omnes* effect,** 204, 208
***espace juridique*,** 137–40
EU law, 29, 33
accession of EU to ECHR, 46–49
autonomy of EU law, 46–47
ECHR, 41–46
European Central Bank (ECB):
global financial crises, 171
European Commission, 174
global financial crises, 171
European Commission of Human Rights, 14
abolition (Prot. 11), 14–15
European Committee of Social Rights (ECSR), 7
European Court of Justice (ECJ), 41–43, 44, 46–49, 53
European Public Order, 56–57, 74, 77, 136, 137–38, 139–40, 206
European Social Charter (ESC), 6–7, 166–67, 174
European Union (EU):
ECHR, relationship with, 41–46
see also EU law
evolutive interpretation of ECHR, 82–90
European consensus, 90–93
expert consensus, 99
internal consensus, 96–99
international consensus, 94–96
living instrument doctrine, 81–82, 90, 98–99, 103
execution of ECtHR judgments (Art. 46), 193
arguments of execution, 199–302
arguments of practicality, 197–99
arguments of principle, 193–95
arguments of the constitution, 195–97
bindingness of judgments, 193
interpretive authority, 204
exhaustion of domestic remedies (ECHR Art. 35), 11, 55–56, 57, 58–59, 70, 190
expulsion from Council of Europe, 30–31
extraterritoriality, 135
climate change litigation, 143–44
Cyprus conflict, 136
Iraq war, 139–42

Russian invasion of Ukraine, 142–43
Yugoslav war, 136–39

feedback loops:
Al-Khawaja and Tahery v UK, 34–35
first-order reasons, 119–20
foreseeability, 113, 116, 129, 144, 210
four-month rule:
admissibility criteria, 57–59, 79
France:
Behrami v France and *Saramati v France, Germany and Norway*, 50
disproportionate security measures, 146
'manifestly ill-founded', 73
Odievre v France, 125
parliamentary decision-making and margin of appreciation, 125
religious dress, 93, 146
SAS v France, 93, 101
Singh v France, 73
free movement of capital, 41
free movement of goods, 41
free movement of workers, 41
freedom of religion, *see* **freedom of thought, conscience and religion**
freedom to provide services, 41
freedom of assembly and association (Art. 11), 75, 108, 109
freedom of expression (Art. 10), 108, 109, 125
freedom of thought, conscience and religion (Art. 9), 73, 74–75, 90–91, 100–1, 108, 109, 112–13, 122
friendly settlements, 72, 77
full-face veils, *see* **religious dress**

gender:
gender equality, 114, 156, 170–71
recognition of gender identity, 10, 83 86–87, 88
general measures, 185, 188–92, 193–94, 197 98
Georgia:
A and B v Georgia, 155
Assanidze v Georgia, 186–87
domestic violence, 155
ECHR and armed conflict, 132–33
extradition cases, 75–76
Georgia v Russia (II), 132–33
illegal detention, 186–87
Shamayev and Others v Georgia and Russia, 75–76
Germany:
balance and proportionality, 110–11, 117
Behrami v France and *Saramati v France, Germany and Norway*, 50
Constitutional primacy, 196
Protocol 16, 16–17
Von Hannover v Germany, 110–11
global financial crises:
social and economic rights, 161–62, 170–75
good faith, 1–2, 84, 149, 153, 164, 210
Grand Chamber, 8–9, 17, 23–24, 26–27, 34–35, 37, 50, 79, 88, 100, 180–81, 203, 208–10
Greece:
Agrotexim and Others v Greece, 65–66
bail-out, 171–72
conditions of detention of asylum seekers, 168–69
corporate victims, 65–66
General Federation of Employees of the National Electric Power Corporation (GENOP-DEI) and Confederation of Greek Civil Servants' Trade Unions (ADEDY) v Greece, 174–75
Koufaki and Adedy v Greece, 172
MSS v Belgium and Greece, 168–69
socio-economic wellbeing, 172, 174–75
withdrawal from Council of Europe, 30–31

headscarves, *see* **religious dress**
healthcare:
MSS v Belgium and Greece, 168–69, 170
right of access to healthcare, 48, 171, 172
right to an adequate standard of healthcare, 163
Holocaust, 83
HUDOC (ECHR case-law database):
Registry of the Court, 29
human dignity, 86–87, 168–69, 194
Human Rights Act 1998 (UK), 139, 196, 205, 207–8
Human Rights Committee (UN HRC), 73, 74–75, 95
Hungary:
ad hoc judges, 24
austerity measures, 173–74
constitutional court, 194
Daniel Karsai v Hungary, 88
evolutive interpretation, 88
Ilias and Ahmed v Hungary, 45

NKM v Hungary, 173–74
same-sex marriage, 123
treatment of asylum seekers, 45
Hussein, Saddam, 51

Iceland, 23
ill treatment, *see* **prohibition against torture, inhuman treatment, and degrading treatment or punishment**
illegitimate children, 94–95
impact cases, 77
***in abstracto*,** 60–61
in vitro fertilisation (IVF), 88
individual measures, 185–88, 202
infringement proceedings, 201–3
insecurity, 51, 53, 131–32
see also armed conflict; domestic violence; war
Inter-American Court of Human Rights (IACtHR), 95
interference:
legality, 108–9
legitimacy, 5, 109
necessary in a democratic society, 109–10
proportionality, 43, 73, 105–6, 107–13
interim measures, 4–5, 94–95, 154–55
International Court of Justice (ICJ), 95
International Covenant on Civil and Political Rights (ICCPR), 3, 73, 161
International Covenant on Economic, Social and Cultural Right (ICESCR), 3, 161
international human rights law, 132–33
international humanitarian law, 132–33
International Labour Organisation (ILO), 75
international law:
consensus based on international law, 94–96
ECHR, relationship with, 49–54
systemic integration, 95–96
see also United Nations
International Monetary Fund (IMF):
global financial crises, 171
interpersonal violence, 132, 159
see also domestic violence
interpretation of ECHR by ECtHR, 81–82
evolutive interpretation, 82–90
European consensus, 90–93
expert consensus, 99
internal consensus, 96–99
international consensus, 94–96
Iraq war:
extraterritoriality, 139–42
Ireland, 196
A, B and C v Ireland, 97, 123
abortion, 97, 123
Airey v Ireland, 162–63, 165
bail-out, 171
Bosphorus Hava Yolları Turizm ve Ticaret Anonim Sirketi v Ireland, 42–43
Bosphorus presumption, 42–43
breach of Article 6 due-process rights, 162–63
constitutional amendment, 198
derogation in time of emergency, 148
European Convention on Human Rights Act 2003, 198, 205, 207
Lawless v Ireland, 148
prisoner voting, 40
socio-economic rights, 162–63, 165
Islam:
disproportionality of security measures, 146
Islamic dress, 10, 100–2
religious beliefs, 112–13
Italy, 195
domestic abuse, 157, 158
Giacomelli v Italy, 108–9
interference, 108–9
Lautsi and Others v Italy, 122
margin of appreciation, 122–23
Oliari and Others v Italy, 123
Pinto Law, 59–60
prisoner voting, 37–38, 100
qualified rights, 122
Scoppola v Italy (No 3), 37–38, 100
Scordino v Italy, 59
Talpis v Italy, 157

Jehovah's Witnesses, 90
Judaism, 113, 173, 180–81
judicial activism, 82–83, 103
judicial independence, 23, 24, 194–95
judicial reasoning, 7–9
European consensus, 90–93
expert consensus, 99
internal consensus, 96–99
international consensus, 94–96
margin of appreciation, 119–21

judicial review, 47–48, 51–52, 59, 115, 117
judicial supremacy, 33–41
judiciary of the ECtHR, 20–23
ad hoc judges, 24
national representation principle, 23–24
tenure, 24–25
Jurisconsult, 21, 28–29, 206
jurisdiction, 2–3, 13, 14–15, 20–21, 30–31, 67
armed conflict, 132–35
extraterritoriality, 135–44
legitimacy, 57–60
subsidiarity, relationship with, 10–13, 16, 106–7, 117, 204
just satisfaction, 183, 185–86, 192

Kosovo:
international peacekeeping, 50

Latvia:
admissibility, 73
Avotiņš v Latvia, 44
Bosphorus presumption, 44
Mentzen v Latvia, 73
legal certainty, 7–8, 58, 61, 63–64, 68, 87
legal reasoning, *see* **judicial reasoning**
legality, 46, 133–35
interference with rights
proportionality, 108–9, 112, 116
legitimacy, 1–2
admissibility criteria, relationship with, 57–60
input legitimacy, 2, 7–9
outcome legitimacy, 2
output legitimacy, 2, 9–10
perceived legitimacy, 2
sources of legitimacy, 2–3
consent as basis for legitimacy, 3–5
effectiveness as basis for legitimacy, 9–10
method as basis for legitimacy, 7–9
moral purpose as basis for legitimacy, 5–7
legitimate aim:
proportionality, relationship with, 108, 109
super-qualified rights, 123
lex posteriori derogat legi priori **principle,** 196
lex specialis, 134
LGBTQ+ rights
Alekseyev v Russia, 72, 109–10
life imprisonment, 156, 157, 203
Lithuania, 24, 205
living instrument doctrine, 81–82, 90, 98–99, 103
see also evolutive interpretation of ECHR
Luxembourg, 24, 41

Malta:
abortion, 97, 123
manifestly ill-founded, 20, 56, 71–74, 79, 173
margin of appreciation, 69–70, 105–7, 128–29
complexity, 128
conceptual limits/boundaries, 121
implicated right defined, 121–24
nature of right, 121–24
definition, 118
democratic legitimacy, relationship with, 118–19, 124–28
determining factors, 124
legal reasoning, 119–21
national authorities' human rights role, 118–19
Prot. 15, 117–18
see also proportionality

marriage, 86, 197
same-sex marriage, 6, 123
meta-function, 69–70, 76–77, 79
method and input legitimacy, 7–9
minimum wage, 174
minority populations:
non-discrimination, 176
religious minorities, 7, 92, 171
unpopular minorities, 40–41, 192
vulnerable minorities, 10, 92, 171
Moldova:
Catan and Others v the Republic of Moldova and Russia, 109
Ciorap v Moldova (No 2), 74
domestic violence, 156–57
FG v Moldova, 111–12
Eremia v Moldova, 156–57
legitimate aim, 109
'manifestly ill-founded', 74
proportionality and positive obligations, 111–12
Monaco:
right to respect for private life, 110
Montenegro, 24
moral legitimacy, 5–7, 31, 78
Muslim communities, *see* **Islam**

'necessary in a democratic society', 90, 101, 108, 109–10
necessity, 109–10, 112, 116, 126, 145, 151, 159
negative obligations, 107–8, 111, 121
Netherlands:
admissibility, 76
'Blonje' v the Netherlands, 76
international humanitarian law, 133, 140–42
Jaloud v the Netherlands, 133, 140–42
Ukraine and the Netherlands v Russia, 142–43
non-discrimination (Art. 14):
domestic violence, 156–58
fundamental importance, 162
socio-economic equality, relationship with, 175–76, 178–81
non-discrimination (Prot. 12), 162
socio-economic equality, relationship with, 176–77, 178, 180–81
non-execution of enforceable judgments of national courts, 189–90, 192, 197, 200–1, 203, 206
non-governmental organisations (NGO), 55, 60–61, 64–65, 67–68
non-pecuniary damage, 74, 185
norm-balancing, 122–23
normalcy, 145–47, 149–50, 152, 159
North Atlantic Treaty Organization (NATO), 50, 136–37
North Macedonia, 24
Norway:
Behrami v France and *Saramati v France, Germany and Norway*, 50
ECHR breaches as part of peacekeeping forces, 50
Folgero and Others v Norway, 74–75
religious education, 74–75

obligation to respect human rights (Art. 1), 131, 135–36, 140
ombudspersons, 58
operative part, 185
Opinion 2/13, 46–48

Parliamentary Assembly of the Council of Europe (PACE):
judiciary of the ECtHR, 20–23, 24
persecution, 10
pilot judgments, 188–92
Pinto Law (Italy), 59
Plenary Court, 19–20
Poland, 194
Protocol, 16, 16
political advertisements, 125
political speech, 105–6
Portugal:
bail-out, 171
climate-change litigation, 143–44
Duarte Agostinho and Others v Portugal and 32 others, 143–44
positive obligations:
prohibition of torture (Art. 3), 167–70
proportionality, 111–12
potential victims, 61–62
poverty, 198
conditions of detention of asylum seekers, 168–70
MSS v Belgium and Greece, 168–70
right to be free from poverty, 6
see also deprivation
practical reasoning, 119
Preamble, 4, 5, 11, 16, 42, 84, 106–7, 118
precedent, 8
President, 19–20, 23
presumptions:
Bosphorus presumption, 42–46, 49, 52
presumption of compliance, 52
presumption of legitimacy, 5
rebuttable presumptions, 93
preventive operational measures, 111, 158
priority policy, 77
prisoner voting:
Anchugov and Gladkov v Russia, 38–39
Frodl v Austria, 37, 40
Greens and MT v UK, 37
Hirst v UK cases, 35–41, 100
Kalda v Estonia (No 2), 36
pilot-judgments, 191–92
proportionality, 36–37
Scoppola v Italy, 37–38, 100
Soyler v Turkey, 39
privacy, *see* **right to respect for private and family life**
process-based review/procedural review, 12–13
prohibition against torture, inhuman treatment, and degrading treatment or punishment (Art. 3), 75, 94–95, 107, 158–67, 168
austerity measures, 172
socio-economic right, as, 167–70, 172

prohibition of abuse of rights (Art. 17), 72
proportionality, 105–7, 128–29
criticisms, 112–15
disenfranchisement, 36–37
justifications, 115–17
positive obligations, 111–12
proportionality analysis and rights adjudication, 107–8
balancing, 110–11
legality of interference, 108–9
legitimate aim of interference, 109
'necessary in a democratic society', 109–10
whether interference, 108
see also margin of appreciation
psychological abuse, 157
public emergencies, 131
see also armed conflicts; derogation in time of emergency
public interest:
deference to parliamentary decision-making, 125–26
margin of appreciation, 118–19, 173
proportionality, 110–11

qualified rights, 107, 122–23
super-qualified rights, 123–24

racism, 171
reasonable suspicion, 152–53
rebuttable presumption, 93
redress, 57, 74–75, 78–79, 190–91, 192
referendums, 60
constitutional amendment, 198
internal consensus, 96–97
reforms, 13–14
Prot. 11, 14–15
Prot. 14, 15–16
Prot. 15, 16
Prot. 16, 16–18
Rules of Court, 18–20
Registrar, 19–20, 25, 27–28
Registry of the Court, 1, 8, 23, 56, 70–71, 79, 208
Directorate of Jurisconsult, 28–29
HUDOC management, 29
independence, 27–28
role, 25–30
religion, *see* **freedom of thought, conscience and religion**
religious dress, 93, 100–2
religious minorities, 7, 92, 171
remedies, 184–85
declaratory judgments, 184–85, 186–87, 192
general measures, 188–92
individual measures, 185–88
pilot-judgments, 188–92
remedy, 58–60
remuneration, 172–73, 174
res interpretata **principle,** 204, 210
Resolution 1483, 51–52, 141
restitutio in integrum, 58–59
Reykjavík Summit, 4–5, 47, 183
right to a fair trial (Art. 6), 12–13, 34–35, 44, 50, 53, 59, 162–63, 178, 189–90, 198, 202–3
right to education (Prot. 1, Art. 2), 14, 74–75, 162, 175
right to liberty and security (Art. 5):
derogation, 134–35
illegal detention, 133, 134–35, 186–87
right to life (Art. 2), 136–37, 141–42, 143
austerity measures, 172
domestic violence, 155–56, 157
no derogation, 145, 150
right to marry and start a family (Art. 12), 122–23
right to participate in free elections (Prot. 1, Art. 3), 36–37, 123–24, 180
right to peaceful enjoyment of your property (Prot. 1, Art. 1), 14
austerity measures, 172–74
Bosphorus presumption, 43
Cyprus conflict, 136
domestic violence, 154
socio-economic rights, 162, 172–74, 179
right to respect for private and family life (Art. 8):
discrimination, 178–79
domestic violence, 154
effectiveness, 175
gender reassignment, 86–87
Hatton and Others v UK, 128
illegitimate children, 85–86
interference, 108
Lacatus v Switzerland, 102
legitimate aim, 109
Marckx v Belgium, 85–86
margin of appreciation, 122, 128
positive obligations, 154–55
prohibitions on begging, 102
proportionality, 110–11, 114–15
religious dress, 92–93

Roman Zakharov v Russia, 62–63
SAS v France, 92–93
socio-economic rights, 175, 178–79
surveillance of telephone communications, 62–63
Von Hannover v Germany, 110–11
Romania:
Association for the Defence of Human Rights in Romania –Helsinki Committee
Calmanovici v Romania, 37
Centre for Legal Resources on behalf of Valentin Campeanu v Romania, 64
deceased victims, 64–65
on behalf of Ionel Garcea v Romania, 65
prisoner voting, 37
rule of law, 7–8, 87, 112, 126, 151, 164, 165–66, 193–95, 199–201
Rules of Court:
Directorate of Jurisconsult, 28–29
pilot-judgments, 188–89
reform of working methods, 18–20
Registry, 25
Rule 18B, 28–29
Rule 47, 58
Rule 61, 188–89
Russia:
admissibility, 66, 62, 75–76
Alekseyev v Russia, 109–10
Anchugov and Gladkov v Russia, 38–39
Burdov v Russia (No 2), 189–90
Carter v Russia, 143
Catan and Others v the Republic of Moldova and Russia, 109
covert surveillance, 62–63
deceased victims, 65
execution of judgments, 189–90, 196
expulsion from Council of Europe, 30–31
Fadeyeva v Russia, 31
Finogenov and Others v Russia, 63–64
general measures, 189–90
Georgia v Russia (II), 132–33
Ilyushkin v Russia, 190
invasion of Ukraine, 30, 135
extraterritoriality, 142–43
judicial imperialism, 143
Kalinkin v Russia, 190
Kondrulin v Russia, 65
Konstantin Markin v Russia, 114–15
legal certainty and effectiveness, 63–64
legitimate aim, 109
Murtazaliyeva v Russia, 12–13
Navalnyy v Russia, 202
'necessary in a democratic society', 109–10
OAO Neftyanaya Kompaniya Yukos v Russia, 66, 186
proportionality, 114–15
Protocol 14, 15–16
right to fair trial, 12–13, 189–90
Roman Zakharov v Russia, 62–63
Shamayev and Others v Georgia and Russia, 75–76
Ukraine and the Netherlands v Russia, 142–43
Ukraine v Russia (re Crimea), 31, 142–43

same-sex marriage, 6, 123
same-sex relationships:
inheritance property tax, 61–62
San Marino:
abortion, 97
second-order reasons, 119–20, 123
self-restraint, 9, 11–13, 89–90, 139
Serbia, 24
socio-economic rights, 173, 180–81
Žegarac and Others v Serbia, 173
sexual orientation, 99, 170–71, 176, 178
Slovakia:
domestic violence, 155
Kontrova v Slovakia, 155
social contract, 164
socio-economic rights:
civil and political rights distinguished, 167–68
ECSR, 7
ESC, 6–7, 166–67
global financial crises, 161–62
ICESCR, 3, 161
rights to education (Prot. 1, Art.2), 162
positive and negative obligations, 165
social constitutionalism, 165–66
protection of property and possessions (Prot. 1 Art. 1), 162
sovereignty, 13, 33, 40, 41, 117, 145, 184–85, 192, 198–99
Spain:
bail-out, 171
special judicial review:
Pinto Law, 59–60
standing, 61, 67
statehood, 164
Steering Committee for Human Rights (CDDH):
fragmentation of rights protection, 49
judiciary of the ECtHR, 21–22
structural problems, 188, 191

subsidiarity principle, 5, 59–60
admissibility criteria, 11
'age of subsidiarity', 10–13
deference to national courts, 11
process-based review/procedural review, 12–13
interpretive authority of ECtHR, 204
Superior Court Network, 206
super-qualified rights, 123
surveillance, 60–61, 63
Switzerland:
Al-Dulimi and Montana Management Inc v Switzerland, 51–52
asset-freezing, 51–52
climate change litigation, 66–67
Lacatus v Switzerland, 102
Osmanoğlu and Kocabaş v Switzerland, 112–13
prohibitions on begging, 102
proportionality, 112–13
Protocol 16, 16
referendums, 198
Verein KlimaSeniorinnen and others v Switzerland, 66–67
systemic integration, 95
systemic problems, 19, 188–89, 191

temporary lawyers, 28
Third World Approaches to International Law (TWAIL):
consent and legitimacy of ECtHR, 3
times of emergency, *see* **derogation in time of emergency**
tipping moments, 81–82
torture, *see* **prohibition against torture, inhuman treatment, and degrading treatment or punishment**
trafficking and sexual exploitation, 10
transboundary harms:
climate change litigation, 143–44
Transnistria, 109
transparency, 9, 21, 30, 71, 76–77, 79, 106, 116
Treaty of Lisbon, 45–46
trials:
detention without trial, 133, 152–53
right to a fair trial, 12–13, 34–35, 44, 50, 53, 59, 162–63, 178, 189–90, 198, 202–3
witnesses, 13
'trumping internal consensus', 97–98, 195
turbans, *see* **religious dress**

Turkish Republic of Northern Cyprus (TRNC), 136
Türkiye:
Aksoy v Turkiye, 152
Civek v Turkiye, 155
Cyprus conflict, 136, 186
Cyprus v Turkey, 186
Demir and Baykara v Turkiye, 95
detention without trial, 152
disproportionate security measures, 146
domestic violence, 155–57
evolutive interpretation, 95
Halime Kilic v Turkiye, 157
infringement proceedings, 203
inhuman and degrading treatment or punishment, 155–56
interim measures, 94
Kavala v Turkiye, 203
lawfulness of detention, 152
Leyla Şahin v Turkiye, 101
Loizidou v Turkiye, 136
Mamatkulov and Askarov v Turkiye, 94
margin of appreciation, 124
Mehmet Hasan Altan v Turkiye, 152
MG v Turkiye, 157
Opuz v Turkiye, 155–56
prisoner voting, 39–40
process-based review, 126
religious dress, 101
rule of law, 194
Şahin Alpay v Turkiye, 152
Soyler v Turkiye, 39
United Communist Party of Turkey v Turkiye, 126
Yumak and Sadak v Turkiye, 124

Ukraine:
individual measures, 187
invasion by Russia, 10, 30–31, 135
extraterritoriality, 142–43
Ivanov v Ukraine, 190
Oleksandr Volkov v Ukraine, 187
pilot judgments, 190
Ukraine and the Netherlands v Russia, 142
Ukraine v Russia (Re Crimea), 31, 142
United Kingdom:
A and Others v UK, 148
Al-Khawaja and Tahery v UK, 34–35
Al-Skeini and Others v UK, 139–41
Animal Defenders International v UK, 125–26
appointment of judges, 21

Brannigan and McBride v UK, 152
Burden v UK, 61
Cameron's criticism of ECtHR, 69
Carter v Russia, 143
Christine Goodwin v UK, 86–87, 88
consensual same-sex relations, 62, 99
deference, 125–26
derogations in time of emergency, 148–49
detention without trial, 152
Dickson v UK, 124
Dudgeon v UK, 62
espace juridique, 139–41
gender reassignment, 86–87
gender recognition, 86–88
Greens and MT v UK, 37, 191
Hassan v UK, 134
Hatton and Others v UK, 128
Hirst v UK (No 2), 35–36, 100, 127, 191–92
Human Rights Act 1998, 139, 196, 205, 207–8
industrial action by prison officers, 75
inheritance property tax, 61
internal consensus, 98
international humanitarian law, 134
LF v UK, 173
margin of appreciation, 124, 128
non-discrimination, 178
pilot judgments, 37
POA and Others v UK, 75
prisoner voting, 35–37, 39, 100, 127, 191–92
right to fair trial, 34
S and Marper v UK, 124
Sander v UK, 178
Sheffield and Horsham v UK, 88
socio-economic rights, 173
Sutherland v UK, 99
territorial jurisdiction, 139–40
Tyrer v UK, 98

United Nations:
ECHR, relationship with, 49–54
Human Rights Committee, 73
UN Charter, 49–50, 51
UN Security Council, 49–54

Universal Declaration on Human Rights (UDHR), 3
universality of human rights, 69–70, 120, 122–23, 161

variable geometry, 126, 127–28
victim requirement, 60–61
corporate victims, 65–66
deceased victims, 64–65
potential victims, 61–62
victims of covert activities, 62–64
Vienna Convention on the Law of Treaties (VCLT), 83–84, 134, 163–65, 199
voting rights, *see* **prisoner voting**
vulnerability, 169–71

war, *see* **armed conflicts**

Yugoslav war, 42–43
extraterritoriality, 136–39